DEMAND

Also by Adrian J. Slywotzky

Value Migration

The Profit Zone

Profit Patterns

How Digital Is Your Business?

The Art of Profitability

How to Grow When Markets Don't

The Upside

DEMAND

Creating What People Love Before
They Know They Want It

Adrian J. Slywotzky

with Karl Weber

CROWN
BUSINESS
NEW YORK

Published in the United States by Crown Business, an imprint of the
Crown Publishing Group, a division of Random House, Inc., New York.
www.crownpublishing.com

CROWN BUSINESS is a trademark and CROWN and the Rising Sun colophon are
registered trademarks of Random House, Inc.

Crown Business books are available at special discounts for bulk purchases for sales
promotions or corporate use. Special editions, including personalized covers, excerpts
of existing books, or books with corporate logos, can be created in large quantities
for special needs. For more information, contact Premium Sales at (212) 572-2232
or e-mail specialmarkets@randomhouse.com.

Tetra Pak, Tetra Pak Classic Aseptic, Tetra Pak Rex, Tetra Pak Wedge, Tetra Pak Hoyer
DeepBlue, and Tetra Pak Prima Aseptic are trademarks of Tetra Pak International.
Yellow+Blue is a trademark of J. Soif, Inc.

Library of Congress Cataloging-in-Publication Data

Slywotzky, Adrian J.
    Demand: creating what people love before they know they want it /
    Adrian Slywotzky.—1st ed.
        p. cm.
    1. Demand (Economic theory).   2. Supply and demand.   I. Title.
    HB801.S56 2011
    658.8'343—dc22   2011009633

ISBN 978-0-307-88732-0
eISBN 978-0-307-88734-4

Printed in the United States of America

Book design by Leonard Henderson
Jacket design by David Tran
Jacket photograph by Mike Kiev, www.dreamstime.com

10 9 8 7 6 5 4 3 2 1

First Edition

For Alexander

Contents

The Mystery of Demand   1

1.
Magnetic
Zipcar Invents a New Kind of Freedom   14

From Ho-Hum to Gotta-Have-It:
Wegmans Makes Groceries Magnetic   34

2.
Hassle Map
The Long, Rocky Road to a One-Click World   55

Better Than a Bonus:
Bloomberg Builds a Service Traders Just Won't Give Up   65

CareMore Connects the Health Care Dots   72

3.
Backstory
It's What You Don't See That Counts:
Behind the Kindle Screen   92

Tetra Pak Steps Out from the Backstory   110

4.
Trigger
Netflix and Its Two-Hundred-Year-Old Secret Weapon   134

Nespresso and the Demand That Almost Wasn't   154

5.

TRAJECTORY

Getting Smarter Faster:
Teach For America's Drive to Reshape Educational Demand 176

The Best Lunch Ever:
Pret A Manger and the Quest for the Perfect Sandwich 194

6.

VARIATION

Selling the Symphony: It's Not Just About the Music 210

The Seattle Opera Grows Its Audience One Member at a Time 219

Demand Variation, from the Corner Store to Eurostar, the Eighth
Wonder of the World 224

7.

LAUNCH

The Achilles' Heel of Demand 250

8.

PORTFOLIO

"Nobody Knows Anything" 275

9.

THE BIGGEST SPARK

Scientific Discovery and the Future of Demand 302

CODA: THE DEMAND CREATORS 327

SOURCE NOTES 329

ACKNOWLEDGMENTS 345

INDEX 349

DEMAND

The Mystery of Demand

YOU LOVE IT as soon as you see it. Something about it resonates inside you, though you can't articulate just why. You rave about it with the same passion that you rant about the things you can't stand. Then you see the long lines forming and hear the excited conversations starting. You realize there are thousands, maybe millions who feel the same as you. And for some reason, something else that seems just as good is met with indifference and dead silence.

Demand is an unusual form of energy. It turns many wheels big and small, from economies to markets to organizations to our paychecks, here and around the world. Everything depends on it. Without it growth slows, economies falter, progress stops. Yet do we understand where demand actually comes from? Can it be *created*, and created repeatedly?

We often think that demand comes from pulling the right levers: more marketing, better advertising, more aggressive sales efforts, distributing coupons, offering discounts. Tactics like these do have their time and place, and they can bring short-term results.

But *real* demand is not about any of these things. Demand creators spend all of their time trying to understand *people*. They are acutely aware of how hopeful, jaded, funny, impulsive, unreasonable, irascible, ambitious, distrustful, enigmatic, enthusiastic, frustrated, and unpredictable we really are. They try to understand our aspirations, what we need, what we hate, what gives us an emotional charge—and, most important, what we might really love. By watching how people actually behave in their own worlds, and by talking to them constantly, demand creators figure out how to solve the big and little hassles we all face—and they make our days easier, more convenient, more productive, and simply more fun. They seem to know what we want even before we do. They wind up creating things people can't resist and competitors can't copy.

Yet they almost never succeed on the first try. They know that real demand comes from connecting the dots between the human factors and a quirky, ever-shifting combination of other elements: financial and emotional costs, social norms, infrastructure, product design, patterns of communication, and many more. It comes from understanding how all these factors interact in complex, unpredictable, and counterintuitive ways. And it comes from a way of thinking that makes the leap from trying to convince people to buy something to human understanding, to seeing the world through the eyes and emotions of the customer. A dozen cylinders have to click into place before the vault door swings open. But when it does, wonderful things happen—for all of us.

In this book we'll tell the stories of an amazing group of demand creators and those who work with them. And while every demand story is unique, they all start in the same place: a person, a problem, and an idea.

❏   ❏   ❏

ONE DAY IN 1997, a man named Reed Hastings was puttering around his house, bundling up old newspapers and sorting through stacks of mail-order catalogs, when, underneath a pile of forgotten junk, he stumbled across an unwelcome surprise. It was a VHS cassette of the movie *Apollo 13*—the same cassette Hastings and his wife had enjoyed one evening six weeks earlier.

The same cassette, he realized with a sinking feeling, he should have returned to Blockbuster the next morning.

His first thought was to calculate the late fee: forty dollars—

almost enough to buy the darned cassette. A petty annoyance, troubling mainly because it represented the penalty for Hastings's carelessness.

Far worse was his second thought: *What will my wife say?* And knowing that she would probably say nothing at all made the situation that much more painful. Hastings could imagine it with utter clarity. Like long-suffering spouses everywhere, she would react with a simple eye roll—"an eye roll that could kill," as Hastings described it.

Millions of us have been there. But for Reed Hastings, unlike the rest of us, the embarrassment triggered a question—a question about the mechanics of movie rentals and the hassles they created.

It happened later in the day, when Hastings, still annoyed over the forty-dollar late fee, was on his way to the gym. "How come," he wondered, "movie rentals don't work like a health club, where, whether you use it a lot or a little, you get the same charge?" And that led to other questions: Could a movie rental business actually work that way—charging a flat membership rate and no late fees? Would the customers ever return the movies without the pressure of a late fee? Could you keep enough movies in inventory to satisfy customers? How would the economics work?

Hastings started tinkering with the idea, first on paper, then in real life. Eventually a business was born—Netflix, which grew into one of the fastest-growing companies of the twenty-first century.

It retrospect, the idea seems obvious. Who *wouldn't* want a movie rental system that eliminated late fees (and the irritation they produce) along with a dozen other petty inconveniences? Yet the growth of Netflix happened under the very noses of the executives at Blockbuster, who watched Netflix grow for *nineteen straight quarters* before they decided to launch their own video-by-mail service. And in the process, Netflix managed to outmaneuver a host of rival companies that seemed far better positioned to take advantage of the opportunity—not just Blockbuster but also such retailing and show-business giants as Walmart, Amazon, and Disney.

How did this happen? Why was Reed Hastings able to see the potential for a billion dollars' worth of demand in the same consumer hassles most of us experienced but ignored or merely complained about?

This mystery is a small example of the bigger mystery that is the subject of this book—the mystery of demand.

In the United States, millions of people inhabit homes that are crowded with things, yet live lives overflowing with frustrations, inconveniences, complications, risks—hassles of every sort. No matter how much we consume, there remain huge gaps between what we really want and the goods and services we settle for. Those gaps represent opportunities for the creation of new demand—as Reed Hastings recognized.

❏   ❏   ❏

WHILE THE IDEA for Netflix was germinating in the mind of Reed Hastings, another demand creation story was taking shape on the other side of the planet. And while the setting and many of the details couldn't be more different from those in the story of Netflix, the underlying mechanism was strikingly similar.

Babu Rajan is a fisherman in Pallipuram, near the southwestern coast of India. By developed-world standards, Rajan is poor. The only significant asset he owns is the one that he and an informal consortium of fourteen fellow fishermen rely on for their livelihood: a seventy-four-foot, steel-hulled boat, the *Andavan,* in which they troll the Arabian Sea searching for schools of sardines, the cheap, plentiful fish that feed millions of hungry South Asians. It's the same way of life that Rajan's father and grandfather followed, right down to the half-mile-long net he uses to gather his catch and the sticks of incense he burns for good luck in the tiny Hindu shrine tucked into the ship's bow.

Some days, Rajan's luck is good. His predawn excursion may yield a catch of ten thousand pounds or more and net $1,800 or more for the boat's crew to share. Other days, their nets come up empty, or nearly so; the lesser haul is barely enough to pay for diesel fuel. The unpredictability of the ocean's harvest makes it doubly important for Rajan to maximize the value of what he catches.

And here is where the relentless power of nature plays a cruel role. After ten or twelve hours at sea, having gathered whatever bounty the ocean has to offer that day, Rajan and his fellow fishermen pull into the nearest port, where they are met at the dock by the local seafood wholesaler. With the fierce tropical sun beating down, both Rajan and the wholesaler know that the fish won't last long. There's no time to travel from port to port, gathering competing offers from rival wholesalers. Rajan has no choice but to accept the dealer's offer, and hope for a larger catch tomorrow. The unyielding logic of the situation is one reason generations of Indian fishermen have been unable to work themselves and their families out of poverty.

At least, until recently. Around 2003, Babu Rajan did the same thing millions of other rural Indians were doing: He managed to scrape together nearly an average month's income to buy a tool his father and grandfather could only have dreamed about—a cell phone. Now his life and work are dramatically different.

Today, as Rajan trails his net in the Arabian Sea, the cell phone, hanging in a protective plastic case from his neck, rings periodically with calls from wholesalers in a dozen nearby ports. "How big is today's catch?" they want to know. "When will you be bringing it in? And have you received any other offers?"

"When I have a big catch," Rajan reports, "the phone rings sixty or seventy times before I get to port."

Now Rajan is able to entertain offers from several wholesale dealers, playing one against another in the classic mode of free markets everywhere. Only after agreeing on the best price available does he select the port to which he'll deliver his catch. As a result, Rajan's family income has more than tripled in the last decade, bringing them a series of luxuries once unheard-of among India's rural poor—electricity, television, schooling for his children.

The impact of the cell phone in rural India extends beyond fishermen. Until recently, farmers in India in need of information to guide their planting relied on the same low-tech tools they'd employed for millennia: guesswork, tradition, word of mouth, even religious rituals. The result: extreme vulnerability to market swings, droughts, floods, crop diseases, and other forms of economic disaster. Each year more than a third of India's fruit and vegetable output would go to waste due to market failures caused by information shortfalls.

Today, this is changing, thanks to the advent of the cell phone. More than 40 percent of farmers in Indian regions from Uttar Pradesh in the north to Tamil Nadu in the south now have access to mobile services providing agricultural information. They can receive voice or text messages with customized market data, such as minimum and maximum prices for a particular crop at specified local markets and the volume of the crop arriving that day. Other voice messages offer how-to advice on topics such as weed control for rice paddies and cultivation tips for bananas.

An American farmer might take such information for granted. But its impact in the developing world is remarkable. Studies show that Indian districts with high rates of cell phone usage climb faster and further out of poverty, creating, in turn, more demand for cars, houses, store-bought clothes and food, and high-end services from health care to education. It's demand fueling demand, with growing society-wide prosperity as the result.

The product driving this trend is the Nokia 1100. Consumers in the developed world are often startled when they learn about the sheer scale of demand for this Finnish cell phone. Consider some of the most impressive high-tech product launches of the past decade:

Within five years of introduction, the Nintendo Wii game system sold 45 million units. In the same time frame, 50 million Motorola RAZRs, 125 million PlayStation 2 consoles, and 174 million iPods were sold. And the Nokia 1100? In that product's first half decade, 250 million were sold, mostly in some of the world's poorest countries. Those numbers make the Nokia 1100 the bestselling consumer electronics device in the world.

Crucial to the success of the Nokia 1100 is its design. Features that make the 1100 an invaluable tool for life in rural South Asia, Latin America, or sub-Saharan Africa have been included; every other feature has been ruthlessly simplified or stripped away completely. At the same time, the 1100 offers options few Westerners would think of. For example, it can store multiple contact lists—essential in a phone that may be shared by many users in a village. The 1100 also allows the user to enter a price limit for a particular call, much like prepayment at a gas station—another feature that supports communal use. There's a built-in flashlight, radio, and alarm clock—valuable accessories where electrical service is unreliable. And the 1100 is available with screen displays in more than eighty languages, or with visual symbols to serve the illiterate customer.

The Nokia 1100 is a triumph of insight and creativity. Nokia's engineers managed to see the world through the eyes of a South Asian farmer, recognized and empathized with the hassles he faced, and designed a product that can dramatically reduce them—transforming millions of lives, and creating huge new demand in the process.

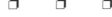

NETFLIX AND THE NOKIA 1100 vividly illustrate the complexity—and the world-altering power—of the art of demand creation. And the more we've learned about these stories, and many others like them, the more we've realized that demand is a lot more complicated and more fascinating than we once thought.

But why does it matter? Why is the mystery of demand important, not just to business executives and economic policy makers, but to all of us? The answer lies in the dramatically changing shape of our world.

We live in a time of two economies. One dominates the headlines and the TV news. It's the economy that became mired in recession in 2008, in which millions are unemployed, millions more are *under*employed, companies are reluctant to invest, factories have fallen silent, and one industry after another—from cars to electronics to airlines to retailing to energy to housing—is experiencing stagnation. In this economy, the once-reliable engine that drove growth and prosperity for decades—consumer demand—has somehow become broken, with painful consequences for all of us.

In the same time and same space, there is another economy in which the demand engine is almost ridiculously strong, operating in overdrive. In this economy, a handful of companies are not just doing better than their competition, they are doing *exponentially* better. They enjoy runaway growth, premium pricing, and extraordinary customer loyalty because they create new products and services that not only attract demand but actually *excite* people. In this economy, companies are growing, profits are robust, customer loyalty is powerful, jobs by the hundreds of thousands are being created, and the lives of millions of people are being enhanced in ways large and small.

What's going on?

We set out to answer this question. To do so, we knew we needed to take a fresh look at the mystery of demand. To look at customers, producers, and the ways they come together in markets without the filters and encumbrances of traditional assumptions. We needed to think about demand as a child would, driven by curiosity and a willingness to ask naïve questions: How does demand actually happen? And how do those who create explosive and sustained demand even in tough economic times do it?

Our curiosity about demand was amplified by a series of

anomalies—odd happenings from the world around us that seemed to make no sense and left us wondering how and why they'd occurred. Surprising stories like those of the birth of Netflix and the Nokia 1100 sparked our interest. And once we began to notice such demand anomalies, they began popping up everywhere we looked.

Before Amazon's Kindle launched the e-book revolution, an almost identical device was introduced by Sony into the avid Japanese book market—and sank like a stone. Why has the Kindle outsold the Sony Reader several times over, despite Sony's three-year head start?

Nonprofit organizations that promote high culture must constantly struggle for funding—yet an opera company in a mid-size city has mastered the knack of generating a deep and ever-growing stream of demand for its programs. How have they done it?

Everyone knows that Americans love their cars, despite their huge economic and environmental costs. How is a fast-growing car-sharing company convincing Americans to give up their beloved cars—and making them *enjoy* doing it?

American health care is an economic disaster zone—yet a little-known health care company in California has figured out how to provide vastly improved services, keep its clients healthier and happier, and simultaneously cut costs—by as much as 20 percent. How is that possible?

The decades-long decline of American education is a familiar story—but a young college graduate launched a rapidly growing nonprofit organization that is transforming American education by generating a revolution in *demand* on the part of students and parents, demand for education that really works. How did that happen?

The unpredictable challenges of the demand creation process produce an endless stream of head-to-head matchups: Facebook versus MySpace, the Toyota Prius versus the Civic Hybrid, iPod versus Sansa, Eurostar versus Air France, and many others. In each case, consumers disproportionately demand one seemingly comparable product over another—not by a few percentage points but by margins of five or even ten to one. Why? What makes demand differ so dramatically when the underlying goods appear so similar?

Closely examining these anomalies and many more like them, we discovered that demand is often created by a special breed of person with a number of unique insights and behaviors—yet the skills these people practice can be learned and practiced by *any* leader and by *any* team.

These demand creators recognize the huge gaps between what people buy and what they really want—and they use those gaps as the springboard for a process of reimagination that you might call the demand way of thinking. They reimagine reality, and then they recraft it. As a result, they wind up creating products that customers can't resist and competitors can't copy.

The process includes several steps that all great demand creators follow.

1. Make It Magnetic

Most of what comes into the marketplace is good, even very good, yet it fails to create an emotional connection with customers. Demand creators begin with a very tough realization: Very Good $\neq$ Magnetic. And they don't stop developing their product until it's absolutely irresistible, generating excitement and conversation everywhere. When it comes to creating demand, it's not the first mover that wins; it's the first to create and capture the emotional space in the market.

2. Fix the Hassle Map

Most of the products we buy are flawed, generating hassles that include time- or money-wasting features, unclear instructions, needless risks, and other annoying bugs and glitches. We rarely get to enjoy *everything* we want: greater simplicity *and* more choices, enhanced automation *and* more personal service, improved quality *and* lower prices. But herein lies enormous opportunity for the demand creator. Mapping the hassles that dominate so much of daily life, and then figuring out how to fix them, provides the path to explosive potential demand.

3. Build a Complete Backstory

What we don't see can make or break the product. As many demand creators have discovered, it's not enough to have 90 percent of the backstory in place—until the backstory is truly complete, demand simply doesn't happen. Demand creators connect *all* the dots needed to fix the hassle map of the customer.

4. Find the Triggers

The biggest obstacles to creating demand are inertia, skepticism, habit, and indifference. Most people who hear about a product remain fence-sitters, unready to buy and stifling the growth of demand until something moves them to act—a trigger. Although it often takes even the best companies years to find the right triggers, great demand creators constantly search for them, always experimenting to find what turns fence-sitters into customers.

5. Build a Steep Trajectory

A product's launch into the marketplace is merely the first step in a series of attacks upon the indifference of the market. On launch day, great demand creators jump into the next phase by asking themselves a very simple question: How fast can we get better? They know that every improvement they make—technical or emotional—will unlock new layers of demand, and leave less open space for imitative, piggybacking competitors.

6. De-Average

"One size fits all" is an appealing idea that great demand creators have discarded—because it doesn't work. Instead, they "de-average" complex markets, recognizing that the "average customer" is a myth, and that different customers (and even the same customers at different times) have widely varying hassle maps. Then they find efficient, cost-effective ways to create product variations that more perfectly match the varying needs of very different *types* of customers, getting rid of overages (things we don't want) and underages (gaps we want filled). They constantly improve their product's fit for very different customer types from 60 percent to 90 percent, or better.

❏   ❏   ❏

GREAT DEMAND CREATORS have not only mastered these six skills; they also know how to transmit them to many other people. They build self-replicating teams that are obsessed with customers and their needs, obsessed with that magical difference between what customers buy and what they *really* want. In this way they are able to reduce hassles and provide life-improving products not just for a handful of people but for the thousands or millions of customers that only a great organization can reach.

Demand creators have a hidden advantage. Many of their rivals are "anti-demand" organizations—organized in disconnected silos, focused on meeting yesterday's demand, and often remarkably immune to the signals that customer behavior is trying to send us.

Demand creators are remarkable people. In trying to decipher the mystery of demand, we've had the privilege of meeting many of them and observing them in action. We've found great demand creators in a surprising range of organizations—not only corporations but small businesses and nonprofit organizations. Some are company founders and CEOs, while others are middle managers, frontline employees, small business owners and entrepreneurs, idealistic reformers, and seemingly ordinary people in many walks of life. They tend to be deeply curious, extremely energetic, thoughtful and self-disciplined, intensely confident yet continually self-questioning, gifted with humility and with a highly evolved sense of humor. And they're always looking for the *next* hassle map of the customer.

Yet perhaps the most important trait this highly disparate collection of individuals has in common is a simple one. When confronted with the same question we've been pondering—Where will tomorrow's demand come from?—they don't point to the government, the Fortune 500, or to macroeconomic forces.

Instead, they look in the mirror.

1.

Magnetic

(mag-NET-ik) *adjective*   1. extraordinarily and irrepressibly attractive
2. combining great functionality with intense emotional appeal 3. capable
of producing a powerful stream of demand

ZIPCAR INVENTS A NEW KIND OF FREEDOM

It was Friday evening, February 14, 2003. Scott Griffith was heading
home from an intense and eventful day. He'd been chosen by the
board of directors of Zipcar to be the company's new CEO, replacing founder Robin Chase.

For the forty-four-year-old Griffith, it was a stressful, tumultuous
moment. He was delighted to be back at the helm of an innovative
young company, a role he'd relished in two previous assignments,
one a failure, one a success. And he loved the Zipcar business for
its uniqueness and its vaulting ambition—to revolutionize the way
people use cars by providing a convenient alternative to ownership,
saving money, eliminating hassles, and protecting the environment.
Yet after four years of hard work by Chase and her dedicated team—
years of research, experimentation, evolution, and struggle—the
business was still on shaky footing. Demand wasn't zero, but it was
low—far too low to be sustainable or profitable.

If Zipcar were a rocket, it was a rocket that had achieved liftoff
but was still unable to reach escape velocity. Time and again it had
stalled and fallen back to earth, grounded by the powerful gravita-
tional force that causes more than 80 percent of new businesses
and new product launches to sputter and fail.

Board members and team members proposed many solutions:

cut prices, advertise more, offer free trial memberships, change the lineup of cars, redesign the website . . . The problem was clear, but the solution was a mystery.

Griffith had always been fascinated by the intersection between technological change and demand. Growing up in Pittsburgh in the 1970s, he'd watched the local economy collapse as its steel industry became outmoded. He was also a natural-born Mr. Fix-It, whose favorite childhood memory was of repairing the family toaster with a soldering gun at the age of nine ("I was lucky I didn't electrocute myself").

Now Zipcar offered Griffith a similar challenge on a grown-up scale: Could he figure out why the rocket wasn't reaching escape velocity? And could he fix it before the company's funding ran out?

❏   ❏   ❏

AMERICANS LOVE their cars. We know it's true, because practically every cultural commentator has told us so. And most ordinary people agree. In a 2001 survey, 84 percent of Americans confessed to loving their cars, 12 percent said they'd named them, and 17 percent reported buying them Valentine's Day presents. Yes, Americans love their cars.

Or do they?

Do Americans love commuting? Do they love the daily traffic jams for which cities like Atlanta and Los Angeles have become infamous, the five-mile-per-hour crawl on New York's Long Island Expressway (sometimes called "the world's longest parking lot"), or the hair-raising adventure that is maneuvering among buses, delivery trucks, battered taxis, and double-parkers on the pothole-filled streets of Manhattan, Chicago, or Philadelphia? Do Americans love trolling for parking spaces, or searching for their cars among three thousand identical slots once they've managed to park them? Do they love paying for insurance, repairs, tickets, registration fees, taxes? Do they love playing gas-price roulette at the pump?

Americans may love their cars. Yet there's another side to the relationship—a side that, at times, looks an awful lot like hatred.

Mary Morgan, a journalist in Ann Arbor, Michigan, has thought a lot about the love/hate relationship between Americans and their cars. In fact, she has lived it, talking with her family about getting rid of their car for a long time. Ann Arbor has excellent public transportation, and the Morgan family could manage most of its daily activities quite nicely without a car. But, Morgan says, "I'll admit that I'm the one who's been dragging my feet. For me, having a car is a habit—an addiction, really—and unable to go cold turkey, I've been edging toward carlessness in nicotine patch–like phases. Part of my reluctance to go car-free has hinged on my sense that owning a car gives me freedom, and that without a car I'll be trapped."

Most telling, perhaps, is Morgan's use of the word *addiction* to describe her feelings about her car. It's a word we reserve for relationships we consider destructive and would desperately love to change . . . but somehow can't. And that addiction is why millions of Americans buy cars: not because they love cars and the hassles that go with them, but because owning a car has been the only way to experience the sense of freedom they *do* love.

Great demand creators are special, in part, because they understand that the things we buy and the things we actually *want* aren't always the same. There's often an enormous gap between the two— and that gap is where the opportunity to create demand originates.

Unfortunately, transforming that opportunity into real demand often borders on the impossible.

Throughout the seventies, eighties, and nineties, as oil spills, price shocks, overseas crises, supply shortages, and the looming threat of global warming exposed the dangers of our dependence on petroleum, progressive political leaders and city planners tried to eliminate or reduce public reliance on cars. They deployed an array of tools, including improvements to urban mass transit, establishment of car-free zones and pedestrian malls, restrictive auto regulations, tough tax and licensing requirements, congestion pricing of tolls, and onerous parking limitations.

Yet most of those efforts foundered. Millions of people *talk* about wanting to break the driving habit; almost none follow through. (As a deadly accurate 2000 headline in the satiric *Onion* put it, "98 Percent of U.S. Commuters Favor Public Transportation for Others.") The missing ingredient has been a powerfully attractive alternative—a form of transportation that eliminates the hassles of car ownership while providing the freedom, convenience, and fun that Americans love about their cars.

In politics they say, "You can't beat somebody with nobody": Even an unpopular incumbent can win reelection when the opposition is lackluster. In the world of demand, it's not enough to identify the failings of existing products—you need to create an alternative that will excite, allure, and motivate consumers to change their behavior. In other words, new demand begins—always—with a magnetic product.*

What is a magnetic product? Here's an easy way to define it for yourself.

Consider the following contrasting pairs of products. Don't think about them a lot—just react quickly. Which product from each pair strikes you as more attractive, interesting, desirable, lovable—in short, magnetic?

Sansa	iPod
Sony Reader	Kindle
Civic Hybrid	Prius
Hertz Connect	Zipcar
Illy	Nespresso

---

* In this context, the word *product* refers to any good offered to customers, including intangible goods often referred to as "services." For the sake of conciseness, and to avoid the frequent repetition of the phrase "product or service," we'll generally call both kinds of goods simply "products."

Air France	Eurostar
MySpace	Facebook
Blockbuster	Netflix
British Air	Virgin Atlantic
Any toy set	LEGOs
Any movie studio	Pixar
Yahoo! Search	Google
Any online retailer	Amazon

You may not be familiar with every product named here. But if you're like most of the thousands of people to whom we've presented this list, you probably feel a much stronger attraction to the products on the right than to those on the left—even though, in many cases, the apparent differences seem not to be significant. As we'll discuss later, magnetism is as much about emotional appeal as about function. And magnetism is one of the crucial elements in creating significant new demand.

In 1999, Robin Chase decided to tackle the challenge of creating a magnetic alternative to car ownership.

A Wellesley graduate with a background in public health and an MBA from the MIT Sloan School of Management, Chase was a dedicated environmentalist who had long fretted about Americans' car addiction, penning earnest articles with titles like "Fossil Fuel Is the New Slavery." In the absence of an attractive alternative, her proselytizing had little impact.

Then, in 1999, while searching for a way to apply her business talents to the mission of greening America, Chase learned about a

little-known approach to the auto dilemma—car-sharing. The idea
was to get needless cars off the road by having multiple people, especially city dwellers, share a single vehicle.

Chase saw that car-sharing could save resources in lots of ways.
Fewer vehicles on the road would mean less steel, rubber, glass, and
other materials expended in manufacturing. Less land would need
to be devoted to highways and parking lots. And drivers relying on
shared vehicles would be less inclined to hop in the car for a five-
block drive to the supermarket, reducing the amount of gas expended
in needless trips, idling at red lights, and round-the-block cruising in
search of a parking spot.

Not-for-profit car-sharing services had already been launched in
cities throughout Western Europe and in a few places in the United
States, such as Portland, Oregon. But these city-sponsored services,
though well intentioned, were clunky and inconvenient. Car keys
were stored in centrally located mechanical lockboxes; driving logs
had to be filled out by hand. Except among hard-core environmentalists, demand for car-sharing was practically nonexistent.

Chase understood that merely replacing the hassles of car ownership with a different set of hassles was unlikely to create much new
demand. But she also recognized that the Internet offered an opportunity to reduce or eliminate the hassles of car-sharing. Chase became convinced that the ecological benefits of car-sharing could be
realized through a for-profit company capable of attracting a serious
stream of demand from mainstream customers.

Armed with this vision, she and a German friend, Antje Danielson, raised $1.3 million from a few venturesome investors and set up
shop in Chase's hometown of Cambridge, Massachusetts. They were
determined to convert car-sharing from a tiny niche into a mass movement capable of having a real impact on the nation's energy and
environmental problems.

Chase's husband, Roy Russell, became the new company's chief
technology officer. He and a team of programmers set about creating

a Web-based system for reserving and tracking cars. Cars would be kept in prearranged parking locations in neighborhood garages or lots, and anyone who paid an annual membership fee could find and claim the nearest available vehicle with a few mouse clicks. A digitally coded card would enable the member to access the vehicle. Billing would be handled online automatically, eliminating paperwork. There would be no insurance forms to fill out—coverage would be included in the hourly fee—and even the cost of gas would be taken care of, with the membership card usable at the pump much like a credit card.

These innovations dramatically improved the functionality of car-sharing—the first half of the magnetism equation. "Our goal was to make access to cars as easy as getting cash from an ATM machine," Chase said, and the new Web-based rental system came impressively close. One early adopter remarked, "I was ten miles down the road at the time I would have been wrapping up the paperwork at the Enterprise counter." Another marveled, "You never have to deal with a live person—just reserve a car through the website." And a third called Chase's system simply "the easiest and cheapest way to get around the city."

The improvements Chase developed were important. A magnetic product must be functionally superb: It works well; it's affordable and convenient; it reduces hassles. But as we've noted, function alone doesn't create magnetism—after all, an MP3 player by SanDisk or any other manufacturer plays tunes just about as well as an iPod. Emotional engagement is required, too—produced, in the case of the iPod, by a combination of unique characteristics, including brilliant design, a superlative user interface, and a system for finding, buying, and organizing content that is practically universal, easy, and fun. That's why for every person who owns an ordinary MP3 player and says, "It works" or even "It's fine," there are ten people who own an iPod and say, *"I love it!"* You can even state the relationship in the form of a simple equation:

M = F × E

That is, magnetic equals great functionality times great emotional appeal. Recognizing this reality, Chase also gave a lot of thought to the company's name, which she knew would help shape public perceptions of the brand. She and Danielson dreamed up several possible monikers and started gathering opinions from strangers on the streets of Boston. One name, Wheelshare, was quickly shot down because it sounded too much like wheelchair.

The next candidate was U.S. Carshare. Asking people about it, Chase was startled to discover that many had a deep-seated emotional aversion to the very concept of "car-sharing." "The word makes people nervous," she later explained.

> They feel they're being scolded or told to wait their turn. At that point I banned my staff from using the phrase "car sharing." Do we call hotels "bed sharing"? That's way too intimate. Do we call bowling "shoe sharing"? Who would want to bowl?

For the idealistic Robin Chase, the term *car-sharing* evoked all that was communal, earth-saving, and virtuous—but for the average American, it sounded weird and distasteful. Chase listened to her customers, and dropped the term.

Eventually Chase named the company Zipcar, evoking fun, hassle-banishing qualities like speed and convenience, and paired it with the slogan "Wheels When You Want Them." She deployed a small fleet of cars—funky lime-green Volkswagen Beetles, chosen for their hip look and eco-symbolism—first on the streets of Boston, then in Washington, D.C., and New York City. Zipcar was up and running.

And in response, nothing happened—the two most dreaded words in the world of demand creation.

Or almost nothing. In the first year, just seventy-five people signed up. Between 1999 and 2003, Zipcar grew steadily but very slowly, plateauing at just 6,000 members and 130 cars in three cities.

Chase labored creatively to infuse greater magnetism into her struggling product. She played up Zipcar's social mission, aiming to create buzz among young city-dwellers who shared her concern for the environment. She launched a company newsletter with community-building features like a "Caption This Photo" contest and letters from readers describing the oddest thing they'd done with their Zipcar. "Making customers feel like they have input and a stake in the game really makes them want you to succeed," Chase remarked. She invited members to a potluck dinner and remained ebullient despite having just twenty-five people show up. What matters, she explained, was "the four thousand people who think, 'How cool—I belong to a company that has potluck dinners.'"

It was all charming and fun. But it wasn't magnetic enough to trigger large-scale demand. Profitability was a distant vision. More deeply wedded to her green vision than ever, Chase remained optimistic. She joked that her vision was "world domination" and that she would consider Zipcar a success as soon as it was hit with an antitrust lawsuit. More seriously, she described her "death bed" dream as bringing the Zipcar system to countries like China, "before the dream of every child becomes what it is here: 'When I grow up and turn seventeen, I will get my own car.'" And she added, "Frankly, I have no doubt that is going to happen."

But as the months passed, Chase's investors began to grow restless. They worried that their zealous CEO was more focused on saving the world than on earning them a decent return on their money. In 2003, a $7 million round of mezzanine financing required to fund Zipcar's operations fell through at the last minute. Although Chase managed to locate an alternative source of funding, the company's board decided they'd had enough. They ousted Chase—the woman whose vision, creativity, and drive had been literally everything for Zipcar—and turned the reins over to Scott Griffith.

❏   ❏   ❏

GRIFFITH HAD WORKED at Boeing and Hughes Aircraft as well as two high-tech start-ups, one (Information America) a success, the other (Digital Goods) a failed early attempt to crack the e-book market. He'd also been a partner and principal at a couple of strategy and investment firms with connections in the world of private equity capital, which promised to be valuable in the ongoing quest for funding (a struggle Zipcar shared with many other would-be growth companies).

But the immediate challenge Griffith had to address was a different one. The Zipcar product crafted between 1999 and 2003 by Robin Chase and her team—call it Zipcar 1.0—was far more attractive than the original car-sharing operations. But its fitful sales growth showed that it lacked the critical characteristics needed to galvanize a really large customer base. The big question was, why?

Scott Griffith's chief job was the development of Zipcar 2.0—the irresistible product that Robin Chase had dreamed of but had been unable to build. It meant broadening Zipcar's appeal beyond dedicated environmentalists, emphasizing the ways it could improve daily life for any urban dweller. "This has to be a lifestyle choice that people make," Griffith declared, "because you're essentially trying to talk them out of a hundred years of marketing that they got from their car companies." It would take a shift of this magnitude to make the company grow into a viable business—in the words of board member Peter Aldrich, to "turn a political movement into a company."

Paradoxically, Griffith started by halting planned expansion efforts. "We had to prove the business model at the city level," he later explained. "The company hadn't really thought through what it would take to get to profitability."

There was no shortage of theories about what Zipcar needed to do to jump-start its growth. Some advocated an aggressive marketing and advertising campaign; perhaps billboards, posters, radio ads, and television commercials touting the benefits of Zipcar would prompt people to test the service. Others favored harnessing the power of free media through publicity events and messaging efforts like interviews and articles that appealed to people's civic sensibilities and environmental values. Still others proposed traditional merchandising schemes—dollars-off coupons, free trial memberships, Zipcar sign-up booths outside subway stations and inside shopping malls.

Instead, Griffith decided it was time to explore the mind-set of customers. To figure out why the Zipcar product lacked magnetism, Griffith held focus groups with fence-sitters—people who knew about Zipcar but for some reason had refrained from joining. What would motivate them to become Zipcar members? Griffith listened carefully to their comments, paying particular attention to the specific factors that were making the fence-sitters hesitate. In the process, he discovered that *growth itself*, if adequately focused, could eliminate many of the lingering hassles of car-sharing and greatly enhance Zipcar's visceral appeal.

With just a few Zipcars in any given city, would-be drivers often found that no car was available on evenings and weekend days when demand was greatest; often the nearest vehicle was parked a ten- or fifteen-block walk from their home. This might sound like a minor inconvenience, but tacking an extra half hour onto the Zipcar rental experience was enough to prevent most consumers from pressing the demand button.

As one Zipcar member told us, "If the nearest Zipcar were more than two blocks away, I would get annoyed having to walk there in the dead of night." Another said, "If the car was more than a five-minute walk from my door, I wouldn't bother." They speak for countless others.

This posed a tricky chicken-or-egg problem. How to make Zipcars plentifully available—and therefore popular—when Zipcar's lack of popularity was itself limiting the number of Zipcars available?

Griffith solved the puzzle by ingeniously redefining it. The key to Zipcar's future, he realized, was *density*. Vehicles had to be available very close to members to make the service a truly convenient substitute for car ownership. If Boston had, say, 200,000 Zipcar members and 8,000 cars, that would be no problem. The real challenge was for the company to *simulate* that level of penetration with a much smaller organization.

To achieve this effect, Griffith decided to concentrate Zipcar's efforts in just a few, carefully selected locations. Almost immediately, the demand-creating power of this approach became evident.

Rather than trying to stretch its fleets across the vast extent of entire cities, Zipcar consolidated them into relatively dense clusters in a few urban neighborhoods filled with prototypical Zipcar members: young and tech-savvy, environmentally conscious, and eager to economize. By focusing on districts where likely customers congregated, Zipcar could create density even while starting from a small base.

Zipcar assigned street teams to promote Zipcar "block by block, zip code by zip code" and launched colorful marketing campaigns tailored to particular neighborhoods. In a Washington, D.C., district filled with young, carless professionals, Zipcar dropped a battered sofa with a sign atop it reading "You need a Zipcar for this." Students from Boston's many universities found the city's T-line transit system plastered with Zipcar posters saying, "350 hours a year spent having sex. 420 hours looking for a parking space. What's wrong with this picture?"

Zipcar was acutely attuned to variations in demand. Different neighborhoods got different kinds of cars: eco-conscious Cambridge was stocked with hybrid Priuses, while Boston's posh Beacon Hill district was seeded with Volvos and BMWs. "We were like the coffee shop or the dry cleaner," Griffith recalls—a local company offering local services catering to local sensibilities. Zipcar was assiduous in identifying many different types of potential customers and tailoring product offerings and combinations to appeal to each of them.

Most important, the hyperlocal strategy enabled "instant density": In the chosen neighborhoods, Zipcars were thick on the ground, making them easily accessible as well as readily recognizable. The math was compelling: Put one Zipcar location in a neighborhood like the ten-square-block area of central Cambridge, and the average customer had to walk ten minutes to reach it. Increase it to seven locations and the average walk was cut to five minutes; grow past twenty locations and the walk shrank to two minutes. With each increase, the value provided to customers soared.

Griffith's instant-density strategy ignited an upward growth spiral. In the chosen neighborhoods, people got used to spotting Zipcars on the street and started asking their friends about them. Once a critical mass of local residents became Zipsters (as Zipcar members call themselves), the company expanded to the next community over . . . then to the next, and then the next.

It's a remarkable truth about demand, and human nature: We let little things govern big decisions. Zipsters save thousands of dollars a year compared with car owners, not to mention countless hours dealing with hassles like parking, maintenance, repairs, and insurance. Yet what catalyzes their decision to go with Zipcar is often the discovery that a car is available five minutes from home rather than ten minutes. The five-minute difference, it seems, is the tiny trigger that's even more powerful than huge savings.

Suddenly people by the thousands began to discover the magnetic properties of Zipcar—and to talk about them to friends, family, and acquaintances. "No more spending eighty bucks and investing time in travel and paperwork to rent a car when I want to visit my friends in the suburb," one Zipster told us. "Now I jump in the nearest Zipcar, spend more time with my friends, and pay less than half as much money."

"My wife's a professional photographer," said another. "She uses

Zipcar three or four times a month to tote her equipment when shoot-ing a wedding. Otherwise, she'd have to buy a car—a big investment she can definitely do without."

"We can do things with Zipcar we could never do without it," said a third. "We've stopped using a grocery delivery service, and we save money by buying a *case* of wine instead of a bottle or two. Last week, we brought home a Christmas tree tied to the roof of our Zipcar. Try doing *that* on the subway!"

"I love using a Zipcar for business meetings," said yet another. "My clients ask about it—they think it's cool!"

Encouraged by the sudden growth spurt, Griffith soon found other ways to achieve instant density and its magnetic appeal. In the process, he also attracted new types of customers to Zipcar.

One approach was to partner with universities by providing cars for use by students and faculty. Most colleges fit perfectly into Zip-car's demographic sweet spot: They were densely populated com-munities with lots of young, tech-savvy, environmentally conscious, and cash-strapped individuals who needed cars for occasional trips and chores. And university administrators typically spent inordinate chunks of time wrestling with the problems of student drivers, such as parking rules; they appreciated any program that would reduce their car-related hassles. ("Customers" aren't just end users of a prod-uct. Zipcar turned college deans into "customers" by fixing the deans' hassles with student drivers. Demand is a highly complex game that can be played on several levels at once.)

In 2004, Griffith worked out a deal with Wellesley College to pro-vide Zipcars with discounted insurance costs for its under-twenty-one drivers. The safety results were so good that Griffith took the data to his insurer, Liberty Mutual, and persuaded them to offer an even better rate at three more colleges. When the results there were just as good, Griffith parlayed them into a series of additional deals.

Now the company has crafted partnerships with more than 150 colleges and universities that offer huge long-term demand-growing possibilities to Zipcar. Students under twenty-five are delighted to discover they are eligible to rent from Zipcar, which is *not* the case with most traditional car rental outfits. When those students graduate, will they automatically switch to Hertz or Avis, or will habit and gratitude combine to keep them as loyal Zipcar customers? Zipcar hopes for the latter.

Griffith also began promoting Zipcar as the "company car" for small businesses that need a vehicle occasionally—to pick up a client or to make a sales call, for example. This new customer type broadened demand for Zipcar's product across another dimension—time. Most of Zipcar's core customers want cars on evenings and weekends, leaving them parked and unproductive during ordinary business hours. The small-company and corporate clients Griffith and his team courted helped pick up the nine-to-five slack, turning those hours into revenue generators for Zipcar and helping to improve the company's finances. By 2009, business customers were producing 15 percent of Zipcar's revenues, and as of late 2010, ten thousand companies had signed on as clients.

Achieving density was crucial to the magnetic appeal of Zipcar 2.0. But Griffith also instituted other changes to eliminate the remaining hassles that discouraged would-be customers. For example, Zipcar customers had been required to pay a per-mile charge after each rental. They hated watching the miles tick away, each tick costing them money. In Zipcar 2.0, 180 free miles were included with each rental.

In its new incarnation, Robin Chase's dream of a car-sharing system that could support a mass-market industry was now showing definite signs of life. While retaining the emotional appeal of being hip and eco-friendly, Zipcar had become increasingly magnetic by reducing or eliminating the hassles of car ownership for a growing array of customer types. As one Zipster puts it, "I like the idea of being green, but I can guarantee you I'm doing this because it puts more green in my pocket." She's typical: Practically every Zipster we spoke to cites the convenience and affordability of the service as its chief attractions, with "the idea of being green" a distant third.

Even seemingly unpredictable hassles are eased by the Zipcar system. One member reported losing his Zipcard halfway through a rental (he was moving from one apartment to another and probably dropped the card while schlepping boxes). He called Zipcar and learned from the service agent that a spare card was hidden in the car. He found the spare and had it immediately activated over the phone.

Another New York–based Zipster recounts this story:

> We were taking a trip with my parents and my kids to do the whole colonial Williamsburg thing, so we took the train to D.C., and reserved a Zipcar minivan in D.C. I did it instead of renting a car because it was actually cheaper because of gas and insurance and the amount of miles that we were going. But then I got an e-mail saying that they were taking the minivan out of service for that weekend because they had to fix it. So I called Zipcar, explained the situation, and they said, "Well, we'll change the maintenance schedule so you can still have it that weekend."
>
> So they changed the maintenance schedule, and then somebody else went online and reserved it before I could. And so I called Zipcar about it again, and they called the other member and explained, "This other person had it first." They did all of that so I could have this one van on this one weekend. I got the swagger wagon and they saved the family vacation. I love them for that.

Later in this book, we'll explore the crucial role in demand creation played by what we call the *backstory*—factors that most customers never see or think about but which contribute to the ease, convenience, affordability, flexibility, and fun of using a product or service. Zipcar works, in part, because it gets the backstory details right. High density in Zipcar neighborhoods guarantees proximity and convenience, the cars are regularly cleaned and maintained, the RFID chips work, the insurance paperwork is taken care of, and the Global Positioning System (GPS) devices in the vehicles ensure that the cars are where the company says they are.

The resulting product is magnetic—incredibly so. When we asked Zipsters whether they'd recommended the service to friends or acquaintances in the past month, an amazing 88 percent answered yes—a full 28 points higher than the closest competing car rental service. And 80 percent agreed with the statement "I love this product"—a 30-point edge over the nearest rival.

When journalist Mary Morgan finally decided, after years of struggling with her car addiction, to give Zipcar a try, density was one of the reasons why: She enrolled in the service as soon as Zipcars popped up within ten minutes of her home. But there were lots of other reasons:

> Zipcar also makes the barrier to joining relatively low. There's a $25 sign-up fee, plus a $50 annual membership fee. Beyond that, you pay $8 per hour for the use of a car.* You have to reserve your car online—a straightforward process that took me less than five minutes—but if it turns out you need it longer than you thought, you can call and get more time. Cars can be reserved and used 24/7.
>
> My first Zipcar trip was impressive in that it was totally mundane. The car I'd reserved was in the exact spot that Zipcar had told me, via e-mail, it would be located—though initially I went to the wrong parking lot, and had to ask a passer-by where the Zipcars were parked. Luckily, she knew. The Zipcard I'd received in the mail, which looks like a credit card, did exactly what it was supposed to: I held it over a spot clearly indicated on the upper-right corner of the front windshield, and the doors unlocked. The key was in a compartment between the front seats,

---

* Zipcar's current sign-up fees, annual membership fees, and hourly rates vary over time and by location.

the car was relatively clean inside and out, it didn't smell like smoke or wet dogs, and the gas tank was half full.

Did I mention you don't pay for gas? Or insurance and maintenance?

The seamless convenience of Zipcar is transforming a vague, inchoate *need* on the part of millions of Americans—the need for mobility without the annoying hassles we usually take for granted— into concrete, actionable *demand* for something entirely new: the ability to quickly and conveniently access a car without owning it.

Even more remarkably, this transformation has been accompanied by a dramatic psychological change on the part of Zipcar customers. Having experienced Zipcar, Morgan now wonders, "How have I come to equate freedom with being encumbered by a costly, 3,000-pound, environmentally damaging machine that's used by pretty much just one person?"

Thanks to Zipcar, Mary Morgan's definition of freedom has actually changed. What's more, *she has a need she never had before*—a need that Zipcar creates and satisfies in a single stroke.

It's the story of demand creation in a nutshell.

TODAY, ZIPCAR and its magnetic product are drawing a growing number of Americans away from their love affair with the car. They are succeeding where generations of well-intentioned social engineers failed, and in the process they've created a brand-new form of demand—to say nothing of one of today's fastest-growing businesses. Since 2002, Zipcar revenues have been growing at 92 percent per year. Today there are more than 7,000 Zipcars serving some 400,000 individual customers and 10,000 corporate clients in more than 50 cities and over 150 universities around the United States and Canada as well as in London. Thousands of Zipsters have given up car ownership altogether. Zipcar has grown into a $131 million business that is projecting growth into the billion-dollar range by 2020.

Now 13 million people live within a ten-minute walk of a Zip-car parking space—4.5 million in New York City alone. In a recent interview, CEO Griffith observed, "Ninety-five percent of people living in the fifteen largest cities don't need to own cars. If we were to sign up just 5 percent of them, that gets us to a million members and a billion dollars. There are already many neighborhoods—in Brooklyn, in Washington, in Cambridge—where 10 to 13 percent of the over-twenty-one population are Zipcar members. And it's not slowing down."

Zipcar still faces challenges. As of the end of 2010, the company as a whole was on the verge of achieving profitability (having gone into the black in each of its most successful city locations). To attract new customer types and continue to enhance their financial results, Griffith and his team are launching several innovative moves.

For example, Zipcar is testing a program to cluster cars at commuter train stations to provide "last mile" transportation for business-people traveling to suburban locations for meetings. It's also providing fleet management services for government agencies. The biggest deal is with the municipal government of Washington, D.C., which reportedly pays Zipcar a one-time $1,500 fee to install its software and technology into city cars as well as a $115 per-vehicle monthly maintenance fee. Washington has already sold off more than one hundred city-owned cars and trimmed expenses by $1.1 million. This new product uses Zipcar's smarts, powered by information technology (IT), to serve a different set of customers and unlock a new layer of profitable demand. As Scott Griffith has said, "We use information as a competitive advantage. You name it—we track it, analyze it, and base every major decision on the information we glean from our systems." Or, as Griffith summarizes the Zipcar business, "At core we're an IT and marketing company—we just happen to have a lot of cars."

In the years to come, Zipcar's leadership of the car-sharing industry it created will face competitive challenges. Car rental giant Hertz has already launched a car-sharing business, a near clone of Zipcar called Connect by Hertz that is currently available in New York, London, and Paris. It'll be fascinating to watch how the rivalry will unfold. Hertz has brand recognition, size, and financial resources on its side. But Zipcar has a decade-long head start, as well as a huge edge in density. As of mid-2010, Zipcar boasted 158 locations in Boston; Hertz had just seven. If you wanted to hop in a car for a quick errand, which would *you* consider more magnetic?

❐   ❐   ❐

WHAT EXPLAINS HOW Zipcar succeeded in creating a magnetic product and attracting a powerful stream of demand when past car-sharing operations had failed?

Zipcar became possible right around the time it happened. In the late 1990s, thanks to technological innovations (including Internet-based communication, wireless telephony, and smart cards), economic developments (such as increasing volatility in the cost of fuel), and social trends (such as burgeoning environmental consciousness among young Americans), a simple and convenient system for car-sharing was finally practical.

In this sense, the success of Zipcar might appear predictable—the inevitable result of external, historical circumstances. But appearances can be deceiving.

Circumstances must be right. Yet demand creation requires much more. Robin Chase was shrewd enough to design her company not from the inside out, based on strategic objectives or financial goals, but from the outside in, based on the enormous gap between what customers were buying—cars, with all their expenses and hassles—and what they really wanted—the freedom of instant mobility. And even then, Zipcar teetered on the edge of collapse for years and might easily have gone under if Scott Griffith and his team hadn't finally figured out how to redesign Chase's creation so as to push it over the invisible dividing line that separates the ho-hum from the gotta-have-it.

Demand creators understand that demand is amazingly fragile. The absence of one critical variable or a flaw in a single crucial detail can negate thousands of hours of hard work, imagination, and perseverance. So great demand creators dedicate themselves to constant experimentation, seeking out and fixing every conceivable weakness in their product and their organizational design.

They know, at a visceral level, that in the world of demand, nothing is really inevitable.

From Ho-Hum to Gotta-Have-It: Wegmans Makes Groceries Magnetic

It was May 1969. Danny Wegman, a young economics major at Harvard University, was putting the finishing touches on his senior thesis, a research study analyzing the business prospects of America's fastest-growing retailing sector—the discount store.

At the time, the discounting phenomenon was relatively new. Traditional department stores still channeled a huge share of the demand for merchandise like clothing, housewares, appliances, furniture, and toys. Giant "category killers" like Toys 'R' Us were just beginning to appear. But a regional chain of discount stores by the name of Walmart, run by a family-owned company that was still a year away from its initial public stock offering, was about to embark on thirty years of explosive growth, during which it would use its unmatched merchandising skills, logistical systems, and ever-growing pricing clout to achieve dominance in one retail market after another.

By the 1980s, the Bentonville, Arkansas–based giant would set its sights on a whole new industry—groceries. Its weapon: a formidable new retailing format called the Supercenter, which combined general merchandise and groceries in the same store. The Supercenter would enable families to make one shopping trip instead of two or more, stock up on everything they needed, and enjoy Walmart's legendary low prices for everything they bought.

In 1969, these radical developments were still far in the future. But young Danny Wegman was already worrying about them.

Wegman's interest in the topic was not academic or theoretical, but personal. Over the last several decades, his family had built a network of unusual and extremely successful grocery stores in northwestern New York state. Landmarks in their communities, the Wegmans stores were beloved by customers and had provided a good living for generations of family merchants. Now the discounters, led by Walmart, were heading their way—not in the next year or two, but surely within the next two decades.

Danny Wegman was acutely aware of what could happen to traditional family retailers in the wake of Walmart's arrival. With its "everyday low prices" and enormous selection of merchandise, Walmart was already looking like an apparently unbeatable competitor. And with just a bit of imagination, Wegman could see how the grocery business must look to the hungry, talented innovators at Walmart: a huge, sleepy industry dominated by a handful of lackluster companies, ripe for the plucking.

What can you do when an unbeatable competitor is aiming directly at the heart of your business?

Wegman typed the final sentence of his thesis—"The mass merchandiser is the most serious outside competitor to ever face the food industry"—rolled the finished page carefully from his typewriter, and tucked the complete manuscript in a manila envelope, ready for delivery to his adviser. He sighed, ran his hands through his unruly red hair, and leaned back in his desk chair.

"Brilliant analysis, Mister Expert," Danny said to himself, his facial expression a curious half grimace, half smile. "An A-plus paper, for sure. But soon the real test begins. *When the discounters arrive, what the heck are we going to do about it?*"

❏   ❏   ❏

IT MAY BE EASY to see how a product like the iPhone, with its sleek design and its remarkable technology, can be magnetic for millions of people. It may even be easy to see—after the fact—how a hip, innovative company like Zipcar could make its lifestyle-enhancing product magnetically attractive for thousands of young city dwellers. But is it possible for people to have the same level of emotional connection with *any* product—even one as mundane and familiar as a grocery store?

If you ever have the opportunity to meet our friend Stephen, simply say one word: *Wegmans.* Then observe as one of the most articulate and analytical people we know struggles to describe his love for a chain of grocery stores he now rarely visits.

Stephen lives in Boston, but he grew up in Rochester in upstate New York, in the heart of the region where the Wegmans stores are located. To this day, twenty years after leaving, he can't quite get Wegmans out of his head. Ask him to explain, and his eyes narrow, his hands move in circling gestures, his sentences falter. "It's hard to describe," he says, "because Wegmans really isn't like any other store—or anything else, for that matter. When I walk in, the total effect—the high ceilings, the subdued lighting, the vast field of fresh produce stretching out in front of me, the glimpse of brick ovens in the bakery on one side and the gleam of coolers with prepared foods on the other side—is just indescribable.

"It's not like a typical competing supermarket," he continues, "because compared to Wegmans even the best leave me wondering 'Is that all there is?' It's not like one of those open-air European markets, because Wegmans is so much cleaner and more welcoming. It's a little like the queuing area to a great theme park attraction, where somebody has thought about every possible detail to capture a mood and fill you with excitement and anticipation. Or like the atrium of a beautiful and well-designed office building or hotel. But it's not really like any of these things. It's like—well, it's like Wegmans!"

If you wonder whether it's possible for a supermarket to be magnetic, just think about Stephen. And we know many more like him—otherwise normal people who get a little emotional when the subject of Wegmans comes up.

To anyone who has visited a Wegmans store, the features that produce its unique magnetic appeal may seem obvious. There's its vast size—for example, the Wegmans we recently visited in Woodbridge, New Jersey, boasts twenty-six aisles of grocery products, not counting the huge sections devoted to produce, meat, fish, baked goods, deli items, frozen foods, prepared foods, cheeses, olives . . .

Then there's the shocking range and variety of goods that this vast size makes possible. Many supermarkets nowadays have a small selection of cooked-on-the-premises foods for quick takeout dinners—but at Wegmans we counted nine different kinds of prepackaged vegetables alone, from crispy roasted potatoes with garlic and rosemary to cauliflower and spinach gratin to soft polenta with parmigiano reggiano. Lots of supermarkets have a few trays of packaged sushi on sale—but at Wegmans we watched two uniformed sushi chefs at work behind a fifteen-foot-long counter displaying dozens of varieties of sushi and an array of Japanese accompaniments like seaweed salads and edamame. Lots of supermarkets have a few exotic fruits for sale, like kiwis, mangoes, and star fruits—but at Wegmans we saw those alongside jicama, rambutan, cherimoya, dragonfruit, fuyu persimmons, tamarinds, kiwano melons, white coconuts, and maradol papayas. We also saw a forty-foot-wide display of various kinds of tea . . . nine varieties of mushrooms . . . fourteen varieties of olives . . . three hundred varieties of cheese . . .

. We could go on, but the point is clear: The *surface* attractions that make Wegmans magnetic are obvious and overwhelming. They are the reasons that last year the chain received more than seven thousand letters from customers in regions where *no* Wegmans store exists, most of them begging the company to come to town; they're the reasons that Wegmans customers crowd Internet food sites like Chow.com with the kind of conversation-starting comments that magnetic products always generate among customers, usually ranging from positive to engaged to excited—comments like "I personally believe that the best of all American grocery stores is the Wegmans chain," and "Simply stated, Wegmans is the category killer to end all category killers," and "Wegmans bends over backwards in customer service. Once I called the store to complain about an error made in the butcher shop. The meat manager recut my six fillets and delivered them to my door one hour later along with a gift certificate for my inconvenience. That's when they won me over for life!"

These reactions raise the question: If the magnetic qualities that attract huge demand to Wegmans are so overwhelming and so obvious, why doesn't every supermarket chain simply do the same?

The answer: The qualities that make Wegmans magnetic may be obvious, but creating them was far from simple. It took some sharply against-the-grain thinking and behavior over a period of decades, starting in the early days when Wegmans was a tiny upstart competing against giant rivals.

The first Wegmans was opened in Rochester, New York, in 1930 by brothers John and Walter Wegman. It quickly won national attention for its retailing experiments, from the first refrigerated display windows and a three-hundred-seat in-store cafeteria to the pioneering use of water vapor sprays to keep counters full of produce fresh. Some of these innovations (like the cafeteria) went by the wayside; others (like the produce sprays) spread industry-wide. But all reflected

Wegmans' reluctance to follow the mainstream in an industry in which the 1930s and 1940s were dominated by store consolidations, chain expansions, no-frills merchandising, cost cutting, and a continual quest for greater sales volume at almost any cost.

It wasn't obvious that Wegmans could survive in such a climate. But it did, thanks to the loyalty it attracted from hometown customers in its relatively small geographic base in western New York and Pennsylvania. From 1950 to 1976, the stores multiplied, slowly but steadily, under the leadership of Walter's son Robert Wegman, a famously brilliant and feisty innovator who described his "philosophy about merchandising" as "To do something that no one else is doing, and to be able to offer the customer a choice she doesn't have at the moment." To this day, Wegmans team members quote that speech, especially its emphasis on doing the *opposite* of what your rivals are doing—and they strive to live by it.

It's easy for companies that achieve great success to become complacent and stop adapting to changing conditions. Wegmans avoided that trap. Part of its secret was simply paying close attention to emerging industry trends and striving to stay ahead of them. That's the significance of Danny Wegman's senior thesis at Harvard. His prediction that creative mass merchandisers like Sam Walton represented the most important challenge to the grocery industry came to pass when Walmart opened its first superstore, with a complete grocery selection, in 1988.

By that time, Danny had already taken over as president and CEO of the company. Under his leadership, the chain has survived the Walmart challenge through continual enhancement of its stores' magnetic qualities, and it has expanded to its current roster (as of late 2010) of seventy-seven stores.

And when changing customer needs demand it, Wegmans is prepared to adjust its business practices in ways that might seem painful but help the product remain magnetic.

When the economic downturn hit in 2008, Danny Wegman

predicted that, over time, the recession would reduce his company's costs, since commodity and fuel prices generally decline in a business slowdown. That would enable Wegmans to hold the line on prices, which in turn would help its customers. Remarkably, however, Wegmans didn't wait for the expected downturn in costs. Instead, it proactively selected hundreds of staple items for price reductions—the equivalent of $12 million worth of discounts—in order to ease the burden of food shopping for cash-strapped families.

"During difficult times like these, it's OK with us if we make a little less money," Danny Wegman explained.

The Wegmans story suggests that creating a magnetic product requires a willingness to take the nonobvious, counterintuitive steps—to "offer the customer a choice she doesn't have," in Robert Wegman's words. But of course there's more to it than that.

We've discovered a half-dozen common threads that link many of the world's most magnetic products and the people who've created them. These behaviors don't add up to a "formula" for creating a magnetic product—nothing so complex can be reduced to a mere formula. But an organization that fails to practice them is highly unlikely to find itself with a magnetic product on its hands.

Let's take a closer look at these six behaviors, one by one, and see how Wegmans has used them to bring an amazing degree of magnetism to an industry largely dominated by me-too thinking and undistinguished offerings.

❏   ❏   ❏

Great demand creators eliminate or reduce the hassles that make most products and services inconvenient, costly, unpleasant, and frustrating. Grocery shopping has more than its share of hassles. From wilted produce, lackluster meats, and out-of-stock specials to hard-to-navigate aisles, malfunctioning shopping carts, and indifferent salesclerks, most supermarkets present an obstacle course of hassles that millions of shoppers dread. Wegmans hasn't eliminated every shopping hassle. But they've made greater progress toward reducing them than others, and they think they're just getting started.

Take the hassle that surveys show irritates shoppers the most (even more than high prices): long, slow checkout lines. You might assume that the vast size of a Wegmans store (over 110,000 square feet versus the industry average 45,000) would make it an inconvenient, time-wasting place to shop. But Wegmans has gone to extraordinary lengths to prevent this. When we visited on a Sunday afternoon, we found nineteen out of twenty-six cash register lanes up and running, each with no more than two customers waiting in line. And fast? Posted on a bulletin board right by the checkout lines, for everyone to see, were computer printouts reporting the number of items scanned per minute by the cashiers on each shift for the past week, with inspirational messages appended, from "12.44—We Can Do Better!" to "14.26—Good Job Everyone, Let's Get 14.5 Next Time!"

Wegmans takes the issue of fast checkout *very* seriously. (Robert Wegman was famous for watching checkout counters and getting very nervous if customers were waiting too long.) As a result, you can get in and out of a giant Wegmans faster than you can at many convenience stores. Our friend Stephen remarks, "Last time my family spent the weekend with my folks in Rochester, I ended up visiting the nearest Wegmans *six times*. It's just the fastest and most convenient place to go. Once I made an emergency run to pick up some cold medicine for my son. It was the middle of the night, but they had six registers working. I was headed back home inside of five minutes."

Wegmans has developed many other hassle-reducing innovations. Toddlers in tow? There are special parking spaces within a few feet of the entrance dedicated to families with small kids, and most stores feature a chaperoned kids' room where youngsters can play while parents shop. Many stores even have checkout aisles marked with "No Candy" signs. Parents can select those lanes knowing that the children propped up in their carts won't be begging for candies temptingly displayed at eye level.

And yet another shopping hassle—a subtle one most consumers take for granted—is the need to visit several stores to get all your food buying done. Wegmans is the single source that is as good as multiple specialized stores. Many Wegmans customers report they can now accomplish as much in one trip to Wegmans as they used to accomplish by visiting a mainstream grocery store, a natural foods store, a butcher, a bakery, a greengrocer, a fish market, and a deli . . . and all without compromising on product or service quality.

In fact, some industry analysts say that Wegmans is leading the evolution of the grocery business toward what they call the "Whole Mart" future—a blend of the best features of Whole Foods (freshness, quality, eco-friendliness, health consciousness, uniqueness) and Walmart (price, size, convenience).

Great demand creators enhance great functionality with emotional excitement. A magnetic product fulfills its essential purpose superlatively well. Then it does much, much more.

In Wegmans' case, selling high-quality ingredients is only the start of what they do. One example among many: the stores' prepared foods, which are a godsend for busy families, working couples, elderly folks, and students with little knowledge of or equipment for cooking. And with their reasonable prices—for example, the rows of four-dollar entrées we saw on display during one visit—Wegmans offers a speedy, healthful, and flavorful alternative to the fast foods many cash-strapped families resort to.

But Wegmans also provides lots of engaging ways to help people become proficient, enthusiastic home cooks. They hire world-class chefs to demonstrate cooking techniques and favorite recipes. They sprinkle the store with signs, flyers, posters, and brochures suggesting menu combinations and offering mini-lessons on planning meals. They train staffers to absorb and share fascinating information about food—where it comes from, how it's grown, imaginative ways to prepare it. They suggest wine and microbrew pairings to enhance meals and, where local laws permit, even display the complementary beverages right alongside the appropriate meat, fish, or vegetable. They publish a lavish four-color magazine, *Menu,* that is sent free to every holder of a Wegmans discount card and features really imaginative, interesting cooking ideas along with chef interviews, articles about great food-producing regions, and nutrition advice. And with the unsurpassed range and variety of products Wegmans sells (an average of sixty thousand items in stock, 42 percent higher than the industry norm), they make it easy for customers to become more imaginative and venturesome when it comes to making menu choices for their families. For many, getting dinner on the table morphs from a daily chore to be finished as quickly and cheaply as possible into a creative pastime in which entire families get happily involved. You don't *have* to become a gourmet to appreciate Wegmans—but thousands do.

Magnetic products enhance the emotional content of people's lives by enabling them to do things better, more easily, and more pleasurably. Zipcar does it for transportation, providing cars that are convenient, fun, and even coolly stylish (with a BMW available for that special night out). Wegmans does it for the enjoyment of great food, helping customers not just to eat better but to participate creatively in the excitement of food culture. And, of course, in the process they generate a huge stream of new demand for the goods and services they sell.

Great demand creators make every employee a demand creator. We're fascinated by successful CEOs and entrepreneurs—people like Reed Hastings, Steve Jobs, and Jeff Bezos. And sometimes a brilliantly creative individual plays a major role in the development of a magnetic product. But the truth is that demand creation is almost never driven by a single person. It's the product of efforts by an entire team of people who understand that creating demand is their chief mission and who use the resources and processes at their disposal to do just that, day in and day out. In fact, in organizations that have mastered demand creation, the process is fractal, following a similar pattern at every level of the organization, from the CEO to the supervisor to the frontline employee.

Robert Wegman, son of cofounder Walter Wegman, understood this truth. The first thing he did after being named president in 1950 was to raise everyone's salary—a hugely symbolic act in the notoriously low-margin grocery business, where skimping on salaries is the norm. This gesture told the world, "At Wegmans, we don't just *say* that people are our most important asset—we intend to *act* like it."

He and the rest of the company's leadership went on to develop a unique set of policies for recruiting, training, compensating, and retaining employees. As a result, they built the most dedicated, best-educated, most highly motivated team of any supermarket in the country. And then they set these remarkable people loose to use their knowledge, creativity, and good judgment in the daily work of caring for customers.

Today, average salaries at Wegmans remain consistently higher than the industry standard. Every Wegmans employee receives benefits that include a 401(k) plan with matching company contributions and a defined-contribution retirement plan funded by the company. Everyone from master bakers to stock clerks gets full medical benefits (although since 2005 employees have been required to contribute a portion of the cost). Wegmans' employee scholarship program will pay a full-time worker up to $2,200 per year for four years, a part-timer up to $1,500. There's no limit on the field of study or the kind of degree being pursued. Since its launch in 1984, the company has supported education for 24,000 employees for a total of over $77 million.

Other benefits are even more unconventional. Senior vice president Mark Ferrera says, "I spend 95 percent of my time helping the employees," and his strategies have included everything from subsidizing monthly bus passes for workers at the Wegmans store in Princeton, New Jersey, to sponsoring an annual Cinco de Mayo celebration that the employees enjoy even more than the customers.

Employee training at Wegmans is also unique in the industry. If you get a job in the meat or fish department, you're expected to pass a thirty- to fifty-five-hour educational program about your specialty. Sometimes the training programs are indistinguishable from perks. Cheese manager Terri Zodarecky was sent on a company-paid ten-day trip to England, France, and Italy to sample new products and learn from master cheese makers. Other department heads have been sent overseas to learn about wines, pastries, and organic farming techniques.

Treating your team members well is important. It may earn you a spot on *Fortune* magazine's annual "Best Companies to Work For" list. (Wegmans has appeared at or near the top of the rankings every single year and in 2005 was named to *Fortune*'s "Best Companies Hall of Fame.") It also makes it easy for you to recruit and retain the very best talent. The star power Wegmans brings to the food business is stunning. Pierre Hermé, once dubbed "the Picasso of pastry" by *Vogue* magazine, has trained Wegmans bakers to make his specialty tartes, pastries, and French toast bagels. Famed chef David Bouley (winner of the James Beard Foundation's Best Chef prize and proprietor of the top-ranked restaurant in Zagat's New York ratings) helped design some of Wegmans' prepared-food entrées. The sous-chef at Wegmans' Pittsford, New York, store is Charles Saccardi, who previously worked for Thomas Keller, proprietor of Napa Valley's French Laundry restaurant.

But even more important, Wegmans gives its many gifted employees the power to meet customer needs using creativity and flair, following their own best judgment rather than rules in a manual. It's hard to overstate the attraction this creates for really desirable workers. A pastry chef who was asked why he'd left a more lucrative career in the restaurant business to join Wegmans replied, with a shrug, "Are you kidding? All my old friends from there want to come and work here. We are doing much more creative work than I ever did in the restaurant game."

Attracting and retaining this kind of team gives rise to the tales of customer service that have become legendary among Wegmans fans—like the time a Wegmans chef rescued a frantic customer whose Thanksgiving turkey turned out to be too big for her oven by roasting it for her at the store. Similar customer-thrilling deeds on a smaller scale are repeated every day—when a salesclerk takes it upon herself to offer a free dinner to a customer who found her last one disappointing, or a team of employees stands waiting with umbrellas to escort shoppers to their cars during a sudden downpour.

Robert Wegman and son Danny have both been great demand creators. But the CEO can't be everywhere. A big part of the genius of Wegmans is a system that turns thirty thousand team members into demand creators in their own right. The ultimate outcome? An unequaled stream of demand for the combination of great foods and amazing services that Wegmans offers.

However, organizational leaders must remember that they can't simply *buy* a team of demand creators. Good pay is important in attracting the best workers. (It also reduces the need for employees to moonlight at second jobs and the time they spend worrying about personal finances.) But as real-life experience teaches, and as many experimental studies have confirmed, an extra dollar or two alone won't unleash employees' passion. The difference lies in what social psychologists refer to as "social norms," which operate separately from the "market norms" that most businesspeople focus on.

Market norms are about paying for what you get. Fair exchange is the driving force, and emotional connections play a minimal role. By contrast, the world of social norms is the world of community, where people help one another out of feelings of friendship, mutual respect, and shared responsibility, without any expectation of immediate payback. In this world, financial reward is only partially relevant to our behavior, and in fact excessive focus on money can easily destroy the positive power of social norms. (Try offering to *pay* your best friend for helping you move a sofa, or your spouse for fixing you dinner, and watch how quickly your relationship gets damaged.) So combining social norms with market norms is an important but delicate balancing act.

Wegmans is one of the few companies that has successfully infused its employee relationships with the leavening power of social norms. Like many employers, it talks about "treating our people like family"—and it actually follows through. Adopt a baby and you get an assistance package including time off to welcome the newcomer and a check to help defray expenses. Start college and you can hand your supervisor your class schedule knowing your hours will be adjusted to match your availability. Stories circulate like the one about the clerk fretting about an overdue electric bill who found out that Wegmans had quietly interceded with the utility company to make sure his lights stayed on.

Having been treated like family, Wegmans employees reciprocate, passing the feeling along to customers. That's why Wegmans stores, and their people, become part of the local community to a far deeper, richer extent than other supermarkets.

Danny Wegman sums up the company's reliance on its people with his comment, "It's our knowledge that can help the customer. So the first pump we have to prime is our own people." And Wegmans executive Jack DePeters makes the same point when he remarks, only half jokingly, that Wegmans is "a three-billion-dollar company run by sixteen-year-old cashiers."

And they run it amazingly well.

Great demand creators have the guts to listen to customers. Practically all of the Wegmans innovations we've mentioned can be traced back to one or more company employees who really listened to customers. But here's an example that illustrates the process especially vividly.

In early 2008, Wegmans launched an online shopping tool to make life easier for their customers. It was pretty good. Customers could use it to build personal shopping lists to ensure they didn't forget the things they needed when visiting their favorite Wegmans store. Sale items were highlighted, you could find online recipes and select ingredients, and lists were easy to print out and save. Customers liked the tool, and Wegmans could have let it go at that. Most retailers would have been proud to have added such a convenient twenty-first-century information-age service to make things easier for customers.

So far, so normal. Then something not-so-normal happened. A few customers who used the shopping tool sent Wegmans e-mails or left phone messages offering suggestions for improvement. Some had complaints about software glitches they encountered. Others provided wish lists of features they'd like to see. And Wegmans actually listened.

With the help of usability experts from the Rochester Institute of Technology, Wegmans convened meetings with a cross section of customers—some enthusiastic users of Wegmans.com, others who found it flawed, and still others who'd never used it at all. Together they crafted a series of changes and improvements to the website and the shopping tools it provided. When the revised version of the list maker was rolled out in February 2009, it boasted a raft of new applications. Now the site lets you add or subtract items from your list with a single click. Tap the "Jump Start Your List" button and you get a starter list to edit with the twenty-six items people buy most often. Use the "Wellness Key" to build a list tailored to your specific health needs—a low-salt or gluten-free diet, for example. Pick a tempting recipe from the site and all the necessary ingredients are added to your shopping list instantly—in the amounts required for the dish. Finally, name the Wegmans store you most often visit and your list will be printed in an order that matches the store's layout, so you never have to retrace your steps in search of an item you missed.

These features and more were added to the website as a direct result of customer input. After using the new online shopping tool, one Wegmans customer, who happened to be an IT professional, wrote the company a note calling it perhaps "the most extraordinary software she'd ever used."

Listening to customers isn't always easy. But it can pay off in amazing ways.

Great demand creators experiment constantly. Creating a magnetic product isn't a one-time challenge. Customers change: They develop new interests, needs, preferences, and problems. The business environment changes, too: New competitors arise, technologies evolve, and economic sectors rise and fall. Great demand creators know that the job of updating and improving their magnetic product begins the same day it goes on sale. Building a steep trajectory of improvement means customers will continue to be excited by the product, and demand will continue to grow.

Wegmans prides itself on leading the grocery business in innovation. Practically every major technological advance in food retailing has landed at Wegmans first. Spurred on by Robert Wegman, the chain started using bar codes on products in the early seventies, and by 1999 it was pioneering (with Nabisco) in the creation of a joint retailer-and-manufacturer program for planning, forecasting, and replenishing supplies. In 2002, Danny Wegman helped launch an industry-wide campaign to reduce costly product data inaccuracies in supplier-retailer systems that has led to, among other benefits, the first third-party certification program for data quality in the food business. And in 2007, Wegmans was among the first supermarkets to test the use of radio frequency identification (RFID) technology to get fresh meat to customers faster.

Wegmans is equally innovative beyond technology. In 2007, spurred by the boom in demand for natural food products, Wegmans launched its own Organic Research Farm not far from Danny Wegman's home in Canandaigua, New York. Although Wegmans has ongoing relationships with more than five hundred local farmers, it has trouble getting reliable year-round supplies of organic produce for all its stores (just as Walmart, Whole Foods, and other large chains do). The goal of Wegmans' research farm is to develop new techniques for growing organic produce in the chilly Northeast that other growers can learn from and emulate.

By 2010, the farm was supplying produce to two Wegmans stores and boasting about unexpected successes—for example, an early season crop of ripe grape and cherry tomatoes grown in an organic greenhouse. "We're excited because one of our goals is to find ways to extend the growing season in the Northeast," said team leader Jim Heberle. "We aimed for ripe tomatoes before Memorial Day and we made it!"

Wegmans team members at every level participate in the culture of experimentation. Frontline workers continually offer suggestions for new products, dishes, and services, many of which are tested and, if successful, retained. "They let me do whatever comes into my head, which is kind of scary sometimes," jokes Bill Garner, a part-timer in the meat department of the Pittsford, New York, store. One day some twenty years ago, Maria Benjamin, who worked in the bakery at the same store, told Danny Wegman about the amazing recipe for "chocolate meatball cookies" her Italian ancestors had left her. "Let's sell them here," he urged. They're a customer favorite to this day.

The open spirit of experimentation at Wegmans ensures that when anyone in the food industry devises an innovation that could make a grocery store even more magnetic, Wegmans will probably be among the first to implement it.

Great demand creators protect their uniqueness. Having developed, through decades of trial and error, a unique food-retailing business model that is a powerfully magnetic creator of demand, Wegmans has also succeeded in meeting one of the most difficult of all business challenges: They've refrained from messing it up.

And the truth is that messing it up would be *so* easy to do.

One of the most surefire ways of dissipating the Wegmans magic would be to expand too quickly. Showing extraordinary restraint, the company has not done this. (The fact that Wegmans is privately held and therefore not subject to the same profit-growth pressures as many publicly traded companies is a helpful factor—but as we'll see, some publicly held companies have resisted the siren song of overexpansion as well.) Despite the clamor from customers around the country who have heard from friends and relatives about the legendary charms of Wegmans, the company opens new stores only at the rate of about two per year—a comparatively glacial pace. They believe it's more important to do it right than to do it fast.

Accordingly, when a new Wegmans is in development, months of research, planning, recruiting, and training are conducted. Managers with decades of experience at other Wegmans stores are recruited to help get the new location off to the right start—a baker from Pennsylvania, a fish expert from Maryland, a meat butcher from New Jersey. Dozens of other Wegmans staffers fly in for temporary assignments. Six weeks before the store opens, new hires

attend a daylong "Living Who We Are" orientation program about
Wegmans values—and at the end of the day they take home an
edited DVD of the day's events, complete with music, to share with
their families.

By opening day, you'd think the brand-new Wegmans you are
visiting has been in operation for years—that's how smoothly it runs.
It's a hugely important achievement, since the opening of a new
Wegmans is a giant community event that attracts intense scrutiny
and often draws more visitors in a single day than the average supermarket attracts in a week.

❑   ❑   ❑

THE WEGMANS STORY makes it clear that creating a magnetic product,
and then *keeping* it magnetic over years and decades, is no simple
matter. Which leads to what may be the biggest question of all, at
least from the perspective of anyone who hopes to become a demand
creator: What's the payoff? Is it possible to lavish resources on employees, invest in enormous stores and vast amounts of inventory,
and provide unheard-of levels of customer service . . . and still make
a decent profit in a notoriously narrow-margined industry like
grocery retailing?

If you do it the way Wegmans does, the answer is yes. Its operating margins are about double what the largest chains earn, larger
even than those of renowned organic merchant Whole Foods. And
weekly sales per square foot run close to $14, well above the indus-
try average of $9.39.

The explanation for Wegmans' economic success is fundamentally simple. It goes back to the theme of our chapter—the power of
the magnetic product—as vividly illustrated by these research findings
from a Gallup organization study of the supermarket business:

In the case of a leading supermarket chain, proof of the importance of an emotional connection can be found in both the fre-

quency of customers' visits and the amount of money they spent during those visits. Shoppers who were less than "extremely satisfied"—those who rated their satisfaction as 1, 2, 3, or 4 on a 5-point scale—visited this chain about 4.3 times per month, spending an average of $166 during that month. Those who were "extremely satisfied" but did not also have a strong emotional connection to the chain (that is, they were not "fully engaged") actually went to the store less often (4.1 times per month) and spent less ($144). In this case, extreme customer satisfaction represented no added value to the store.

However, when Gallup looked at customers who were extremely satisfied *and emotionally connected* to the store— customers Gallup calls "fully engaged"—a very different customer relationship emerged [emphasis added]. These customers visited the store 5.4 times and spent $210 a month.

Apparently, not all "extremely satisfied" customers are the same. Those with strong emotional connections visited the grocery chain 32% more often and spent 46% more money than those without emotional bonds. Satisfaction without engagement? Worthless. Satisfaction with engagement? Priceless.

Gallup attributes the difference between mere "satisfaction" with a supermarket's offerings and "engagement" with them to the customer's "emotional connection" to the store. And as we've seen, emotional appeal is the key ingredient that great demand creators integrate into their functionally excellent products to produce magnetic appeal. When customers are engaged, they become advocates and sources of new ideas for great products and services. The amount of money the company must invest in advertising and marketing goes down; the revenues available to serve customers even better go up; innovative improvements based on customer suggestions help Wegmans become even better, and the excited conversation about the company attracts even greater streams of demand. The power of this positive spiral is potentially limitless.

It all begins with a magnetic product. That 46 percent edge Gallup discovered in sales enjoyed by "emotionally engaging" stores like Wegmans is the Magnetism Gap. It represents the huge stream of extra demand that results when a product is more than just good—even very good. It's magnetic.

2.
Hassle Map

(HA-sul map) *noun* 1. a diagram of the characteristics of existing products, services, and systems that cause people to waste time, energy, money 2. (from a customer's perspective) a litany of the headaches, disappointments, and frustrations one experiences 3. (from a demand creator's perspective) an array of tantalizing opportunities

THE LONG, ROCKY ROAD TO A ONE-CLICK WORLD

When plans for an unprecedented New York–Paris auto race were announced in August 1907 by the publishers of the cities' leading newspapers, the *New York Times* and *Le Matin,* even car enthusiasts were astonished by its audacity. The sponsors projected a twenty-two-thousand-mile journey nearly spanning the globe, with legs including the great American desert, the wilds of Alaska, and the Siberian tundra (with a Pacific crossing by steamer). As the race kicked off in Times Square on February 12, 1908, only five driving teams—one from Italy, one from Germany, two from France, and one from the United States—were brave or mad enough to dare the venture.

Disasters beset all five. The American car, the Thomas Flyer, piloted by a debonair celebrity driver named Montague Roberts and a resourceful young mechanic named George Schuster, got stuck in snowdrifts and could advance only as fast as shovel-wielding volunteers could clear its path. The huge Protos, steered by Lieutenant Hans Koeppen of the German army and resembling a modern pickup truck more than a race car, had to be extracted from a swamp by a team of twelve horses. And this all happened while the competitors were still in New York state.

Weeks later, after Roberts, the driver with matinee idol good looks, had abandoned the crazy quest in Nebraska, young Schuster found himself pleading with officials of Union Pacific to classify the Flyer as a train so it could rattle over the railroad tracks rather than navigate the trackless wastes of the West. When crossbars on a Siberian horse-cart bridge snapped beneath the Flyer's weight, Schuster avoided a thirty-foot plunge into foaming rapids only by adroitly steering the car onto the creaking wooden support rails at the edge of the bridge. Eventually, Schuster won the race, arriving in Paris after 169 grueling days—one of just three competitors to complete the trek.

Such was the state of car travel in 1908 . . . fully thirty years after German engineer Karl Benz invented his four-stroke gasoline engine and, with it, the modern automobile. For decades after the invention of the automobile, car travel was strictly for adventurers, even in relatively well-developed North America. Drivers donned special gear—hats, goggles, gloves, voluminous dusters—to shield them from the fumes, sparks, and dirt churned up on rutted country lanes. A tool kit was standard equipment in every vehicle, and motorists were advised to be expert in basic repairs (including, when necessary, the *manufacture* of spare parts). The earliest guides for tourism by car assumed—quite correctly—that motorists would have to find their way through a formless chaos of unmarked roads, half-cleared trails, and cattle crossings.

The automobile itself was just one piece of the puzzle that needed to be completed before the United States could become the hypermobile country it is today. Standardized highway signage, modern road design guidelines, the Interstate Highway System, and vast networks of supporting businesses from gas stations and repair shops to roadside eateries, motels, and parking garages all had to be conceived and built before the hassles of auto travel were truly tamed.

Only then could the age-old desire for mobility be expressed in demand for cars—cars by the hundreds of millions.

Today, in the twenty-first century, the infrastructure that supports car travel is still being refined and expanded. Only in the past decade have E-ZPass and other automated networks reduced the hassles associated with driving on toll roads, bridges, and tunnels. The car-sharing revolution launched by Zipcar is finally addressing the hassles faced by the urban driver. A generation from now, automated guidance systems that maintain buffer zones between cars and dangerous obstacles may make deaths by collision almost unheard-of . . . and in time, drivers may marvel, and shudder, at the callous inhumanity of a civilization that tolerated forty thousand annual deaths in car crashes. We've lived in an internal-combustion world for more than a century, yet even today some of the lingering hassles of that world continue to baffle our best efforts to solve them.

So perhaps it shouldn't be surprising to observe that today—six decades after the onset of the electronics revolution (with William Shockley's invention of the transistor) and almost three decades after the advent of the PC—the world of digital communication and information is still hassle-ridden, plagued with mutually incompatible systems, buggy programs, unresponsive networks, and products that don't quite work as intended. Like the internal-combustion world, the digital world will likely take a while to thoroughly de-hassle.

What's more surprising—indeed, almost shocking—is the fact that very few people are thinking about, let alone building, the new products, services, and systems needed to make the world's digital resources available to everybody in easy, hassle-free form. Which makes the handful of exceptions rather amazing in their own way.

The exceptions are people who focus not just on the brilliant potential of new technology but on the hassles that prevent us from taking advantage of it—the high-tech equivalent of unmarked roads, undrained swamps, and axle-snapping potholes. In any arena, hassles like these are often the first clues—the earliest flashing signals—of unrealized potential demand. That's why, in case after case, the creation of a magnetic product has begun with someone drawing a map of the hassles and points of friction in customers' lives—and then figuring out a way to reduce or eliminate them.

You remember the story we told, in the introduction, of one man's frustration with video-store late fees, and his determination to do something about them. Many of us experienced similar annoyances—but only Reed Hastings recognized those hassles as an opportunity to create the demand generator known as Netflix.

Or consider another observer's comment about one of the ubiquitous hassle generators of the early 2000s: "We all had cell phones. We just hated them, they were so awful to use. The software was terrible. The hardware wasn't very good. We talked to our friends, and they all hated their cell phones too. Everybody seemed to hate their phones." You know what he means: the awkward message interfaces, inadequate Web browsing, hard-to-read screens, time-consuming procedures, and unfriendly applications that plagued (and still plague) countless cell phone users. Only Steve Jobs (who of course is the "observer" we just quoted) understood that those hassles were crying out to be solved by a new kind of device—the iPhone.

Jobs and his team at Apple set to work at fixing those hassles. They invented "visual voice mail," which allows users to scan their voice mail messages like e-mail and pick the items they want to listen to, in the order they prefer. They made reading text messages and scanning the Internet more pleasurable by making the iPhone capable of multitasking, building in the Safari browser, and enabling the iPhone to rotate horizontally, creating an easy-to-read widescreen effect. And they applied Apple's trademark talent for simplifying and clarifying user interfaces, reducing the number of key clicks needed to download a song (for example) to just five—as compared to the eighteen to thirty-nine clicks required on other devices.

The launch of the iPhone, announced in January 2007, created the smartphone industry and tapped a flood of latent demand. To this day, no competitor has succeeded in fully beating its array of hassle-fixing features.

And think about the sheer frustration of wrestling with digital tools that do only a fraction of what you'd like them to do and were apparently designed with anyone *but* the end users in mind. One Wall Street trader recalls complaining to the engineers who supplied electronic data-managing equipment to his firm, "All of you people keep producing devices where the letters and numbers are much too small for me to read, and the buttons are too small for my big fingers." Petty problems? Not when a trade is in the balance and a mistaken digit may cost millions.

That trader was Michael Bloomberg, who parlayed his experience with the hassles of using financial data into the information empire that bears his name.

The kinds of insights that led Hastings, Jobs, and Bloomberg to create big new streams of demand seem obvious in retrospect—but only in retrospect. These three great demand creators made their discoveries by immersing themselves in the lives of customers—indeed, they *were* the customers—and becoming experts in the hassles that ordinary products and services generated. It's a form of intense, problem-solving exploration that is *both* objective and subjective, often better couched in intuitive, emotional terms than in statistics. Maybe that's why most business executives find this kind of exploration difficult to master—especially those immersed in the high-tech world, where it's so easy to fall into the trap of putting *devices* rather than people at the center of the universe.

Hastings, Jobs, and Bloomberg are all masters of the hassle map—the array of frustrations, inconveniences, complications, and potential disasters lurking in most customer experiences. Think about the last time you traveled by plane, challenged an erroneous cable TV bill, or dealt with any large and unresponsive bureaucracy. That's the definition of a hassle map. Each needless step, wasted moment, and disappointing outcome is a friction point on the hassle map—and each represents an opportunity to create new demand by eliminating the friction or even reversing it, turning hassle into delight.

A hassle map may be a purely mental construct, or it may be a literal map—a physical, visual representation of the hassles a customer experiences. If you want to master the discipline of demand creation, drawing the hassle map of the customer you seek to serve is an invaluable exercise. It's a crucial step toward *seeing differently*—glimpsing, for the first time, both how bad the present reality is and how much better it can become.

Some hassle maps are lists of the steps involved in a process, often including too many activities that are needlessly complicated or whose value and purpose are unclear. (Filling out your income tax return might be an example.) Other hassle maps chart the people, organizations, suppliers, and sources a customer must engage to complete a given task, often leading to confusion, waste, excess choice, and information overload. (Renovating a kitchen, for instance.) And still others graph the trade-offs between consumer needs that are equally desirable yet apparently mutually exclusive: In one arena after another, customers are told they can have low cost *or* quality, convenience *or* variety, personal service *or* speed—but never both.

As they sketch the hassle maps of their customers, the smartest demand creators ask themselves probing questions like:

"What is the psychology of customers? What do they want out of life? How do existing products meet those desires? And if they don't, why not?"

And also: "Which hassles drive customers crazy? Are there hassles they barely notice because they're so familiar—but which we might be able to fix?"

Hassles are everywhere. But people with the clarity of vision to understand them and the tenacious creativity to fix them are few and far between. That's why it took decades for auto travel to become (relatively) safe, easy, and efficient—and why it may take decades more for the digital information revolution to achieve its full potential.

❐   ❐   ❐

TODAY—at long last—we're witnessing the start of a transformation of the digital landscape driven by a handful of pioneers who recognize the crucial importance of hassle map thinking. In the process, they are creating incredible floods of demand for their magnetic, life-changing, hassle-reducing products . . . as well as changing the rules of the high-tech industry game.

Hassle map thinking has a way of turning traditional perspectives upside down. Accordingly, the transformation of our digital world by masters of the hassle map has produced business outcomes that look like startling anomalies.

In this transformed world, a computer company (Apple) makes the best cell phones and leads the music distribution business. An online company (Netflix) is the most powerful emerging rival for the demand currently flowing to the television networks and the cable companies. Another online company (Amazon) is the world's second most valuable retailer (despite having *no* retail stores), one of the most innovative makers of electronic devices, and an increasingly powerful player in book publishing. And a data technology company (Bloomberg) is a major force in the media universe once dominated by companies like NBC, the New York Times, and Dow Jones.

These outcomes make little sense when we try to sort companies under neat, familiar labels like "computer company," "media company," "telecom company," and "consumer electronics company." But they make perfect sense when we consider all of them under the heading of "hassle-fixers." The companies that are creating the greatest demand streams in today's high-tech world are the ones that do the best job of fixing customer hassles by using technology from *any* source—regardless of labels. Today's digital hassle-fixers are reaching beyond individual technologies like the PC or the cell phone, redesigning these devices and the infrastructure that surrounds them to make them more responsive to customer needs.

Sometimes this involves merging technologies; in other cases, it involves connecting the dots among devices or information streams; in still other cases, it involves creating new tools, technology-based or otherwise, that make digital devices more convenient to use. But in every case, the hassle-fixers understand that the new key to success is developing innovations that are centered on *customer problems*, not device capabilities.

The emerging result of this new, customer-centric approach is the erasure of the neat divisions that once separated technologies from one another. We're now moving rapidly toward a One-Click World in which customers take for granted easy, instant, ubiquitous access to digital products and services—and in which the industry boundaries that once defined demand spaces are no longer operative.

Hundreds of companies are now grappling in the resulting worldwide scrum. Yet only a few seem to fully understand what is happening. Consider, for example, the contrasting paths of two great corporations—Sony and Apple.

Sony could have been an early player in the one-click game. It had expertise and experience in all the industries that today are merging. Starting as a consumer electronics company, Sony took positions in the computer industry (Vaio), the telecom industry (Sony Ericsson cell phones), and the media industry (Columbia Pictures, music, games). But all these positions were "siloed"—that is, there were no links between these businesses that would benefit or even impact a consumer's experience. Owning a Vaio laptop had nothing to do with using a Sony Walkman to listen to music or watching a movie from Columbia. Sony owned places in all four industries, but (despite the much-discussed notion of "synergy" among these positions) it didn't integrate them for the consumer or create new tools to improve anybody's hassle map.

By contrast, Apple's Steve Jobs has been a pioneer of One-Click World. When he entered the consumer electronics world with the iPod, he integrated the iPod with iTunes, the world's first (and still its best) system of software and online retailing for buying, organizing, and enjoying music and video. Then he entered the telecom space with the iPhone and integrated *that* product into an even bigger and more powerful system of apps and services (including iTunes). Today the iPad is connecting touch-screen technology with video created by movie and television producers, digital content from book and magazine publishers, and many other sources of information and entertainment.

Rather than simply participating in four separate industries, Apple integrated them. Even more important, it connected the dots between the digital technologies and a world of desirable content, redrawing the consumer's hassle map and providing a seamless, unique, and powerfully magnetic experience.

The business result: an extreme and unforeseen reversal of fortune. In December 2000, Sony had a market value of $63 billion, Apple less than $5 billion. Today, they've swapped positions. Apple's value (as of March 2011) is $330 billion, while Sony's is just $36 billion. The demand result: Consumers the world over associate the name Apple with products and services that are not only cool, elegant, and powerful, but also intuitive, easy, and fun to use—hassle-fixers par excellence.

In One-Click World, we customers increasingly *assume* that products will ignore technological boundaries to bring us convenience, accessibility, and fun. When offerings remain trapped within traditional technological or corporate walls, we are poised to reject them—and more so with every passing month.

Another example: The first version of Sony's Reader, launched in the United States in September 2006, was a well-designed, even revolutionary consumer electronics device, using E Ink technology to create the best-looking digital book reader anyone had ever seen.

But you almost certainly didn't buy one. Why? Because Sony didn't find a way to merge that wonderful technology with affordable, instantaneous, ultraconvenient wireless access to most of the world's favorite books. Fourteen months later, Amazon's Kindle made that connection happen, making Amazon the early winner in the e-reader race.

The e-reader contest illustrates the Curse of the Incomplete Product. The rule is simple: *In One-Click World, a new product that offers only part of what customers want will miss the target.*

Imagine the iPhone without the App Store and the thousands of loyal software developers creating cool, useful tools to enhance the phone's value—it would be just another cell phone (though well designed) for people to complain about rather than a lifestyle accessory people fall in love with.

And mentioning Apple, Netflix, Amazon, Kindle, and other successful one-click demand creators suggests a second reality of the new competitive universe—the Three Dimensions of Design. *In One-Click World, design has become ten times more important—in terms of device design, yes, but also in terms of experience design and the design of the business system that supports it.*

The great one-click companies take the physical design of products very seriously. You know about Apple's superlative aesthetics. But did you know that Netflix ran through more than one hundred fifty redesigns of its iconic red mailing envelope before finding the design that served its customers most effectively? Have you ever really examined the brilliant combination of form and function that is the Amazon website (and which Netflix frankly admits it imitated when creating its own superb pages)? Or noticed all the subtle differences, such as perfectly positioned buttons, that made the Kindle easier and more fun to use than the original Sony Reader?

Even more important than device design, however, is the artistry that these companies deploy in designing the experiential connections between them and us, their customers. Think in terms of hundreds of adjustments, large and small—in systems, interfaces, information flows, service protocols, intercompany alliances—each of which reduces the amount of time wasted, effort expended, or frustration experienced by customers by a fraction of a percent. Add up all those differences and you have a (practically) hassle-free experience that we customers love and will happily pay for, rather than one we remain indifferent to.

And then there's the third dimension—the design of the business, which nails the difference between success and failure. Successful one-click companies understand that a world-class business design is not available ready-made but must be custom-built with at least as much creativity as an innovative new product, including a value proposition that's unique, a profit model that captures a share of the value delivered to buyers, and strategic control to protect those profits.

So the emergence of One-Click World is a fascinating phenomenon with all kinds of implications for the future of demand. But it starts in a very simple place—with a few unusual people who share both a clear-eyed focus on customer hassles and an unrelenting determination to eliminate them, no matter what technological boundaries they must violate in the process.

BETTER THAN A BONUS: BLOOMBERG BUILDS A SERVICE TRADERS JUST WON'T GIVE UP

As long ago as the early 1970s, Michael Bloomberg was exploring ways of fixing the hassle maps that bedeviled Wall Street traders. His mission: to make timely, vital data more easily accessible and really *useful* to men and women for whom information equaled profit. It was a mission for which his background and personality made him ideally suited.

Bloomberg's first job, in high school, had been a part-time stint at an electronics company in Cambridge, Massachusetts. He went on to study engineering at Johns Hopkins before attending Harvard Business School and becoming a floor trader at Salomon Brothers— by all accounts a particularly impatient and irascible one. ("He was always screaming," recalls one former colleague. "He'd call me, put me on hold, then three minutes later he'd come back and yell, 'Whaddayawant?' I'd say, 'Bloomberg, you called me!'") Bloomberg appreciated the value of any tool that could save traders time and help them focus on their number one job—making money. He was also quick-witted, strong-willed, self-confident perhaps to excess, and fond of the spotlight. These traits exasperated Bloomberg's colleagues at Salomon but ultimately served him well in his later careers as a One-Click World demand creator and a precedent-smashing independent politician.

At its root, success on Wall Street is all about information—about being quicker to recognize market-moving trends, price shifts, imbalances, and anomalies than the trader around the corner, or, today, around the world. So investment banks, brokerage houses, and investment managers had always been among the early adapters of new information technologies, from the telegraph and the telephone to the telex and fax machine.

By the early 1970s, Bloomberg was already using his engineering background to figure out how computers could make securities trading more hassle-free. Having been put in charge of Salomon's information systems, he talked the company into providing every trader with a computer workstation wired to a back-office mainframe—a step that was revolutionary at the time. Then he recruited programmers to devise ways of connecting the dots so as to make this infrastructure more useful to traders. Having been a trader himself, Bloomberg understood the trader's hassle map, even down to the physical elements of infrastructure—hence his obsession with details like the legibility of characters on monitors and the size of buttons on keyboards.

Unfortunately, Bloomberg's fellow partners at Salomon Brothers didn't fully appreciate the value of his insights (or, perhaps, the high-voltage combination of those insights with his combustible personality). When the firm merged with commodities-trading company Phibro Corporation in 1981, the irascible Bloomberg was "not invited to stay"—or, as Bloomberg less genteelly put it, "They threw me out after fifteen years."

Being ungraciously canned stung Bloomberg's sizable ego. But it also unleashed his powerful entrepreneurial streak. Together with a handful of partners, Bloomberg used the nest egg he carried away from Salomon to launch a company dedicated to bringing electronic information tools to Wall Street. Three forms of value would be provided: streams of up-to-the-moment financial data, from stock and bond prices to currency valuations; electronic systems to connect traders with back-office systems to facilitate rapid execution of trades; and software tools to perform analytic tasks like identifying arbitrage opportunities or comparing the relative values of securities.

These were the kinds of services Bloomberg himself would have lusted for during his trading days, and they looked and were impressive even on the primitive electronic equipment then available. A Wall Street veteran recalls seeing an early demonstration of the service using "an old IBM Selectric typewriter hooked up to a terminal"—dated technology even at the time. But savvy traders understood its power.

The first order was from Merrill Lynch—an ideal business fit, since Merrill was not then a major player in the capital markets and was looking for any unique advantage to spur its growth. Merrill assigned two traders to provide detailed, real-time feedback on the technology. According to Bloomberg himself, their "nit-picking" played an important role in the service's success by facilitating a steady stream of improvements. Increasingly impressed with the trading edge Bloomberg's data feeds were providing, Merrill invested $30 million in the business with the proviso that no sales be made to Merrill competitors for five years—a restriction Merrill waived when it realized the huge profits to be enjoyed once the floodgates of demand were opened. Bloomberg LP was up and running.

It didn't take a prophetic genius to see, in the 1980s, that electronic IT tools would be increasingly important for financial professionals. Bloomberg had at least twenty potential rivals, chief among them Reuters and the Dow Jones electronic news service, Telerate. But these competitors assumed that generic data was all their customers needed. Bloomberg knew better. He began hiring analysts to transform generic data into proprietary information with unique value to traders.

Some of those value-adding transformations might seem mundane—for example, converting company data compiled for different fiscal years and based on different financial assumptions into uniform formats for easy, accurate comparisons. But they dramatically simplified the trader's hassle map by eliminating time-consuming steps from the investment decision-making process. Others were more sophisticated—for example, continually updated yield-curve analyses, an array of portfolio-planning tools, "what if" systems that allowed traders to extrapolate the results of alternative investments, and programs to support "black box" trading systems that made investment decisions electronically. Thousands of traders who tried using such Bloomberg tools quickly found it difficult to imagine ever having to live without them.

Ask the Bloomberg people why they outlasted the better-connected, better-funded Telerate in the battle for demand, and they'll tell you, "Telerate didn't *do* anything with the data." Bloomberg did. By 1997, its Princeton center employed nine hundred analysts. Traders flocked to Bloomberg. A year later, Dow Jones threw in the towel, selling its Telerate unit for more than a billion dollars *below* its purchase price. Reuters found itself forced to invest hundreds of millions to match Bloomberg's offerings.

Since then, Bloomberg LP has steadily increased the range, depth, variety, and quality of the information it provides for its subscribers. The company started with data on bonds, the business area Bloomberg himself specialized in during his trading days. Then it expanded into stocks, mutual funds, commodity futures and options, foreign exchange, real estate, and an array of complex derivative securities based on mortgages, indexes, interest rates, and more—5 million financial instruments in all. (Like Zipcar, Bloomberg quickly recognized the value of demand variation—understanding that hassle maps differ for different kinds of customers and developing unique products designed to fix hassles for all of them.) To match the breadth and depth of financial information now provided by Bloomberg, an individual trader would need to access up to two hundred exchanges and thousands of other research sources around the world. Bloomberg is the single, dot-connecting source that makes it all instantly accessible.

Bloomberg didn't slow down. "Any news that touches money" was aggregated to flow through Bloomberg's custom-designed monitors. A video link in one corner of the proprietary screen offered press conferences, Senate hearings, and news-making interviews by TV host Charlie Rose (whose PBS show moved into a studio at Bloomberg's New York headquarters). In 1990, Bloomberg launched his own news service, covering business, political, social, economic, and other news. Today it employs 2,300 people in dozens of bureaus around the world, produces radio and television interviews and flash news spots, publishes its own business magazine (*Bloomberg Businessweek*), runs a cable network and a radio station, and produces a news feed carried by more local papers than Associated Press, Reuters, or any other news service.

Bloomberg proves that a business product can be so magnetic that customers refuse to give it up even when *bribed* to do so:

Figuring unhappily that the cost of a Bloomberg [terminal] was $18,000 annually and not believing that his value-investing analysts could be getting that much out of it, [the head of an East Coast money management firm] told each of 12 analysts that he would raise their individual bonuses by $15,000 if they would give up their Bloombergs. Eleven out of the 12 said no. One analyst said he would actually prefer to see his current bonus cut by $15,000 rather than give up his Bloomberg.

Mike Bloomberg has not been directly involved with running his company since he was elected mayor of New York City in 2001, but the intense demand for his product continues to grow. There are now more than three hundred thousand Bloomberg machines installed in offices around the world, each generating revenues for the company of about $1,500 per month. Unlike competing firms like Reuters, Bloomberg offers no volume discount, except a single price drop from $1,800 when a company installs its second monitor; the giant Wall Street firm that buys a thousand subscriptions pays the same rate per monitor as the two-person shop. Additional charges are levied for services like execution on stock trades.

In return, Bloomberg delivers a level of service befitting a brand that people casually compare to Mercedes or Rolex. "Our products don't have a manual," is Bloomberg's justified boast. "They have more than ten thousand people ready to help; highly trained and multilingual, providing help twenty-four hours a day, seven days a week." If the problem takes a few hours to solve, you'll be handed off from one expert to the next, one time zone to another, receiving help in whatever language you like, from Japanese to Urdu.

And some elements of Bloomberg's service are so intensely personalized and valuable that it's easy to understand the magnetic appeal they generate. Our favorite example: Customers who lose their jobs get to keep a Bloomberg machine at home for four months—free of charge, with no diminution of service. Perhaps only a onetime trader who'd been unceremoniously sacked, like Bloomberg himself, would have the intimate understanding of the customer hassle map required to even *imagine* making such an offer. Think of the psychological boost this service offers a trader battered by a firing—and of his improved odds of finding a new job with the Bloomberg information stream keeping him current. When Amaranth Advisors, a $9.5 billion hedge fund, went out of business in 2006, Bloomberg let its 221 employees keep their machines. Within months, 180 of them had landed new jobs—and insisted on new Bloomberg subscriptions as part of their employment packages.

Bloomberg LP itself is not immune to economic challenges. When Wall Street retrenched during 2009, Bloomberg's subscriber base actually fell by some 11,000. But the company's leadership stuck to its agenda of providing more to its customers, purchasing *Business-Week* magazine, and introducing more than two thousand new functions on the Bloomberg terminals. In 2010, the upward march of the subscriber base resumed. "We've actually picked up market share," says chairman Peter Grauer. And they did so without cutting prices.

Bloomberg LP illustrates the huge demand-creating potential in just one corner of One-Click World. Hundreds of other nooks and corners of the demand universe are waiting to be settled by *their* pioneers.

And this suggests the *ultimate* goal for all the thousands of people and companies at work in the world of technology: to transform every corner of today's often disjointed digital world into One-Click World, where the information tools that surround us become so simple to use and so integrated into our very consciousness that they are, finally and delightfully, hassle-free.

CAREMORE CONNECTS THE HEALTH
CARE DOTS

Ellen S., an eighty-two-year-old widow, lives in Anaheim, California, just outside Los Angeles. One Wednesday morning, she got on her scale, as she did every morning. One hundred and forty-six pounds—wasn't that a little high? Ellen felt vaguely troubled as she poured herself a bowl of oat bran in the breakfast nook.

Half an hour later, the phone rang. It was Sandra at the clinic.

"Good morning, Ellen. Did you notice anything different today?"

"I think my weight's up a little . . ."

"That's right," Sandra said. "One forty-six. That's three pounds more than yesterday."

"I had a feeling it was high."

"We need you to come to the clinic this morning."

"I can't, my daughter's away this week."

"No problem, we'll send a car for you. Can you be ready in an hour?"

"Sure, I'll be ready."

For Ellen, who had a history of congestive heart failure, an overnight weight gain of three pounds was bad news—a possible sign of fluid buildup. Ellen's treatment started that very morning and continued for two weeks until she was out of danger.

Ellen's friend Rebecca has a different health care provider. Six months earlier, Rebecca had experienced the same weight gain as Ellen. But without a wireless scale transmitting her daily weight to the clinic, it went unnoticed and unaddressed for days. A week later, Rebecca was rushed to the emergency room with shortness of breath and heart palpitations; she ended up suffering a long, painful hospitalization.

Dan A., a retired letter carrier, is eighty-seven and frail, his once-sturdy legs now weak and unsteady. He was at the clinic for two reasons: a session of light-weight training to strengthen his arms and legs, and his usual monthly toenail trimming.

Dan was a classic candidate for a fall. Many of his friends had already been devastated by broken legs or hips, requiring weeks in the hospital and months in rehab followed by years of pain and reduced mobility. But Dan's doctors knew that weak limbs, long toenails, and shag carpets are contributing factors to falls among the elderly. They'd already visited Dan's apartment and made sure that his daughter replaced the eighties-vintage shag carpets with low-pile rugs. Now they were following up his regular muscle-toning sessions at the gym with periodic toenail clipping. As a result, Dan and his fellow clinic patients are reducing their fall risk by 80 percent.

Joseph S., a seventy-nine-year-old diabetic, had gotten a cut on his foot (banged it against a door). When it didn't heal after a couple of days, he limped into the office of his family physician. Dr. Naylor glanced at the cut and sent Joe immediately to the clinic in Whittier, California.

A nurse practitioner there cleaned and dressed the wound. And she told Joe, "I want to see you here in two days so I can fix you up again. And two days after that, and two days after that, until the cut is healed. Understand?"

Joe grinned ruefully and nodded. He'd been through this routine before.

For a diabetic, even a small cut is a serious matter. Untended wounds often fail to heal and contribute to an alarmingly high rate of amputation. But Joe's foot was saved. And Joe's wasn't the only one. Patients served by his clinic experience more than 60 percent fewer amputations than those served by other providers.

Dr. Naylor had started working with Joe's clinic a couple of years before.

"To be honest, I didn't like them at first. They had a lot of very definite ideas about how things should be done, and I don't like to be told how things should be done.

"But after a year or so, I came to appreciate what they have to offer.

"You have to understand my situation as a PCP—a primary care physician, that is. I see sixty or seventy patients every day. Everything you can imagine, from toddlers with ear infections to pregnant teenagers to older folks who are starting to lose their memories. I'm pressed for time and limited in options. When my patients run into serious problems, I have only two choices—send them to a specialist, or send them to the hospital.

"The clinic provides a third option. When it comes to elderly patients, the clinicians know exactly what they're doing. They're well staffed. They're very responsive. They'll pick patients up if they can't get transportation. And they're obsessively focused not just on treatment but also on prevention.

"And you know what else? They understand *my* problems, too. They help me do a much better job for my older patients, and you just can't imagine how good that feels."

Ellen and Dan, Joe and Dr. Naylor are all real people, though their names have been changed. And the clinics that serve them are also real, and are all parts of CareMore. Based in Cerritos, California, CareMore is a combination insurance carrier and health care provider with twenty-six centers in California, Arizona, and Nevada, serving more than fifty thousand Medicare patients. These patients drive health care demand by being able to choose from any Medicare Advantage plan they like. But CareMore isn't like other plans. Through its unique approach to caring for the elderly, CareMore is routinely achieving patient outcomes other providers can only dream about, preventing needless deaths, reducing hospitalizations, and improving lifestyles.

It's a level of enhanced care for which most people would gladly pay extra. And yet these outcomes are produced, not through high-tech procedures, intrusive interventions, or exclusive "concierge service" that only the wealthy could afford, but rather through simple, commonsense routines that put a premium on the human connections among doctors, nurses, therapists, and patients—so that lives are greatly enriched and prolonged while overall costs are *reduced* by nearly 20 percent.

CareMore is an American health care story that nobody knows—but that everybody should. People hearing about CareMore for the first time always come away with the same questions: "How do they do it?" And "Why isn't the same kind of care available for me, or for my parents?"

❏   ❏   ❏

THE CAREMORE STORY started almost two decades ago, with a man named Sheldon Zinberg—a gastroenterologist who was deeply concerned about the changing economics of health care in Southern California.

Here as in other U.S. markets, health maintenance organizations (HMOs) had come to dominate the landscape. The theory behind HMOs sounded attractive. "Managed care" was supposed to coordinate and guide treatments so as to maximize both patient well-being and economic sustainability. But under pressure from corporate health insurance sponsors and government agencies (as well as investors seeking profits), the HMOs were increasingly focused on reducing costs by any means necessary—including short-term fixes that often led to worse patient outcomes and, in the long run, even *higher* medical expenses. The hassle maps of patients were growing ever more complicated, doctors were getting squeezed, and costs were still spiraling upward.

Sheldon Zinberg was alarmed. Back in the 1960s, he'd founded a large internal medicine group that had grown to include some twenty physicians in a range of specialties, from cardiology and oncology to rheumatology and nephrology. Internal Medicine Specialists, Inc., had provided excellent care, and its members had thrived.

But by the late 1980s, with a small number of HMOs growing more dominant, referrals were dwindling and service restrictions were multiplying. Zinberg and his colleagues were being
forced to spend more and more time on the phone with "benefits
coordinators"—hassle creators whose main job was to find reasons
to deny coverage: "Why do a colonoscopy? The patient's only forty
years old. We won't pay for it."

Internist Charles Holzner worked for one of the HMOs. He
describes its behavior in scathing terms. "It was a complete non-
integration of care," he says. "I could get the patients out of the hospital in two or three days, but they would go right back in because
they would disappear into the ether and get none of the follow-up
care they needed."

It was the worst of both worlds: uncoordinated, low-quality patient care combined with punishing economic results.

Sheldon Zinberg was appalled by the destructive impact of managed care. Already in his early sixties, he could have simply retired
and walked away from the problem, as many of his colleagues were
doing. Instead Zinberg rose at a 1988 meeting of his group's board
to make a fateful declaration: "The only answer is for someone to
start a *good* health care program."

He spent the next several years figuring out how to do it.

Zinberg was acutely aware of the incredible hassle map that dominated the patient experience. He'd long been mulling the elements
of a coordinated care system centered on reducing hassles for patients rather than simply cutting costs. A personal fitness aficionado,
he spent time every day in his home gym devising specialized exercise routines to strengthen specific physical systems—the kind of
nonmedical wellness program few doctors were knowledgeable
about. Traditional medicine tended to view patients as mere collections of organs, symptoms, and conditions rather than as the integrated beings they are. Zinberg began to envision a health care
organization in which teams of doctors, nurses, therapists, trainers,

and other professionals worked together, continually sharing information and insights about their mutual clients and providing whatever services were needed to keep those clients in the best possible physical and mental health. The organization would connect the dots for the patient, who would be at the center of the system.

This was the kind of care any physician would want for himself, or for a member of his family. But would it work financially? And would doctors whipsawed by the economic changes of the 1990s—and long accustomed to making patient care decisions autonomously rather than as members of a team—be willing to take a chance on Zinberg's new concept?

Zinberg spent almost two years struggling to recruit physicians to his program. "During 1991 and 92 my wife barely saw me," he recalls.

> I was having dinner four nights a week with groups of doctors, explaining my concept. I was begging them, literally begging them, to help me develop the first integrated system of health care. A lot of them turned me down. "This is a huge job," they would say. "We're too busy to take on something like this." Others were so capitalistically minded they didn't want to have anything to do with the project. I wanted them to throw their hearts and souls into an organization that we would all jointly own and that would be focused exclusively on what was best for the patient. "If we put people before profit," I would tell them, "we *will* profit." But the idea made them nervous.

Fortunately, a few doctors understood what Zinberg was trying to do. Charles Holzner was one of those early converts; today he is a senior physician at CareMore. Other long-term colleagues of Zinberg's were moved to join by their personal connections with him—some were even patients of his—and by the depth and sincerity of his commitment to the cause. And eventually one of Zinberg's impassioned after-dinner speeches would lead to a breakthrough. Halfway through one presentation at an Italian restaurant, an oph- thalmologist jumped up and interrupted Zinberg. "Hey, guys," he yelled. "This is what we should have been doing all along. This is why we became doctors! Can we all try to remember that?" Several more doctors signed up that evening.

By 1993, physicians operating twenty-eight separate medical of- fices had agreed to become affiliates of Zinberg's new system. In June, CareMore Medical Group opened its doors.

Zinberg had always seen his vision of coordinated care as espe- cially suited to the needs of the elderly, where investments in co- ordinated care programs lead to lower costs and much better outcomes. As a gastroenterologist, his practice naturally included a high percentage of older patients, and as he himself grew older, his interest in the physiology of aging deepened. (His insights into the subject, including not just his unique exercise programs but also his ideas on nutrition, genetics, and memory retention, would lead to his 1993 book, *Win in the Second Half.*) And Zinberg recognized that elderly patients covered by Medicare—the patients normally regarded as the greatest drain on the health care system—could benefit the most from special attention. Due to the system's failure to connect the dots, they experienced the worst set of hassles in American health care: avoidable hospitalizations, duplication of ef- fort, misdiagnoses, patient confusion, needless suffering, and sheer neglect. In short, wildly *misplaced* demand, with costly, uncoordi- nated treatments leading to complications, poor outcomes, and still more treatments.

But at first, under pressure from a few investors, including one community hospital, CareMore accepted all kinds and ages of patients, including some covered by employee medical insurance ("commer- cial plans," in industry parlance). For four years, CareMore operated on this basis, and like most other medical practices, it struggled to make ends meet even as its membership rolls slowly grew. But in

1997, the commercial insurers, perhaps feeling threatened by Care-More's growing presence, insisted that the company promise it would never introduce a commercial insurance package of its own. When Zinberg and his board of managers hesitated to accept this demand, the commercial insurers abruptly canceled their contracts with CareMore.

It was a huge short-term financial blow. But it proved to be a long-term blessing. It provided Zinberg and his team with the opportunity to restructure CareMore around his original concept—a specialized health care system that focused on the elderly and put the patient at the center of the system. It also had the important benefit of creating a single funding source for the business model—Medicare. Medicare's payment system provided CareMore with what's called "an acuity adjusted aggregate payment" for all its patients. In other words, CareMore received an annual per-patient fee, adjusted according to each client's risk profile. This replaced the distorted incentives of the fee-for-service model, allowing CareMore to be rewarded for driving health care innovations for its elderly patients.

"The concept was much simpler than a lot of people seem to think," Zinberg says. "It didn't require the brain of Socrates. You start by listing the needs of the senior population. Then you ask, to what extent can we meet those needs? And you figure out ways to provide what they need to get healthy and stay healthy."

Like all demand creators, Zinberg had the guts to listen to customers. But there are limits to what customers can tell you. Sometimes they won't talk about their real desires or motivations ("I bought a Mercedes to make my next-door neighbor jealous"). Other times—particularly in a technical field like health care—they don't really know what they want, or lack the language to explain it clearly. This is why smart demand creators supplement their conversations with customers with plenty of observation, looking especially closely at the gaps between what people say and what they do.

As if guided by Yogi Berra's dictum "You can observe a lot by just watching," Zinberg, Holzner, and their colleagues set about doing something rather unusual in the world of health care: simply *looking* at the root causes of the hassles that were creating needless suffering among their elderly patients. They analyzed how these upstream events led to often catastrophic downstream consequences. Then they set about eliminating those hassles, one by one.

In this upstream-downstream analysis, CareMore was applying an old systems management principle first developed at Bell Laboratories in the 1930s and refined by management guru W. Edwards Deming in the 1950s: You can fix a problem at step one for a dollar, or fix it at step ten for thirty dollars. Or, as one physician put it, "The American health care system is built around waiting for train wrecks and then cleaning up the damage. At CareMore, we wondered what would happen if we tried preventing the train wrecks in the first place."

One of their first discoveries was the simple realization that up to *one-third* of their elderly patients failed to show up for doctor's appointments.

Why? Charles Holzner explains: "About forty percent of the elderly people we were taking care of were home by themselves. They'd outlived their family resources, they couldn't drive, and their kids lived out of town. So when they got sick, they ended up calling 911. And when it comes to routine doctor visits, they sometimes just couldn't make it at all."

CareMore came up with an unconventional idea: providing transportation, at no charge, to get patients to their medical appointments. Local car service companies were happy to have the business. It cost CareMore money—but it saved a lot more. It meant that simple problems were recognized and treated in their early stages; complications were avoided; rates of hospitalization and nursing home admittance began to fall. Providing free transportation for patients isn't the kind of thing most physicians would consider doing; focusing on *nonmedical* challenges that might be harming patients is not a subject taught at medical school. Perceiving such problems, much less solving them, required Zinberg and his colleagues to alter old mental habits developed over decades.

But once they started seeing and thinking in this new way— seeing health care hassles from the patient's perspective and connecting the dots to eliminate them—they discovered more and more opportunities to improve the system and provide the kind of care patients actually wanted. And the Medicare payment model allowed CareMore to translate these health care improvements into increased margin, fueling growth, innovation, and improvements in care.

Another example: In the world of health care, "noncompliance" is a serious problem, including not just missed appointments but prescriptions unfilled, medicines untaken, exercise and diet regimens unfollowed, and symptoms unreported. Health care professionals grumble about noncompliance, but given the myriad demands on their time there's little they can do about it.

CareMore invented a different approach. As Zinberg puts it, "Noncompliance is *our* problem, not the patient's." CareMore found that adding nonmedical services to its routine care could improve compliance rates—for example, sending health care professionals to patients' homes to make sure they had scales to keep tabs on their weight, to look for loose throw rugs that might cause falls, and to provide "talking pill boxes" that automatically remind patients to take their medicine.

Each of these innovations led to a small improvement in patient wellness and a corresponding improvement in the economics of providing care. For the first time in anyone's memory, health care costs began to decline rather than steadily increase.

But CareMore was just getting started.

Next, the professionals at CareMore began to focus on diabetes, one of the most widespread and debilitating illnesses suffered by elderly patients. When they investigated how the worst complications of diabetes occurred, they learned exactly how important early

detection and proactive action are in caring for frail elders—and
how that makes both clinical and economic sense.

Take amputations. The typical chain of events would begin with
a small cut (on the foot, for example) self-treated, maybe with a Band-
Aid. If the cut resisted healing for a week or more, the patient might
visit her family doctor (called the primary care physician, or PCP).
The doctor might clean the wound, change the dressing, and advise
the patient, but the advice might or might not be understood or followed. A week later, with the wound getting worse, a second doctor
visit would lead to a referral to a surgeon—the average oversched-
uled PCP's only real resource for this kind of problem.

After the typical two-week delay in arranging an appointment,
the surgeon might discover that gangrene was beginning to develop
and recommend a consultation with a specialized vascular surgeon.
And after another two-week delay, the wound would have become
so serious that an amputation was now inevitable—at a cost of many
thousands of dollars and untold suffering. All beginning with a single,
scarcely noticeable cut.

No one taking a patient's-eye view of the problem would ever
design a system like this. No patient would ever demand it. But
this is the nonsystem that had grown up in the wake of America's
unconnected-dots approach to health care. With most of the U.S.
health care system working under a fee-for-service payment model,
fragmented transactional care is promoted, and no payment is provided for many of the kinds of proactive engagements the CareMore
team has built into their system.

CareMore responded by creating a wound clinic, staffed by nurses
whose primary job was to care for diabetic patients with small cuts.
They'd change the dressing every other day and spend a few minutes talking with the patient, making sure the wound was healing
on schedule.

Amputation rates for CareMore's diabetic patients fell by more
than 60 percent.

The HMOs whose draconian policies had so appalled Drs. Zinberg and Holzner had behaved as if *excessive demand* was the main problem in American health care—and that the solution was simply to say "No" as often as possible. CareMore's approach to diabetes exposes the flaw in that thinking. Elderly diabetics—like virtually all patients—don't actually *want* lots of medical treatments. In fact, they are prone to putting off doctor visits and avoiding care for as long as possible, often resulting in needless complications and enormous long-term costs. The coordinated care provided by Care-More recognizes this reality. Rather than taking the route of "No, no, no," it reduces costs *and* human suffering by providing patients with the effective, early-stage treatments and diligent follow-up care required to keep them healthy and vigorous. And that, after all, is what our demand for health care is *really* all about.

❑   ❑   ❑

ONE OF THE MOST important innovations pioneered by CareMore is the Extensivist. A patient is a unified being, not a collection of disconnected symptoms. Yet mainstream health care generally ignores this reality. One study of the care received by patients with chronic conditions like diabetes, heart disease, and asthma found that 40 percent of them were visiting an average of eleven different physicians; the upper quartile in the study actually averaged sixteen specialists from nine different practices. This regiment of doctors rarely speak to one another, coordinate plans, or consult on the possible interactions among their treatments.

It's an ineffective way to deal with so delicately balanced and complex a mechanism as a human being. But whose job is it to sort out the confusion? It falls to the patient, the only one who knows everything the various physicians are doing and therefore the only person in a position to raise the issues of how they all interact—except that very few laypeople have the time, energy, and expertise to play that role. And when the patient is frail and elderly, the likelihood of communication failure and ineffective care skyrockets.

Extensivists are connect-the-dots experts—specialists in coordination and integration whose goal is taking the hassles out of health
care and ensuring that what patients need, want, and get are one and
the same.

Charles Holzner explains how this new type of medical specialty
came into existence:

> When we started CareMore, we found we needed programs to
> keep the elderly frail out of the hospital. A sizable fraction of our
> patients would inevitably get readmitted over and over again if
> you treated them like routine patients. But no one wants to spend
> time in the hospital, and needless readmissions are a huge waste
> of energy and resources.
>
> So to keep our patients out of the hospital, I began seeing
> them myself every week or two. I basically became their per-
> sonal doctor, making sure they understood their post-operative
> regimen and were following it correctly. But very rapidly I be-
> came overloaded. So I told Dr. Zinberg, "We need more people
> like me."

And that's how the concept of the Extensivist was born. The
CareMore team realized that elderly patients commonly have many
interdependent clinical conditions. Without an integrated care plan,
problems will inevitably fall through the cracks. Whole person integrated patient management is a new kind of job in the health care
field. It equips a doctor with an array of powerful tools that make
it possible for the needs of the whole patient to be considered together. These tools include Patient QuickView, a system of unified
electronic health care records of the kind that the Patient Protection
and Affordable Care Act, which became law in 2010, aims to foster
on an experimental basis around the country, but which is already
up and running at CareMore. The Extensivist doesn't rely on a patient's memory or the hand-scrawled notes of his fellow physicians;

each CareMore patient's complete background data are available at the touch of a button.

Another set of tools is a series of interlocking protocols for treating the most common chronic conditions, incorporating the latest insights from the burgeoning science of "evidence-based medicine." Let's go back to the example of diabetes. A patient in CareMore's diabetes program receives a comprehensive medical assessment, wound care management and supplies, routine foot care to avoid needless amputations, the Diabetes Health Planner regimen, the "Shape Up and Levels Down" exercise and strength training program, and a personally tailored and monitored nutrition plan. Several dozen metrics are monitored at least monthly, and care plan adjustments are made accordingly.

The Extensivist makes sure that all these pieces of the puzzle are in place—in fact, that's her sole job. As a CareMore brochure puts it, "Integration and coordination of care is not voluntary." That means *it actually happens*. And because frail elder patients need integrated whole person care, the Extensivist role is the cornerstone of Care-More's clinical and economic success.

CareMore has developed similar programs for other chronic conditions like end-stage renal disease, chronic obstructive pulmonary disease, and hypertension and congestive heart failure. Having studied the evidence about what combination of practices yields the best impact on patient well-being, CareMore doesn't leave the choice of treatment up to chance or even to the whim of an individual physician—it provides a road map and a to-do checklist, much like the checklist airline pilots follow to make sure that *every* step in their preflight routine is completed before the jumbo jet leaves the runway.

The Extensivist must be a knowledgeable physician, of course. But people skills and a talent for clear, effective communication are even more important. "It's all about trust," Holzner emphasizes. "I saw that when I got involved in a patient's care, if I gained his trust he would do anything I told him to do. So showing patients that we have their best interests at heart is key to a strong and healthy relationship."

Today, whenever Holzner hires a new Extensivist, he recommends journalist Daniel Goleman's book *Emotional Intelligence* and urges him to apply its lessons to his work.

The Extensivist focuses on the sickest 15 percent among CareMore's client base, partly because those relatively few patients traditionally generate 70 percent of health care costs. One of his chief goals is to avoid needless hospital stays. "When a patient goes into the hospital for an unplanned reason," says CareMore executive Leeba Lessin, "we consider it a failure." Providing the frail 15 percent with efficient, complete, and coordinated care helps prevent small problems from becoming huge ones, reduces the number of five-figure bills that CareMore must pay, and has cut readmission rates by a third. And that frees up resources to improve every patient's care.

This all sounds startlingly like common sense. As CareMore's Dr. Balu Gadhe asks, "What's the point of spending up to three hundred thousand dollars on complicated in-patient care for congestive heart failure when you discharge the patient to a home where there's no family support, no food in the fridge, and no money for medication?" But mainstream medical care produces exactly this outcome thousands of times a day, since current fee-for-service Medicare programs leave gaping holes in coverage, incentivizing fragmented transaction medicine and exacerbating the cost problem at the expense of frail patients. It's another example of the gigantic gap between the health care people want and need, and the care they end up buying for lack of a better alternative.

At times, the CareMore intervention team even goes beyond what common sense would dictate. Gadhe recounts the case of a patient who refused a needed stay in an assisted-living facility because she couldn't bring her dog along. Her CareMore social worker solved the problem by adopting the dog and bringing it to visit the patient regularly.

The work of Extensivists helps produce some of CareMore's remarkable outcome statistics—for example, a rate of hospitalizations that is 24 percent lower than the industry average, average hospital stays that are 38 percent shorter than the norm, and a dramatic reduction in bedsores, that scourge of hospitalized patients that is one of the leading causes of iatrogenic (medically induced) deaths. (In a country where thousands of elderly people in nursing homes suffer from bedsores, CareMore's nursing home residents have reported, over the past two years, a total of *one* bedsore.) At-home follow-up care helps patients maintain the health benefits they received in the hospital and reduces readmission rates, now one-third lower than the Medicare average.

CareMore provides care to its members in several settings: hospital, home, and the CareMore clinic. All patients have access to the CareMore clinical center, where an array of services is available under one roof: health assessment, self-management skills training, mental health and social services, wellness and nutrition guidance, diagnostics and lab services, and counseling on the total package of benefits available through CareMore. Patients no longer have to trek from one clinic or doctor's office to another by car, cab, or bus, often toting X-rays, lab results, or folders of documents that are easy to lose, damage, or misplace. CareMore even provides toenail trimming for patients—because research shows that old folks with well-tended feet are better at keeping their balance.

New programs are constantly being tested. Two recent innovations are wireless monitoring for patients with congestive heart failure (CHF) and hypertension. Scales automatically send a CHF patient's daily weight to medical assistants at CareMore, so that an increase of three pounds or more (which may signal dangerous fluid accumulations) can be quickly noticed and dealt with. Blood pressure cuffs transmit readings for hypertension patients back to CareMore.

The patients like knowing that someone is paying attention to their condition every day. And in the first six months of testing the wireless scale system, CareMore found that hospital readmissions for CHF had fallen by 56 percent. Now similar systems for diabetes monitoring and the use of camera phones for daily conversations with a nurse practitioner are being tested.

❐   ❐   ❐

THE STRENGTH of CareMore's connect-the-dots system is that it produces a cascade of benefits for everyone involved.

The patient, of course, is the chief beneficiary. Health care that considers *all* aspects of an individual's well-being lifts the burden of planning, organizing, coordinating, and tracking dozens of variables off the shoulders of the patient and lets her focus on her role—getting well and staying well.

CareMore's member satisfaction rates reflect these benefits. Ninety-seven percent are either very or somewhat satisfied with their CareMore health plan. Eighty-two percent report that their customer service representative is "always courteous"; 74 percent say they are "always satisfied" with member services; more than 80 percent have recommended CareMore to a friend.

Physicians benefit, too. For many doctors, the opportunity to work with a company like CareMore, one that actually puts patient needs at the center of its practices, is very appealing. And having CareMore's expert help with some of the most challenging patient problems increases the effectiveness of the average PCP, leading to greater satisfaction for both patients and their caregivers.

And what about the issue that dominated the reform debates of 2009–2010, and that forced Sheldon Zinberg and his colleagues to launch CareMore in the first place—the unsustainable economics of health care in America?

Zinberg had convinced other doctors to join with him in creating CareMore by promising them, "If you put people before profit, you *will* profit." During its years as a more or less conventional health care provider (1993–1997), CareMore accumulated losses of around $11 million. But as the system of coordinated care Zinberg had dreamed about rose into place, the economic benefits he'd envisioned gradually emerged. By 2000, CareMore had turned the corner, showing a $24 million profit. It has remained solidly in the black ever since.

The economic logic behind CareMore is unconventional. Professionals at CareMore take on tasks and responsibilities physicians don't traditionally assume, and CareMore staffers spend more time with patients and their families than health care workers normally do. But every dollar CareMore spends saves multiple dollars down the line. As a result, overall member costs are 18 percent below the industry average. By reversing the cost curve, CareMore has created an economic model for health care that creates a path toward a sustainable private health care marketplace.

In January 2006, a group of private equity investors purchased CareMore, and Alan Hoops became CEO in March of that year. The investment premise: Replicate the CareMore model and build a national business by bringing differentiated health care services to the elderly around the country. The key challenge is making the model replicable while preserving its unique, patient-first focus. If CareMore can achieve this, it will be almost unique in the annals of U.S. health care.

Hoops emphasizes the importance of thinking about this challenge clearly. "It's not about 'growing to scale,'" Hoops explains.

The phrase implies we need huge numbers of patients to make our system work. That's not so. We can set up shop in a community, attract three to five thousand patients, and begin having an impact in terms of reduced costs and improved patient outcomes right away. So the word to use is "replicating." We're now in the process of replicating our model in communities in

Arizona and Nevada as well as elsewhere in California. The problem is no longer proving that the system works—it's bringing the system to more people . . . hopefully, in time, to millions of people.

Hoops's main focus has been on making the replication strategy work—and it has. CareMore has established new clinics while improving its health care impact and growing the number of satisfied members.

This success hasn't come easy. It required codifying the best practices and systematizing them for simple, accurate replication. It required creating and applying clear standards for measuring improvement and encouraging it. Most challenging, it meant transplanting the *heart* of CareMore—its passionate, patient-centered culture—from one location to another, through strong leadership, communication, and training.

Easy? No. But it's achievable—and it's working. Between the new clinics and the growth in CareMore's original network, membership has grown at an annual rate of more than 15 percent from 2005 to 2010. And designs for new clinics to serve additional communities are already in the planning stages.

The importance of the CareMore experience for our troubled national health care system is clear. CareMore concentrates its efforts on a particular subset of American consumers—the old and frail. But this subset is an especially important one when it comes to defining demand for health care. They consume an outsize share of the health care dollar invested by the country, whether willingly or not—and a lot of evidence suggests that much of the health care they get is not what they want or need. Simply giving the old and frail the kind of health care *they actually need and desire* would go a long way toward solving the national crisis.

Is CareMore's system a complete solution to America's health care crisis? Not in itself. But Alan Hoops believes the CareMore model, with appropriate adaptations, could be effective with any high-risk population, including chronic disease sufferers, drug and alcohol abusers, and the disabled. The same basic principles could be applied to them as to the elderly: treat patients as whole people, not as collections of disconnected systems; integrate care through all the specialties and the nonmedical behaviors that impact health; emphasize early intervention and prevention of medical problems, and follow through meticulously; monitor and measure results continually, and make accurate patient information readily available to every professional who needs it; help patients improve their health status through diet, exercise, and other lifestyle changes; and develop and apply consistent, evidence-based protocols defining effective care for every major health care problem that commands resources and impairs lives.

Above all, give patients what they *really want* from their health care providers—a few caring doctors who actually know their patients and are focused solely on their well-being.

If we ever have a national approach to health that meets the real demands of *all* Americans, it's likely to embody the CareMore experience, writ large.

3.

Backstory

(BAK-sto-ree) *noun* 1. elements beyond the product itself that help to make a product magnetic 2. unseen, often-overlooked factors, including infrastructure, ecosystem, and business design, that are essential to creating demand

IT'S WHAT YOU DON'T SEE THAT COUNTS: BEHIND THE KINDLE SCREEN

For decades, inventors had been dreaming about the electronic book—a handy way of making an endless stream of great reading conveniently accessible anywhere, any time. Imagine, they said, a slim, lightweight e-reader that was easy to read, fun to navigate, and had a long battery life. Such a magnetic product would entice avid readers, excite technology lovers, and unleash a powerful new stream of demand.

Wouldn't it?

This was precisely the dream that haunted Yoshitaka Ukita of the Sony Corporation.

Ukita was one of Sony's most gifted product designers as well as one of its most visionary experts on consumer demand. He'd developed the Sony Discman, which had revolutionized the CD music business back in 1984 much as its legendary predecessor, the Walkman, had done for the music cassette. He'd participated in shaping Sony's development of technologies for the Internet in the mid-nineties, produced early smartphones in the late nineties, and led the creation of a pioneering online music distribution network known as Music Clip in the early years of the new millennium.

Now Ukita was engaged in a project that he believed had greater potential to reshape the media landscape than any of these.

"Sony had already invested in the Japanese movie business," Ukita told us, "which at the time was approximately a three-billion-dollar industry. And we had invested in the music business, which was worth four to five billion dollars a year. But for a long time we had been looking for a way to apply our technology to a different kind of content—what we referred to as the data business. And this was a much, much bigger business. When we examined all kinds of publishing content—books, magazines, comics, and so on—the value added up to around twenty-six billion dollars in Japan alone. So, yes—we were very excited about the idea of an electronic device that could do for this content what the Discman had done for music."

In 2003, inspired by this vision, Ukita invited representatives of the ten most powerful publishing companies in Japan to a top-secret meeting at Sony's headquarters in Tokyo. As arguably the planet's best-respected and most-innovative electronics company, Sony had access to the world's most advanced technology. But the publishers owned the content. If Ukita's vision was to come to pass, an accord between Sony and these ten dark-suited men around the Tokyo conference table would be absolutely essential.

The meeting opened with the usual ritualized pleasantries. But it really began when Ukita revealed the purpose of the gathering—by pressing the power button on a small, putty-colored plastic device and conjuring to life a display screen that made the publishers gasp.

They'd seen countless video displays of Japanese characters before, including those affixed to would-be electronic readers. They were flickery, distractingly pixilated, glare-prone, low in contrast, and difficult and unpleasant to read. But the screen on the device in Ukita's hand was very different. Its pale gray background was adorned

with neat rows of crisp, black kanji characters, glare-free and effort-
less to read. When Ukita brought the device to the window and
exposed it to the full sunlight of a Tokyo morning, the executives
were shocked to discover that it looked exactly the same—unlike
the display on a laptop computer or mobile phone, which was practically impossible to read in direct sun. At a glance, you might think
you were looking at ink on paper—not an electronic screen at all.

"This is the Librié," Ukita declared proudly. (A world traveler,
he'd come across the word during a visit to Spain and had jotted
it down as if with this very moment in mind.) "One day, millions
of people will read everything you publish on a device like this
one."

As the pale-faced executives exchanged glances, Ukita began to
explain the technology behind the Librié. He'd first seen a display
like this after being tipped off by a call from a friend: "I just met an
American named Wilcox who has a new toy you will really want to
see." The very next day, Ukita had arranged a hotel room meeting
with representatives of a company called E Ink, where he'd become
one of the first executives to see the latest version of the company's
unique "microcapsule" display technology.

Ukita had been thrilled. For over a decade—ever since he'd tried,
and failed, to create demand for an information machine called the
Data Discman back in 1992—he'd been looking for a better way to
let people read on a screen. Now he'd found it. Ukita and E Ink's
Russ Wilcox quickly negotiated a deal to let Sony become the first
company to use E Ink in an electronic reader. Months of teamwork
between the Americans and the engineers and designers at Sony
had resulted in the sample device now being passed from hand to
hand in the conference room.

"The Librié is easy to use, compact, and convenient," Ukita told
the assembled publishers. "It can hold up to five hundred books at
a time. The contents are protected so that no one can make unau-
thorized copies. And the whole device, including batteries, weighs

three hundred grams. The average book you publish weighs three hundred *and nine* grams. Our machine is lighter!" He tapped the screen. "This is the future," he declared. "And Sony wants you to be our partners in creating it. And in profiting from it."

For a long moment, the publishers stared at the table in silence.

They had no reason to doubt the accuracy of anything Ukita had said. Just the opposite: Their attitude toward Sony was one of admiration bordering on reverence. They knew that no company in the world had a greater tradition of technological innovation—and demand creation—than Sony. If Ukita-san believed that Sony was on the verge of transforming their industry, they believed it, too.

And that's why, when they broke their silence, all ten publishers broke into smiles of approval and eagerly began describing how they could work in close partnership with Sony on shaping the new market for electronic books distributed through the Librié.

They understood all too well that collaborating with Ukita-san and with the great corporation he represented might be their last chance to participate in the electronic publishing revolution—and, they desperately hoped, to smother it in its cradle.

ONE OF TODAY'S most impressive demand stories is the boom in electronic reading devices that is reshaping one of the world's oldest industries, the traditional publishing business launched by Gutenberg nearly six centuries ago. Yet few people even in the publishing industry understand the *real* story behind this demand explosion.

Most attribute the runaway success of Amazon's Kindle to the E Ink technology incorporated in its clear, highly readable screen. But if the advantages of E Ink explain the success of the Kindle, what explains the little-known story of Sony's Librié, which used the same E Ink technology and was launched, with much fanfare, in the vibrant Japanese book market three full years before the Kindle—only to fail completely?

As usual, the key to unraveling a demand mystery is the anomaly—the piece of the puzzle that makes no sense at first glance.

In this case, the true explanation for the triumph of the Kindle is not the E Ink technology but something far less obvious—the behind-the-screen elements that make the Kindle into a powerfully magnetic product while its near twin created almost zero demand in Japan (thanks largely, as we'll see, to the smiling sabotage practiced by those ten Japanese publishers after their fateful meeting with Ukita-san).

Such behind-the-screen elements—easy to overlook yet crucial in the creation of demand—make up a product's *backstory*.

Think, for example, of the last great movie you saw. Your attention was riveted by the action on the screen: the charismatic stars, the compelling plot twists, the amazing visual spectacle. Yet insiders know that the *real* secret to a movie's greatness frequently lies in the backstory elements whose existence audiences can only guess at. They include the deals made and not made, as well as the contributions of the hundreds of professionals whose very titles are mysterious to most moviegoers—"Sabre artists" and "Foley artists," "location mixers" and "ADR editors," "gaffers" and "grips" and "best boys"—yet who give a movie its distinctive look, sound, texture, pacing, and drive. Without them, and the incredibly complex backstory they build, all the more obvious contributions of headliners like Julia Roberts and James Cameron would go for naught.

In the same way, it's the unseen and unheralded backstory elements that make the Kindle magnetic, while Sony's failure to support the Librié with an equally compelling backstory led to an epic demand failure.

The telltale pattern emerges in one demand story after another: What you *don't* see is often what makes or breaks the product.

❑   ❑   ❑

LIKE SO MANY tales of electronic innovation, including those of the computer mouse and the graphical user interface, the story of the Kindle begins in the 1970s at Xerox's legendary Palo Alto Research Center (PARC) in California. Nicholas K. Sheridon, a PARC researcher, was frustrated with the dim, low-contrast, hard-to-read display screens then used with computers. So he devoted eighteen months to experimenting with alternatives. Sometime in 1973, he came up with a device he called the Gyricon, which used microscopic balls embedded in fluid to create recognizable images with high contrast and no flickering.

This was the technological breakthrough that would ultimately produce the e-reader. But Xerox did nothing with Sheridon's invention. We could chalk it up to managerial shortsightedness, but the real point is a broader one: New technology, all by itself, almost never leads directly to demand. Most often, the path connecting innovation and demand is a circuitous one, depending on serendipity, luck, insight, persistence, and the fortuitous coming together of numerous, seemingly unrelated circumstances—including the eventual discovery and deployment of the backstory elements that are often the secret keys to demand.

In the mid-seventies, the backstory required to make the e-reader a success was still decades in the future.

The big step toward a practical application was taken in the mid-nineties by Joseph Jacobson, a young physicist at the MIT Media Lab, and a pair of research assistants, J. D. Albert and Barrett Comiskey.

Jacobson, a voracious reader, had long been intrigued by the idea of an electronic book—a device that would be as comfortable, convenient, and pleasant to read as a traditional printed book while being able to display an endlessly changing array of texts or images. In 1996, he asked Albert and Comiskey to experiment with Sheridon's approach. By 1997, the concept was well enough developed to become the basis of a new company: E Ink. Cofounded by Jacobson, Albert, and Comiskey along with Russ Wilcox, then a recent graduate of Harvard Business School, and Jerome S. Rubin, a former president of Lexis-Nexis, E Ink began developing prototypes for paper-like electronic displays.

From the start, the basic E Ink technology was highly promising, enabling the company's founders to draw some $150 million in start-up capital from companies like Intel, Motorola, Philips, and Hearst Interactive Media. But the circuitous path from innovation to demand would prove to have many more twists and turns.

With the benefit of hindsight, E Ink's CEO Russ Wilcox has described the "naïveté" he and his colleagues brought to the start-up process:

> We understood that it was probably going to take two years to make something that people wanted to buy. And in terms of making something that looked good, we did that. But what we didn't see in the beginning, and learned over time, was that it would take another two years to go from something that looked good to something that would look good for many years under all operating conditions—in other words, to achieve stability and robustness. And then it would take *another* two years to get something that you could reproducibly manufacture, at an affordable cost point. . . . It's a very complex system design that combines chemistry, materials science, electronics, optics, and mechanical engineering.

By 2004, E Ink had been developed to a point where something close to Joe Jacobson's early dream of an electronic book was feasible. Sony's Yoshitaka Ukita had licensed E Ink technology to create the Librié for the Japanese market. E Ink, which had been running on fumes, saw its revenues soar that year. Finally the company had a chance to put its technology in the hands of thousands of customers.

And, once again, the magical link between technology and demand failed to materialize.

The crucial factor, as Ukita told us years later, was the nature of the support given to the Librié by the Japanese book industry. Mindful of Sony's reputation as a brilliant creator and marketer of electronic products, the publishers assumed that the Librié marked the beginning of the end for the print-on-paper era in their industry. And they hated the idea. Fearing loss of control over their own products and their elimination as needless middlemen, the publishers decided they had to battle the e-book with everything they had. And they chose to do so in characteristically oblique Japanese fashion—by supporting it.

When Ukita met with the publishers, they were outwardly positive. They praised the technology and complimented Sony on its coup. They promised to provide access to their publishing libraries, and they even offered to invest in the new product. To all appearances, Sony had succeeded in creating a powerful network of allies in its quest to revolutionize publishing in Japan.

But in reality, the publishers had quietly resolved to provide Sony with just enough cooperation to kill the Librié altogether. Each of the ten leading publishers agreed to give Sony access to one hundred book titles. A thousand books might sound like a lot. But visit any bookstore and count off a thousand titles from the shelves that surround you. You'll soon realize that this amounts to perhaps one corner of a typical bookstore or Barnes & Noble outlet—enough to engage the interest of a browser for five minutes or so, but not much more.

It didn't help that the Librié had to be physically tethered to a PC to download books, which was awkward and inconvenient, or that ownership of an e-book expired after an arbitrary sixty-day life span. But it was the passive aggression of the Japanese publishers that delivered the fatal blow. Sony's device was well designed and technologically remarkable—but what good is an e-reader that provides access to just a handful of books and snatches them away if you don't read fast enough? It was the Curse of the Incomplete Product—the cardinal error of One-Click World—spelling doom for a technically superb device from one of the world's great consumer electronics companies.

A cool piece of technology with a badly designed backstory is like a movie that features big-name stars . . . along with ludicrous dialogue, impossible-to-follow editing, and laughable special effects. Neither one is destined for box-office glory.

◻   ◻   ◻

WHICH BRINGS US, at last, to the breakthrough success of the Kindle— an overnight sensation thirty-five years in the making.

Many CEOs are every bit as smart, knowledgeable, and hard-working as Jeff Bezos, founder of Amazon. But Bezos has a couple of qualities that distinguish him as a great demand creator.

One is that he is incurably inquisitive about how things really work. He is also obsessively customer-oriented. He summarizes his business strategy this way: "Whenever we're facing one of those too-hard problems, where we get into an infinite loop and can't decide what to do, we try to convert it into a straightforward problem by saying, 'Well, what's better for the consumer?' "

This isn't just lip service. All the elements of Amazon—from the crystal-clear design of its website and the simplicity of its single-click shopping system to the seamless incorporation of offerings from thousands of other retailers and the unobtrusive but always-available value-added features such as customer reviews and individualized product recommendations—all are tailored to make the consumer experience as easy, pleasant, complete, and satisfying as possible. They apply this principle even when it appears to hurt sales. For example, recognizing that customers with large collections of books or CDs sometimes mistakenly order a product they've previously purchased, Amazon provides a warning before the "confirm order" button gets pushed. Yes, this discourages a few sales, and some in Amazon considered it unnecessary. But Bezos said, "We know this is a feature that's good for customers. Let's do it." In the long run, happy customers will return to Amazon.

Bezos and his company have followed this approach from the beginning, when they were running yearly deficits because they offered services that seemed impossible to turn a profit on, and have maintained it to this day, having become the world's second-most-valuable retailer (trailing only Walmart) and one of the most profitable.

The other special quality Bezos exhibits is a certain kind of eyesight that few people have.

Back in 2004, an ordinary person looking at Sony's Librié might have said, "Oh, that's a cool device. Wonder if anyone'll buy it?" A typical book retailer would probably have turned up his nose, sniffing, "We've seen these electronic readers come and go. My customers love the feel and smell of *real* books." Both responses would have been understandable.

But Jeff Bezos looked at the Librié—evidently he first glimpsed it at a business conference where E Ink's Joe Jacobson was demonstrating it—and said, "Uh-oh—*this is a machine that could destroy my business.*"

Now, this wasn't literally true—a Japanese-only reader with access to a rental library of just a thousand books posed no threat to Amazon. But with just a little bit of imagination, Bezos could envision a next-generation Librié—one with multilanguage capabilities, a wireless connection to the Internet (so that books could be purchased almost instantly rather than being downloaded through a separate computer link), and access to a vast online bookstore like the one Amazon itself maintained, or (and here Jeff Bezos might have shuddered just a bit) the one Barnes & Noble had launched in 1997. In other words, an e-reader that backed up its amazing display technology with an equally brilliant backstory.

Such an e-reader would have the potential to revolutionize book buying, sweeping away the remaining hassles that Amazon itself had been unable to remove. "I've got millions of customers who love getting books from me in two days," Bezos must have thought. "What if somebody else can deliver them in *two minutes*?"

Bezos ordered thirty Libriés for his staffers to play with, to study, maybe to disassemble and tinker with. And soon he was in touch with the E Ink people to ask, "How can we work together to build a better e-reader for the U.S. market?"

In a way, it was an utterly bizarre project for Amazon to tackle. Amazon wasn't a maker of electronic gear, like Samsung, or of computers, like Apple, or of wireless-enabled phones or equipment, like Nokia—any of which would have seemed a more natural partner for E Ink. But Bezos was doing what he does best—working backward from the customer's hassle map, sussing out the new forms of demand that map implied, and then asking, "What will it take for Amazon to meet that demand?" If the answer was "Building a great e-reader," then that's what Amazon would do.

Bezos set up the project carefully. When a company is successful and growing rapidly, it's hard to fund and manage a potentially revolutionary product or service within the mainstream corporate environment. There's too much potential for internal rivalries, budgetary pressures, imagined threats, ingrained assumptions, and habitual behaviors to subtly derail the project. So Bezos assigned the job to his right-hand man, Steve Kessel, a person whose visibility and recognized clout meant he'd have little trouble marshaling the attention of people within and without the company. He gave Kessel a new title (senior vice president of digital) and created a separate business unit to house the project, giving it the Ludlumesque name of Lab 126.

Located in the technology hotbed of Cupertino, California (both for access to the best talent and to insulate it further from the pressures at corporate headquarters in Seattle), Lab 126 was handed over to the day-to-day leadership of Gregg Zehr, a wunderkind with previous stints at Palm, Linux, and Apple. Zehr in turn hired a collection of other brilliant technology types. They set to work designing the world's best e-reader—including the backstory elements that the Librié had failed to deliver.

"If anyone is going to destroy our online shopping business model," Jeff Bezos had decided, "it's going to be us."

◻   ◻   ◻

MEANWHILE, SONY'S UKITA hadn't given up on his e-reader dream. Even as the team at Lab 126 set to work, Sony was tackling the flaws of the Librié. The new Sony Reader was introduced into the American market in 2006. Although the Reader still didn't have its own wireless link, it did boast a large (six-inch diagonal) screen with improved contrast and readability as compared to the Librié. The buttons were better designed and the device felt comfortable in the hand. Reviewers waxed poetic. Descriptions like "beautiful," "extraordinary," "elegant," and "amazing" were tossed around.

In an attempt to upgrade the Librié's disappointing backstory, Sony worked assiduously with publishers to assemble an attractive list of book titles to sell through Connect, its corporate version of the Apple iTunes Store. There was just one problem: By the time the Reader was introduced, Connect was already moribund, having failed dismally in the competitive race against iTunes. The resulting shopping experience, though an improvement over the Librié, was less than scintillating. One reviewer wrote in 2007:

> Though Sony threw in the towel on the music side of its online store Connect earlier this year, the e-books division is still alive and healthy. Well, it's alive, anyway . . .
>
> Sony claims more than 20,000 titles for the store, and the selection certainly seems varied enough to keep readers occupied. The store is simple to use, if spartan, with capsule reviews from *Publishers Weekly* and space for user comments. Unfortunately, that space is largely empty; even such popular titles as *Freakonomics*, *The Tipping Point*, and Stephen Colbert's *I Am America (And So Can You!)* have no comments yet. This sort of thing makes Connect feel like a ghost town filled with vending

machines; you can get what you want, and you know that people must come through to top up the supply of Cokes, but boy, it sure looks empty.

We can't help but wonder what the history of demand might have been like if Sony had teamed up with a major bookselling chain such as Barnes & Noble or even with a big independent bookstore like Powell's, in Portland, Oregon, or Denver's Tattered Cover, rather than using its own retail site. The Sony Reader, preferably equipped with a wireless connection for downloading contents and coupled with an online book source nearly as extensive as Amazon's, might have opened the floodgates of e-reader demand while Amazon was still perfecting its own device.

But it didn't happen. Sony failed to fully grasp the make-or-break importance of backstory to the future of the e-reader—despite having witnessed how backstory weakness had spelled the doom of the Librié. The new backstory Sony crafted was improved, but not by enough. Another near miss was added to the lengthening saga of the e-reader. Would *this* be the fatal blow that finally spelled the end of E Ink and, perhaps, of the quest for the holy grail of electronic book publishing?

No—because fourteen months later, in November 2007, Amazon released the Kindle.

Strictly as a reading device, the Kindle offered no significant advantages over the Reader; in fact, it was slightly *less* sophisticated than the Sony device. (For example, the Kindle offered just four shades of gray rather than the eight boasted by the Reader.) But the screen-to-screen standoff paled in importance against what you saw when you looked *behind* the screen.

Kindle's advantages began with its wireless connection for downloading books—a crucial infrastructure link previous e-readers had failed to include. In truth, using a USB cable attached to a PC is not terribly onerous. But every added step, every extra restriction, every additional piece of gear needed to perform an activity makes a product dramatically *less* magnetic. Unplugging the PC wire gave Kindle users freedom—and gave the Kindle an essential touch of magic.

More important was Amazon's unmatched catalog of e-books for sale. After more than a decade building the world's biggest online bookstore, Jeff Bezos had developed working relationships with every major publisher—and having pioneered Amazon's "Search Inside the Book" feature in 2003, he'd even amassed experience with digitizing texts. Now he deployed these advantages to make the e-book experience unforgettable. On the Kindle's launch day, there were 88,000 e-books available for download, including practically all the current *New York Times* bestsellers—more than four times the number available from Sony. Better still, anyone with an Amazon account could buy them with a single click. Most were priced at ten dollars, a significant discount from the typical cost of a trade paperback or especially a new hardcover book. Subscriptions to the *New York Times* and other online periodicals were also available, making the Kindle a handy alternative to the familiar laptop for keeping up with the news online.

Yet another backstory strength available to Bezos was his company's ongoing relationship with some 65 million online shoppers—including several million avid book readers whose buying habits (and e-mail addresses) were known to Amazon. If visitors to Sony's online bookstore felt they'd wandered into a "ghost town," Kindle users found themselves in a friendly, familiar setting where book recommendations tailored to their preferences and lively reviews by readers with similar interests jostled happily for their attention.

Look at the Kindle, and you don't see the wireless connection, the relationships between Amazon and publishers, the vast and easy-to-use online bookstore, or the personalized book recommendations. But all these backstory elements—invisible yet powerful—dramatically enhanced the e-book experience, giving the

Kindle the magnetism its predecessors lacked. Despite the hefty price tag of $399 (and the fact that the device was available only through Amazon, not in any stores), the first production run of Kindles was sold out within five and a half hours.

Suddenly—after thirty years of trying—e-reading technology had tapped a mother lode of demand, thanks mainly to the multiple advantages that Amazon offered to consumers over and above the E Ink screen itself.

Based on our interviews with dozens of readers, we believe another factor contributed to the emergence of demand for an e-reader in 2007: the growing ranks of green-minded consumers. A significant number of our interviewees volunteered, unbidden, the fact that they *hated* thinking about the trees sacrificed to print the newspapers, magazines, and books piling up in their apartments.

There are still traditional book lovers who refuse to touch e-readers because "I love the feel and smell of paper in my hands." But their numbers may now be matched or even exceeded by those who feel *guilty* about the old-fashioned pleasures of paper. This was probably a modest factor in the successful launch of the Kindle—but a real one whose importance is still growing.

For all these reasons, the Kindle achieved the demand breakthrough that E Ink had been searching for. By the end of 2008, one analyst estimated Kindle sales at 500,000 units, making it a roughly $200 million business—a startling leap forward for the nascent e-book industry.

True to its nature as a customer-centric, demand-focused company, Amazon didn't stop at Kindle 1. Within fourteen months (in February 2009), an improved Kindle 2 was released, featuring a modest price reduction (to $359), a sleeker and more ergonomic design, quicker refresh times for the E Ink display, and new text-to-speech technology that enabled the device to "read aloud" the texts of books. Like its predecessor, the Kindle 2 flew off the shelves.

In October—just in time for holiday sales—pop culture icon Oprah Winfrey declared on her show that she had "fallen in love" with the Kindle 2. (E Ink employees today grin when they recall the thrill of gathering in the company's big central workroom-cum-meeting space to watch TV images of Jeff Bezos handing out free book-filled Kindles to the cheering members of Oprah's studio audience . . . and the sudden terror of realizing that their new biggest problem would be manufacturing E Ink displays fast enough to keep the machines in stock.)

In May 2009, a third Kindle model was added to the lineup. The Kindle DX has a larger (9.7-inch) screen, can read PDF files (as well as Kindle-format digitized books), and can be rotated for use in either portrait or landscape mode. And in August 2010, yet another model appeared, with modest performance improvements and a dramatically reduced price—$139 with a Wi-Fi connection, $189 with 3G.

Perhaps most important, Amazon's Steve Kessel, now known as senior vice president of Kindle, claims that Kindle owners buy books at a rate 2.7 times greater than when they were shopping via mail, the old-fashioned way. To adapt the familiar razor/razor blade analogy, imagine if Gillette could come up with a way to make its customers want to shave *2.7 times as often*! Talk about creating new demand—and building a company's bottom line.

And now, with Amazon having demonstrated beyond doubt the latent demand for an electronic reader with real hassle-reducing magnetism and a powerful backstory, other players in One-Click World are moving to claim spaces in the burgeoning e-reader industry.

Sony is still in the game. In August 2009, it released a new version of the Reader, known as the Daily Edition, which boasts an increase in the number of grayscale tones from eight to sixteen, making more detailed images possible. And Sony has put a lot of work into improving its backstory. The Daily Edition offers—at last!—free 3G wireless service, as well as a greatly enhanced bookstore. Though still a distinct number two to Kindle, the Sony entrant now enjoys its own steady stream of demand.

Meanwhile, in October 2009, Barnes & Noble launched the third major entrant in the E Ink reader field—the Nook. It closely resembled the Kindle, but added a small color touch screen below the E Ink display as an input device. The Nook's content source was the vast bookstore of B&N.com, second in size only to Amazon's.

In March 2010, Apple weighed in from a very different direction with its long-awaited, much-ballyhooed iPad, which eschewed E Ink's monochrome look in favor of a brilliant full-color, multitouch LED screen. And as we might expect from a master one-click company like Apple, the iPad-as-reader is supported by a magnificent backstory. Apps for both the Nook and Kindle bookstores are available, giving the iPad access to a larger array of e-books than any other device. By the end of 2010, more than 7 million iPads had been sold, and me-too touch-screen tablet devices were beginning to proliferate—including a new Barnes & Noble e-reader with an LED screen, dubbed the Nook Color.

Finally (for now), December 2010 also witnessed yet another major entry into the e-books universe—the launch of Google eBookstore. This new online bookselling site boasted the world's largest e-book catalog—nearly 3 million free books in the public domain as well as hundreds of thousands of other titles. Google e-books were offered in device-neutral formats suitable for reading on the iPad, the iPhone, the iPod touch, the Nook, the Sony Reader, and on personal computers—in fact, practically any reading device *except* the Kindle (although hackers quickly created software designed to convert Google e-book files for Kindle use). And in a fascinating backstory twist, Google announced its intention to partner with independent booksellers around the country, providing them with immediate, low-cost access to the e-book marketplace—and a possible way to combat the steady decline in sales they'd suffered at the hands of Amazon and the big chains.

The revolution Amazon sparked back in 2007 is likely to spin off even more new and unpredictable developments. But for now, the Kindle continues to lead the way among electronic readers. By the end of 2010, an estimated 8 million Kindles had been sold (precise figures are proprietary). And as the number of Kindles grows, so do sales of electronic books. Amazon reports that, for books available in both e-book and hard copy formats, Kindle sales now represent almost half of its unit sales.

The e-reader demand breakthrough has happened—in a very big way. But who will capture the lion's share of demand as this new world of reading evolves? The answer will depend, in part, on which device book lovers find most magnetic in the long run. But it will depend even more on the power and completeness of the backstory each company creates and the strength and creativity of its network of publishers, booksellers, designers, distributors, programmers, and other collaborators.

In the decade to come, as e-books become more and more ubiquitous, what's behind the screen will loom larger than ever. And this means that the fears some "old media" players have expressed that the digital age may render them irrelevant are groundless—provided they take full advantage of their unique experience as creators and deliverers of compelling content.

Imagine publishers employing the speed and flexibility of technology to multiply the inherent power of well-crafted words—unforgettable stories, amazing characters, mind-expanding insights, passionate and evocative poetry—and provide opportunities for millions of young people to fall in love with reading through the new medium of the e-book. The great publishing phenomena of the past generation, from Oprah Winfrey's Book Club to J. K. Rowling's Harry Potter series, offer just an inkling of the demand that can happen when the right reading experience comes along in the right way at the right time. Enabled by powerful backstory connections, the e-reader can multiply the kinds of reading experiences in ways we're just beginning to understand.

Imagine all this, and then ask: Is there any limit to the future demand for books?

TETRA PAK STEPS OUT FROM THE BACKSTORY

One of the minor culture shocks Americans experience when visiting Europe comes when helping to make after-dinner coffee in a friend's apartment, whether in Paris, Berlin, or Rome. "Where's the milk?" they ask, peering into the surprisingly undersized refrigerator.

"In the cupboard" is the reply. And sure enough, there on the shelf is a square carton of milk—alongside cartons of orange juice, scrambled egg mix, yogurt, pudding, and other items no sensible American would dream of storing at room temperature.

What's going on here? Are Europeans unaware of the basic rules of food safety as American families have practiced them for generations?

The real explanation leads us to one of the more fascinating corners of the demand universe—and a story that illustrates vividly how culture and psychology influence the shape of demand.

Think about the rich flavor of classic hollandaise sauce, made with fresh egg yolks, butter, and a touch of lemon juice, in a dish like eggs benedict or served as an accompaniment to steamed asparagus spears or a poached salmon fillet. How would you react if hollandaise sauce were poured onto your plate straight from a cardboard box stored on an unrefrigerated pantry shelf?

If you're like most Americans, you might insist that you'd never eat such an unappetizing and possibly dangerous item. But the fact is that you probably *already have*. A hollandaise sauce containing the traditional ingredients is now available in special cartons that can be stored without refrigeration, just like the milk in our European friends' cupboards. The sauce contains no preservatives or other chemicals, meets every health and safety standard, and obviously is much faster and easier to prepare than hollandaise sauce from scratch.

Most shocking, it tastes good—really good. After tasting it, one American chef admitted, "It is very hard to tell the difference between the hollandaise sauce I make and this product." And ready-made hollandaise sauce is just one menu item from an expanding array of liquid foods in boxes that are increasingly being served, and savored, in restaurants, hotels, and catering halls across America.

Is this some recent scientific breakthrough that has jumped straight from the laboratory to the pantry shelf? Not exactly. The new wave of demand for boxed foods in the United States has taken more than *fifty years* to develop. And to this day, there are millions of American consumers who simply *don't want to know* that part of their gourmet dinner came from an unrefrigerated cardboard carton.

In response, the remarkable company behind this innovation— lauded as the most important food packaging invention of the twentieth century and exhibited in the permanent collection of New York's Museum of Modern Art as an example of brilliant design— has been carrying out a kind of "incognito revolution," transforming the way we eat while remaining almost completely obscure. And while very few American consumers have heard of Tetra Pak, executives at the companies that produce the foods you enjoy know the company well and rely on it more with every passing year, creating an enormous stream of demand for Tetra Pak's unique expertise.

Most intriguingly, today a new chapter in the Tetra Pak story is beginning—one that tests whether a unique and amazing product that almost no one has heard about can step out of the shadows and begin to attract demand, not just as part of someone else's backstory, but in its own right.

❏   ❏   ❏

ASEPTIC CARTON PACKAGING was the brainchild of Sweden's Ruben Rausing. While studying business at New York's Columbia University back in the 1910s, Rausing was struck by the spread of modern food retailing techniques, including national product distribution, self-service shopping, and the first supermarkets. Convinced that the same trends would eventually revolutionize Europe, he began thinking about ways to address the challenges they'd produce.

Back in Sweden, Rausing teamed up with an investor named Erik Åkerlund to found Åkerlund & Rausing, a company devoted to creating packaging for the new-era retailing of the twentieth century—for example, a consumer-sized flour package to replace the old barrels formerly used for shipping and selling flour in bulk.

In the 1930s, Rausing's attention was caught by another traditional commodity whose packaging and distribution badly needed updating: milk. At that time, milk in Sweden was sold either in bulk, using unwieldy metal canisters, or in heavy consumer-sized glass bottles (much as in the United States). Neither system fit well into the emerging world of self-service food stores. Rausing began experimenting with new ways of packaging milk that would eliminate hassles for milk consumers and producers alike.

He first needed to address the problem of sealing the milk flow into the container so that it was not exposed to contaminants that would dramatically limit its shelf life—a surprisingly thorny engineering challenge that took Rausing years to solve.

In 1943, Rausing was chatting about the issue with his wife, Elisabeth, over lunch. Suddenly she exclaimed, "Why don't you continuously fill milk into the tube and then seal it *through* the milk?" The idea was that the uninterrupted flow of milk would eliminate air pockets within the package, which were the troublesome source of impurities.

Rausing was dubious. "It seemed impossible," he later recounted, "as the hot clamps [used] for hot sealing would give the milk a burnt taste."

But his wife responded with a question: "Have you tried to do it?" Rausing later described this as "a typical, logical answer from this remarkable woman." After lunch, he returned to the lab, tried sealing several paper cylinders filled with milk without interrupting the fluid stream, and found that no burnt taste could be detected. The sealed-off, milk-filled portions of paper cylinder took the form of a tetrahedral (four-sided) container that Rausing dubbed a *tetrapak*.

But solving the problem of continuous milk flow and airless packaging wasn't enough. A number of other innovations were required, including a multilayered paper, plastic, and foil material that was light, flexible, odorless and tasteless, and leakproof; a method for quickly sterilizing both the package and the contents and keeping them sterile; and an interlocking system of machines to perform all the necessary processes quickly, efficiently, and automatically. Even the question of how to pack a batch of tetrahedrons for shipping posed a puzzle. Rausing's associate Harry Järund solved that one by designing a six-sided "basket" that neatly and compactly held eighteen of the little tetrahedrons.

It took almost a decade to get all these pieces right. (As Rausing later remarked, with Nordic understatement, "Doing something that nobody else has done before is actually quite hard.") The new Tetra Pak company, originally a subsidiary of Åkerlund & Rausing, delivered its first Tetra Pak machine for tetrahedron-shaped cartons to the Lund (Sweden) Dairy Association in September 1952. Two months later, the dairy began shipping cream in one-deciliter, aseptic tetrahedral packages.

The Tetra Pak system immediately enhanced the dairy industry's backstory. Some of the benefits flowed directly to consumers. Unlike a can, a Tetra Pak carton required no special tool for opening; the consumer simply tore off a corner of the paper pack and poured out the contents or drank them directly.* Unlike a bottle or jar, a Tetra Pak carton was unbreakable, preventing the loss of contents and the danger posed by shards of splintered glass. Because of the unique flash-sterilizing method Tetra Pak developed, which required fifteen seconds or less of heating, the contents (milk or other liquids) were kept in a close-to-nature state, with minimal effect on their taste and texture. And the sterilized Tetra Pak carton didn't impart the tinny or "off" flavor sometimes experienced with cans or bottles, even when partial contents were refrigerated after opening in the original package.

Other benefits of Tetra Pak cartons were experienced mainly by food processors, wholesalers, and retailers. Shipping costs were sharply reduced because of the light weight of Tetra Pak packages as well as their unusual geometric design—a fully packed basket held more liquid in a given space than a batch of cylindrical bottles or cans. Even more significant, the fact that perishable products like milk packaged in Tetra Pak remained fresh and wholesome without refrigeration for up to a year eliminated the need to maintain a "cool chain" from processing plant to grocery store. No more refrigerated trucks or train cars were needed. As a result, the practical radius within which products could now be shipped was dramatically expanded, making it possible for a single plant to service a much larger customer base, producing further savings. And the energy savings meant Tetra Pak containers had what today we call a much smaller carbon footprint—an economic benefit whose importance would only grow over time.

In short, Tetra Pak redrew the dairy industry's hassle map through a dramatically improved backstory—and it soon began to do the same for producers of many other kinds of food.

---

* This is not a negligible issue. A bizarre fact from the history of packaging: The metal can was invented in 1813; the first can opener was not invented until 1858. For forty-five years, people used chisels or pickaxes to open cans.

In its own quiet way, the Tetra Pak was a magnetic product—gratefully accepted by consumers and positively embraced by the businesses whose operations it improved and whose bottom lines it enhanced. Food companies soon began using the refrigerator-free packaging to bring the benefits of prepared foods to a wider marketplace, including in the developing world. The first Tetra Pak Classic Aseptic machine outside Europe went into operation in Lebanon in 1964. The technology arrived along with a training center in Kenya in 1972, in Brazil in 1978, and in China in 1979; the first products to be packaged in China included sugarcane juice and chrysanthemum tea. Today there are Tetra Pak facilities in 170 countries, on every inhabited continent in the world.

Creating this demand wave made Ruben Rausing one of the most successful—and richest—entrepreneurs in the world. By 2010, Tetra Pak boasted annual revenues of 8.95 billion euros (about $12.5 billion). Tetra Pak produces 145 billion packages a year—twenty for every man, woman, and child in the world. And as noted above, Rausing's original Tetra Pak design enjoys a spot in the permanent collection of the Museum of Modern Art, alongside such other icons of twentieth-century design as Frank Lloyd Wright's Fallingwater and the Eames chair.

YET THERE'S ONE market where demand for Rausing's brainchild has lagged—and it happens to be the richest, most important consumer market on the planet. When it came to the United States, the magnetism of Tetra Pak, and its demand-creating potential, were almost completely lost in translation.

For six solid decades, Americans resisted buying most foods or beverages in aseptic packaging, with one exception: single-serve juice boxes for kids, known as Tetra Brik cartons—the kind with a little straw for insertion into a tiny foil-lined opening in the top—which became enormously popular in the United States in the 1980s.

Tetra Pak's other carton types, from the gable-topped Tetra Rex to the Tetra Wedge, struggled to attract demand from U.S. consumers.

Why? What makes Tetra Pak magnetic to Europeans, while Americans shy away?

The cultural and social factors behind these divergent attitudes make a fascinating study. Chief among them is the early U.S. adoption of refrigerators, which became fixtures in millions of American homes beginning in the 1930s. By contrast, as late as the 1960s, technology historian David Landes could write about how demand for home appliances in France was depressed by homemakers "who contend that the taste of refrigerated food is necessarily altered for the worse." By 1970, 99 percent of U.S. households had refrigerators; in Western Europe, the rate was just 72 percent.

The physical structure of American kitchens, dominated by giant refrigerators, shaped our behavioral infrastructure—deeply ingrained habits surrounding the purchase, storage, and use of food that profoundly affect demand. Unlike European town and city dwellers, who often shop for food daily, visiting several small local shops and markets to pick up fish or meat, vegetables, cheese, bread, and wine (as well as the latest neighborhood news), Americans are accustomed to making a big once-a-week shopping trip to a giant supermarket—and storing the bagsful of foods they bring home in their huge refrigerators and freezers. As a result, Americans have been raised for generations to mistrust perishable foods not stored at low temperatures.

It's a principle we've seen at work before: Different types of customers define magnetism differently. One of the big challenges faced by companies like Tetra Pak that serve a wide array of customers is finding cost-effective ways to provide *all* those customers with products they'll consider magnetic.

Under the circumstances, with Americans burdened by a vague sense of unease regarding the safety of foods stored at room temperature, a direct assault on the U.S. market by Tetra Pak would not have worked. To the extent that American shoppers are aware of Tetra Pak cartons at all, they associate them with juice for kids— not a great image if you'd like to sell boxes filled with sophisticated products like hollandaise sauce.

So Tetra Pak's first forays into the American consumer market have followed an indirect path. Tetra Pak is playing an increasing role in the backstory of more and more companies that serve food to U.S. families, whether at home or in restaurants, getting aseptically packaged foods onto the plates of millions of Americans without their knowing it.

You might call it "unseen demand."

❏   ❏   ❏

THE CHALLENGE of building a great backstory company like Tetra Pak is amazingly complex, requiring an understanding of how demand works on at least three distinct levels. At one and the same time, Tetra Pak needs to think about its immediate customers—the food-packaging businesses that buy its goods or services; its customers' customers—the retailers (like grocery stores) that buy products from the packagers; and its customers' customers' customers—the product end users who, ultimately, provide the dollars that drive the whole complicated machine.

This kind of thinking is essential in today's complicated multi-level global economy. And it's exactly the kind of thinking at which Tetra Pak has learned to excel.

To foster demand at the food packager level, Tetra Pak has developed a remarkable array of innovations that go way beyond the aseptic carton itself.

The ten-year process of solving the complex combination of problems that Ruben Rausing and his team had to master before the first Tetra Pak system could be installed in a Swedish dairy helped Tetra Pak develop a tremendous array of talents in process management, equipment design, materials science, microbiology, and techniques like homogenization, evaporation, and filtration. Today they put those skills to work on behalf of their corporate customers, developing ways of trimming costs, improving efficiencies, reducing downtime, and, most important, opening up new revenue opportunities by developing new products for new markets.

An example is Tetra Pak's development of the Tetra Hoyer Deep-Blue Ice Cream Freezer, a system for improved ice cream production that grew out of Tetra Pak's close relationships with its dairy customers. Based on a design created by Swiss scientist E. J. Windhab that transforms the freezing process during ice cream manufacture, DeepBlue offers companies a fairly remarkable list of benefits, including a shorter and simpler production process, reduced capital expenses, less downtime, and less waste. Even more impressive, the creamier taste and smoother "mouth feel" of the ice cream produced by DeepBlue allows manufacturers to reduce the amount of cream or butter fat in their products by as much as 40 to 50 percent. As consumers grow increasingly health conscious, this is a huge business advantage—and a fantastic backstory driver of demand for healthier frozen desserts.

Those who savor the new low-fat ice creams that DeepBlue makes possible will never see Tetra Pak's innovative freezer design. But it's just one of many bright demand creation ideas that Tetra Pak has generated that have made it a crucial part of many food companies' backstories.

And Tetra Pak's magnetic appeal for food processing businesses runs even deeper than technological creativity. If Magnetism = Function × Emotion (M = F × E), the emotional tug exerted by Tetra Pak derives from the intimate work relationships it establishes with the client companies it serves.

Here is where Tetra Pak's unusual approach to business design becomes crucial. We noted that masters of the backstory always ask, "Is my organization optimized to serve customers and to learn from them?" The executives who run Tetra Pak have asked that precise question repeatedly, and redesigned the company as necessary to improve the answer.

Most business-to-business relationships run through departments labeled "sales" and "procurement." In effect, two people are involved: a salesperson and a procurement officer. Others in both companies have to request, design, build, ship, use, and service the products, but these individuals don't generally consider themselves part of the business-to-business connection, nor do they behave that way.

Tetra Pak operates quite differently. When it takes on a new client—a dairy in China, a juice producer in Spain, or a nectar company in India—it sends a team of food processing and packaging experts to work at the client facilities, examine their operations, and analyze their needs. They study the flow of products into, through, and out of the factory, typical production goals and shipping schedules, causes of bottlenecks and equipment failures, rates of waste and spoilage, and opportunities to reduce costs and maximize efficiencies. Tetra Pak employs several thousand scientists, engineers, and design and development specialists who work intensively on-site with client companies, mapping their hassles in excruciating detail and searching for ways to reduce or eliminate them. ("Wherever waste is being produced," a Tetra Pak spokesman says, it indicates "a non-perfect system"—and that's something Tetra Pak considers unacceptable.) Finally, specific Tetra Pak equipment is recommended for installation—along with thorough training of client staff and continuous monitoring and upgrading, as needed, by Tetra Pak's own experts. Actual manufacturing of packaging equipment is outsourced to several hundred locally based "system suppliers" and "component suppliers"—but Tetra Pak's unique contribution, its proprietary understanding of food processing systems, remains in-house.

The result isn't a typical sales relationship—transactional, centered on "the deal"—but rather a profound *embedding* in the life and work of the client company, centered on a continuing relationship with many touch points, whose purpose is to find new ways to make things work better. Sales and procurement departments are involved, but so are engineering, product development, quality control, marketing, customer service, inventory management, logistics, finance, human resources, training . . . and dozens or scores of individuals who work together constantly, not just two people negotiating a contract once or twice a year.

All of this changes the role of the sales manager for Tetra Pak as well. "Unlike a [traditional] salesperson," a Tetra Pak spokesperson explains, "the key account manager goes beyond mere sales. He holds responsibility for helping the customer grow his business, not just pushing his company's products. . . . His attitude has to be, 'I am your partner in growth.'"

It's important to stress how unusual Tetra Pak's customer-centered business design is. The leading competitive company, the Swiss-based SIG Combibloc, has a more traditional structure in which so-called line functions (production, technology, procurement, and so on) operate separately and in parallel with market-centered functions (such as sales, service, and business development). In most companies organized this way, the result is "dotted-line" connections between customer-facing managers and the engineers, scientists, and designers who actually create the products, often leading to unclear roles and confused priorities. Perhaps this is one reason why SIG Combibloc is a distant runner-up to Tetra Pak in the race to satisfy global demand for aseptic packaging.

Tetra Pak's customer-centered business design penetrates very deep into the organization. Even the company's research and development arm was reconfigured in the early 1990s to abolish traditional functional units based on technologies and expertise, replacing them with cross-functional teams organized around specific projects for particular customers. Partially as a result, demand for Tetra Pak's research and development services increased several-fold between

1994 and 1999, as did the number of patents earned by its engineers.

For an example of how Tetra Pak's unique design helps it enrich the backstory of its business customers, consider how the company has helped to shape and build the booming Chinese dairy industry. Beginning in 1998, the company has worked with government health officials and educators to make milk drinking part of the daily routine in schools around China. The design of packaging systems for Chinese dairies—operational infrastructure—is just one part of Tetra Pak's contribution. Other programs focus on the behavioral infrastructure surrounding dairy products, educating families and teachers about the nutritional benefits of milk for schoolkids and training dairy workers to improve the quality of the raw milk produced and processed in China. In 2008, for example, 260 farmers attended a "dairy school" supported by Tetra Pak to learn new, productivity-enhancing techniques for cattle raising. And in 2009, Tetra Pak opened a technology center in Pudong (near Shanghai) that specializes in researching and solving engineering, business, and marketing challenges specific to the Chinese food market—for instance, analyzing rural road conditions to provide expertise and guidance on local transportation issues.

China is not the only location in which Tetra Pak is actively shaping demand for its client companies' products—and even creating new demand where none previously existed. School milk programs similar to the one in China have been set up in cooperation with government agencies, nonprofit organizations, and local dairies in more than fifty countries around the world, improving children's access to milk and the nutritional benefits it offers. Ulla Holm, the director of Tetra Pak's Food for Development program, describes the goal as creating a "milk-drinking generation" as well as developing business for both Tetra Pak and the companies it serves.

Reviewing the breadth of Tetra Pak's involvement in China's

social, educational, and health ecosystems, one Chinese newspaper observed that the company has been "so often dubbed by the media as a 'nosy person'" (that is, an intrusive external force). But the article went on to say, "However, people seem willing [for] Tetra Pak to be a 'nosy person.'"

The lesson: A company's intimate role in shaping a customer's backstory *might* be seen as threatening—but when the results lead to magnetic products and ever-growing demand, such intimacy is appreciated rather than feared.

In fact, this kind of connection is the source of the emotional energy that makes Tetra Pak a magnetic backstory company. A consumer product like Wegmans, CareMore, or the Kindle sparks an emotional connection by making daily life better in unexpected and delightful ways—more delicious, more creative, more fun, more healthy, more convenient—and provoking customer comments like "I love it so much that I can't imagine living without it!" A business product like the service provided by Tetra Pak sparks emotion in its customers through the power of its people to multiply a client company's productivity, efficiency, and innovation, generating reactions like "My Tetra Pak team is so valuable that I can't imagine tackling a production problem without them!"

Different contexts, different benefits—and an equally powerful emotional appeal.

Building an enduring emotional tie between companies based on human connections can require thousands of employees with an unusual array of attributes—technical talent, yes, but also strong people skills, broad business insights, and intense personal commitment to the goals of both companies. And while Tetra Pak is a privately held company that shares few of its organizational secrets, it's possible to catch glimpses of the system it's created to nurture just such a team.

For example, Tetra Pak recently hired its first full-time vice president of internal communications. Her mandate is to ensure that every employee has a deep understanding of Tetra Pak's business strategy, knows how that strategy relates to specific assignments, understands the goals of client companies, and is intensely dedicated to helping them achieve those goals. Many companies pay lip service to these concepts; few give them the level of importance and concrete investment that Tetra Pak has.

For another example, the LiVE Tetra Pak program is a four-hour employee engagement and team-building event that includes speeches, music, games, interviews, question-and-answer sessions, slide presentations, documentary-style films, and audience-participation activities. It's a huge investment that has been presented around the world and translated into twenty-five languages, and it will eventually reach all twenty-one thousand Tetra Pak employees—an investment of eighty thousand participant hours, which suggests how seriously the company takes its internal communications mission.

Talk to Tetra Pak customers and you begin to get a sense of how this commitment translates into results. Phil Mazza and Nick Marsella are executives with Byrne Dairy, which has been in business in upstate New York since 1933. They talk about how, when Byrne enlisted Tetra Pak's help to expand into extended-shelf-life milk and cream products, the relationship got off to a slightly rocky start. "We felt their service wasn't strong enough," Nick recalls. Tetra Pak's response was to send their North American vice president to meet with the new client and jointly develop an action plan for improving the alliance. Then Tetra Pak sent its entire service department to Sweden for retraining and skills upgrading—and not for a day or two, but for a full month.

Now Tetra Pak not only addresses Byrne's problems swiftly and efficiently, it proactively works with the dairy to help it become more efficient, sustainable, and profitable. "We had some issues last year where there really weren't any issues," Nick explains with a smile. "We just wanted to learn more. So Tetra Pak sent in a team just to brainstorm—three people spent two days with us, walking through our operation, meeting with our people, figuring out ways to improve our operations." The shared goal: to understand the challenges Byrne faces and to devise innovative ways to help it succeed.

Hear me, know me, grow me—this is the message Tetra Pak executives say is implicit in every customer conversation. It's also the customer service mantra that Tetra Pak swears by. The six words certainly seem to capture the dynamic of the company's relationship with Byrne Dairy.

Like Wegmans and many other great demand-creating organizations, Tetra Pak understands that its team members are the key source of its magnetism—and it invests in them accordingly.

❏   ❏   ❏

TETRA PAK HAS GROWN enormously, and generated huge flows of demand, working almost exclusively behind the scenes with client companies. Its customer-centric approach to creating manufacturing systems that enhance its clients' businesses has worked brilliantly. But it requires a continual stream of innovations and improvements in response to market changes. As CEO Dennis Jönsson points out, the nine thousand production lines that Tetra Pak has developed over the decades are both the company's greatest strength and its greatest vulnerability. "With an average age of thirteen years," he notes, "a very large part of our machines [will need] to be replaced in the near future. It opens the door to competitors unless we can offer new solutions that lead to increased profitability for our customers."

There are also limits to growth as a pure backstory company—especially in the vast American market, where customers have been reluctant to sample products packaged in aseptic cartons. If Tetra Pak wants to bring the benefits of its know-how to U.S. companies other than juice makers, it needs to step out of the backstory and help consumers discover the safety, convenience, cost savings, and improved taste that aseptic packaging can provide.

Today the company is working on several fronts to make Tetra Pak as magnetic for American consumers as it is for Europeans.

One approach has been to seek a foothold for Tetra Pak in emerging product categories where the behavioral infrastructure is unformed. Contrast the dairy aisle in your local grocery with the display of soy milk. The former section is refrigerated and filled with traditional plastic or cardboard cartons; the latter is (mostly) nonrefrigerated and features brightly hued Tetra Pak containers. It's tough to persuade Americans long accustomed to chilled milk to switch to aseptic packaging; we have no such limiting expectations regarding soy milk, which was unknown in the United States until 1979, when Hong Kong–based Vitasoy introduced the first soy milk in a few stores in San Francisco's Chinatown. That virgin market represented an opportunity for innovation, which Tetra Pak seized.

Today the gourmet foods market offers another opportunity. In the mid-nineties, a Florida-based company called Chef Creations was searching for a better way to offer its specialty food items to restaurants, caterers, hotels, cafeterias, and other food service providers. Deploying the backstory magic they'd perfected in Europe, Tetra Pak offered to support them. A team from Tetra Pak worked with Chef Creations to adapt the Tetra Brik technology to their sauces and dessert items. The taste quality had to be high—a restaurateur serving hollandaise sauce from a Chef Creations pack had to be sure that customers would accept the product as worthy of a gourmet kitchen. And of course there could be no question of spoilage, since nothing destroys a food business faster than a safety issue.

Food packaged in Tetra Pak cartons from Chef Creations has now built a significant presence in the U.S. gourmet foods market. You've almost certainly enjoyed some of their sauces or desserts when dining at fine restaurants around the country. Spokesmen for

Chef Creations like to tell stories like the one about the caterer who needed three hundred crème brûlées for a wedding—a demand he would have been hard-pressed to satisfy a few years ago, but which the arrival of Tetra Pak cartons made possible.

Tetra Pak cartons have also found their way into other back-story niches. Restaurateurs are serving puddings, soups, even eggs from Tetra Pak cartons. Carol White, a Houston coffeehouse owner, says she uses soy milk packed in aseptic boxes because "it's shelf-stable and I want to save refrigerator space." And then she adds, sotto voce, "My customers don't see it. They don't know the difference."

But for the leaders at Tetra Pak, today's big question is, Can Americans learn to love aseptic packaging when they *do* see it?

Little by little, the old *No* answers are changing to *Maybe*, then to *Yes.*

Americans are finally beginning to warm up to the idea of grown-up food and drink in boxes. Self-proclaimed foodies—chefs, gourmets, and adventurous eaters—are leading the way.

In 2004, one of the foodies' favorite magazines, *Cook's Illustrated,* performed extensive comparisons between boxed chicken broth and the traditional canned variety. Executive editor Jack Bishop declared, "The broth in a box clearly tasted better. You can really tell the difference." And he added this advice to would-be home chefs: "Get rid of your can opener."

Soon thereafter, Kate Murphy, a *New York Times* reporter, conducted her own experiments: "I compared chopped tomatoes in a box (Pomi from Parmalat) to chopped tomatoes in a can (Del Monte). The boxed tomatoes had better consistency, flavor, and color. I also made the crème brûlée from Chef Creations, a brand available only to restaurants and other food service companies, for a gathering of food snobs. They all loved it and asked for the recipe."

Murphy's reference to Chef Creations is just one link in an in-

triguing tale of new demand in the making. At the time of her article (March 2004), the company's boxed specialty foods were sold
only to restaurants and other wholesale food purveyors. Today, the
retail market—consumers and home cooks—is slowly making room
for Tetra Pak. Six-and-three-quarter-ounce Tetra Wedge Aseptic
pouches of alfredo sauce, poultry gravy, and—yes—hollandaise sauce
are now available at Kroger, Safeway, Winn-Dixie, and other grocery
chains. So are a growing number of other specialty items in Tetra Pak
containers, from Wolfgang Puck soups and Brazil Gourmet fruit
nectars to Souk Wild Garden hummus and ArteOliva extra virgin
olive oil. (On your next shopping trip, keep an eye out for Tetra
Pak containers. You'll be surprised at how many grocery aisles are
now home to these once-unfamiliar packages.)

Tetra Pak goes to amazing lengths to study the wants of consumers and to test and demonstrate the appeal of its innovative solutions. The company maintains twelve research and development
centers in locations around the world, as well as a Consumer Concepts Lab, based in Modena, Italy, where cross-functional teams that
include industrial designers, psychologists, graphic artists, and engineers study real-world customer behaviors around packaging. For
example, ethnographers employed by Tetra Pak visit grocery stores
armed with clipboards and video cameras to record the reactions
of consumers to the appearance, shape, size, and style of food packages as well as their ultimate purchase decisions.

Marketing director Chris Kenneally describes the mission of Tetra
Pak's R&D team in classic hassle-fixing terms: "A new product solution requires many concepts to be evaluated before the best one is
found. The team's work starts with compiling an inventory of consumer needs, comparing them to the current product portfolio and
identifying any gaps." Based on this research, the designers create
a multitude of new product prototypes—9,436 in 2008 alone—which
are then winnowed through testing to a collection of workable

concepts (626 in 2008) and then, finally, reduced to a small set of products to be launched (a total of nine).

The story of Tetra Recart is a particularly vivid example of how Tetra Pak uses direct consumer contact to enrich its demand creation skills. Introduced in 2004, Tetra Recart is the first aseptic carton designed for retort sterilization—a way of purifying particle-containing foods that aren't suitable for Tetra Pak's traditional continuous flow packaging method. The carton made its debut holding Hormel chili. But sales were disappointing, and Hormel pulled the line.

Undeterred, Tetra Pak tackled the consumer challenge head-on. Working with packagers at Del Monte, Tetra Pak created its own line of crushed tomatoes, diced tomatoes, and tomato sauce using the brand name Corelli. Then it arranged a twelve-week test at selected retailers. The results were encouraging: Consumers said they felt that food in a carton seemed "fresher" than in a metal can, store managers liked the fact that rectangular cartons shelved more efficiently than cylindrical cans, and (most important) sales were 29 percent higher than for comparable canned products. Armed with this data, Tetra Pak has been educating food packagers about the benefits of Tetra Recart, and foods ranging from sweet corn kernels to moist cat food are beginning to find their way into this new packaging.

Tetra Pak's efforts are gradually making aseptic packaging acceptable to consumers in more and more food categories. Another sign of the nascent shift in attitudes is the growing acceptance of another "high-class" product in aseptic packaging—wine. And here, one inherent characteristic of Tetra Pak—its European roots—links up with another characteristic—its modest environmental impact— to create a package that increasing numbers of American consumers find appealing.

Matthew Cain, founder and president of wine importer J. Soif,

Inc., turned to Tetra Pak for a container for a new wine made from certified organic Malbec grapes. It was the enviro-economics of wine importing that convinced him.

"Over a period of time I came to the realization that the wine business just doesn't work," Cain explains. "Eighty percent of wine is drunk within a week. It doesn't make sense to put nine liters of wine in a forty-pound box and ship it thousands of miles."

Cain was hesitant to consider Tetra Pak for wine, despite the popularity of what he calls "alternative packaging" abroad, even for fine vintages. "Here in the U.S.," he notes, "it's only been used as a gimmick." But in 2008, with gas prices soaring, the economy tottering, and consumers looking for opportunities to save, the economic logic of Tetra Pak became compelling—especially when bolstered by a green rationale.

Today, the eco-friendly characteristics of aseptic packaging, when compared with heavy glass bottles, are a significant element in Tetra Pak's appeal to well-informed wine lovers—and a vivid example of the kind of three-level thinking (about manufacturers, retailers, and consumers) that Tetra Pak has mastered. Capitalizing on this benefit didn't come easily. In fact, for a time, Tetra Pak and other companies came under attack from environmentalists because of the lack of recycling systems for aseptic packaging. The state of Maine even passed a law in 1989 banning aseptic cartons. Uno Kjellberg, then the CEO of Tetra Pak, called for an unprecedented cooperative effort with rival firms. The jointly formed Aseptic Packaging Council (now known as the Carton Council) worked with environmental scientists and engineers to develop recycling programs and reduce their products' footprint. Not only did these efforts get the Maine law overturned in 1991, but Dennis Jönsson, then Tetra Pak's U.S. chief, was invited to the White House by Vice President Al Gore in 1996 to receive the Presidential Award for Sustainable Development.

Going green wins friends for Tetra Pak at all three levels of its demand chain. As CEO Jönsson puts it, "Retailers are leading the growing environmental awareness and they are tapping into the concerns of consumers. This is here to stay and it is something that will be part of the day-to-day way that we conduct our business if we want to remain preferred suppliers to retailers."

Matt Cain's line of certified organic wines, sold under the brand name Yellow+Blue (since yellow plus blue makes green), now include a Malbec and a Torrontes from Argentina, a Sauvignon Blanc from Chile, and a Rosé from Spain. All have won praise for their flavor from wine aficionados. But their environmental impact—or lack thereof—makes them unique. Cain draws the comparison to traditional glass bottles in stark terms:

> Yes, glass can be recycled. But the process is expensive. And very few people actually recycle it. In the United States, 15 percent of wine bottles are recycled—the rest go into landfills. The recycling rate of glass and Tetra Pak is now just about the same. And in a landfill, thirty Tetra Paks are equivalent to one wine bottle. There's just no comparison.

Cain offers another statistic that's even more startling: "When you ship a glass bottle, half of what you're shipping is packaging. With Tetra Pak, it's 93 percent wine, just 7 percent packaging." That beats even the egg—long regarded as nature's "most perfect package"—where the shell represents 13 percent of the total weight. Imagine that: green packaging that even outperforms Mother Nature herself.

Eco-friendliness is playing a growing role in emotionalizing Tetra Pak and energizing consumer demand. But so is aesthetics. Eye appeal is behind the company's introduction of the Tetra Prisma Aseptic, a recent variant on the Tetra Brik that is taller and slimmer, features six-sided indents on two corners, and can be printed with a "metallized" effect. Taken together, the visual innovations of the Prisma add up to a package vaguely resembling a contemporary office tower or even a Frank Gehry museum design, "making it ideal," as Tetra Pak puts it, "for all sorts of consumer situations." The striking design creates a whole new customer set for Tetra Pak: packaged goods companies eager to give their products a uniquely attention-grabbing, upscale appearance.

With the addition of a practical screw cap, called StreamCap, that is shaped to be easy pouring, tamper-evident, and resealable, the Prisma makes an attractive container for wine. The Canandaigua Wine Company, now known as the Centerra Wine Company, introduced new red and white Sangrias in Prisma packages in 2005. Encouraged by the results, they've now come out with a line of Vendange varietals using similar Prisma packages.

For Tetra Pak, today may be the perfect time to be making a concerted push on behalf of wine-in-a-box for the U.S. market. Combine gradually spreading acceptance of the concept of aseptic packaging with the rise of the green consumer as an avid, vocal, informed element of the market as well as the enhanced price sensitivity in the aftermath of the Great Recession, and you have the formula for a potential mass shift in demand—one for which Tetra Pak is ideally positioned.

❐   ❐   ❐

THE STORY OF Tetra Pak offers several intriguing lessons about demand.

First, it's a fascinating reminder of the sheer *complexity* of most significant demand breakthroughs, even those that are seemingly simple. Ruben Rausing began to think about a new way to package milk back in the 1930s. It took him several years just to come up with the *idea* for a new system—and after that, it took another decade to actually make it practical. The saga sends a sobering message about the massive investments in time, patience, and money that are required to bring great ideas for stimulating demand to fruition—and reminds us again that the best time to begin working on a brilliant innovation is, always, yesterday.

A second lesson is the *interdependence* that exists between demand and the backstory element of infrastructure. The demand for convenient movies-by-mail that Netflix creates and satisfies couldn't exist until the infrastructure of DVDs and DVD players was in place; the demand for grab-and-go urban car rentals by the hour that Zipcar creates and satisfies couldn't exist until the Internet infrastructure for tracking and reserving vehicles existed.

In the same way, the demand for lightweight, convenient, non-refrigerated food packages couldn't exist until Tetra Pak developed machinery to create such packages. But by the same token, the Tetra Pak infrastructure—which today includes factories around the world producing packaging materials for a wide variety of aseptic packages in quantities of billions—could never have been built if Rausing's package hadn't generated magnetic appeal for its first set of customers. Rausing would have been relegated to a footnote in business history as a tinkerer with a funny concept that never found its market, and we wouldn't today be talking about— or shopping for—cardboard-and-foil cartons of soup, juice, or wine. Infrastructure and consumer demand grow hand in hand; each depends on the other, and the unfolding development of each over time determines the long-term shape and health of our economy.

Finally—and perhaps most important—the Tetra Pak story suggests the powerful ultimate dependence of the entire structure of demand on the individual consumer. As one of the world's great backstory suppliers, Tetra Pak makes its profits by selling to corporations like dairies and food processors. But those profits would be scanty if not for Tetra Pak's understanding of what families want from their foods—qualities like convenience, freshness, flavor, and affordability. Perhaps the biggest benefit that Tetra Pak brings to its business clients is its ability to sense and provide what its customers' customers want, and *will* want in the months and years to come.

Because in the end, the whole vast pyramid of demand for food all comes down to your family sitting down at the kitchen table and wondering, "What's for dinner?"

4.
Trigger

(TRIG-er) *noun* 1. the difference between hearing about a product and buying it 2. a critical element in the business design that makes it easy for people to get truly excited about a magnetic product and transform themselves into customers 3. something that *helps me buy* something I really want 4. something that turns fence-sitters into customers

NETFLIX AND ITS TWO-HUNDRED-YEAR-OLD SECRET WEAPON

It was 2001—four years after entrepreneur Reed Hastings was embarrassed by a forty-dollar fine for a long-overdue movie, and three years after that hassle inspired him to launch a company that pioneered a new way of renting movies—Netflix.

As a Bowdoin College math major, a Stanford computer science graduate, and the founder of a software troubleshooting company called Pure Software (later sold to a larger business and now part of IBM), Hastings understood both the science and the business of high technology. As an alert consumer, he understood its human aspects as well. He'd launched Netflix based on a simple core insight: that this newish thing called the Internet might be the basis for a faster and more convenient way of choosing movies, just as it already was for buying books, thanks to Amazon.

A second recent innovation, the invention of the DVD, had intrigued Hastings further. Thin and light, a DVD looked a lot easier to deliver to a customer than a videocassette, which was heavy, bulky, and breakable. To test the concept, Hastings bought a bunch of CDs (since DVDs weren't readily available), stuck them into stamped envelopes, and dropped them off at the local post office. A couple of days later, the discs arrived in his mailbox—not, as he'd feared, in shattered fragments, but intact and playable.

Hastings would later learn that shipping DVDs through the mail wasn't quite as simple as this first experience suggested. But his initial success excited him. Maybe, he thought, the combination of the Internet and the DVD would make it possible to do away with the cumbersome retail model of companies like Blockbuster, Movie Gallery, Hollywood Video, and ten thousand mom-and-pop video rental stores. Maybe they could reduce or eliminate the countless annoying hassles of movie rental: the difficulty of finding the right movie to rent (Which picture will my spouse like? Is this movie kid-friendly? Does this adventure flick have "real" violence or just "fun" violence?); the frustration when the hottest movies are out of stock; the inconvenience of having to drive to the local rental store twice, once to rent a movie and once to return it; and, above all, the irritation of those punitive late fees.

Hastings got to work. He and the other members of his team crafted the first version of the Netflix website for selecting movies, built a warehouse for shipping DVDs near their company head-quarters in the northern California town of Scotts Valley, purchased a varied array of movies, and began marketing their service.

But their first product was far less than magnetic. Like today's version, the ur-Netflix offered Internet movie selection and DVD de-livery by mail. But it charged traditional rental fees, starting at four bucks per movie, and even imposed late fees like those that had irritated and inspired Hastings in the first place. In search of buzz, the start-up also wangled deals to sell "hot stuff" available through no other retailer—things like advance tickets to upcoming concerts and entertainment-related posters and merchandise.

Most customers who heard about this package of offers responded with indifference. At this point, Netflix was a little better than a storefront video rental—but only a little. It takes more magnetism than that to tug people out of their habitual orbits and into a new pattern of consumption.

Hastings quickly got the message. The number of reinventions the company went through in subsequent months illustrates just how complicated demand creation really is.

Hastings changed Netflix to a simple one-charge subscription model no matter how many movies you watch, eliminated late fees, and dropped the nonvideo product assortment, which had generated some publicity but scant demand. He also invested in vastly expanding the number of movie titles available, thereby addressing one of the worst hassles of video rental—the frustration of searching your local store in vain for a movie you want to watch. And he experimented with many pricing systems and several price levels.

Perhaps most important, Hastings inaugurated a tradition that Netflix maintains to this day: *Don't do anything irrevocable until you've tested it, run the numbers, tested it, and then tested it again.* Hastings loves to conduct clinical trials examining new ideas—to see what really works, and how well. That's why those who know Netflix best often describe it as "an entertainment company run by a computer scientist."

After dozens of redesigns, Hastings finally arrived at a business model roughly similar to today's Netflix—the company that has generated an amazing stream of demand with its magnetic, fun-to-use product.

Yet as of 2001, that stream of demand was still just a trickle. Netflix subscribers nationwide were fewer than half a million—a respectable number for a young company, but only a minuscule fraction of the 130 million movie-viewing households in America. The company's revenues ($76 million) were dwarfed by those of Blockbuster ($5.1 *billion*).

Hastings *knew* Netflix's product was better than Blockbuster's— more convenient, cheaper, almost hassle-free. His modest cohort of customers loved the service, and surveys showed that significant numbers of potential members had heard about Netflix. But growth remained slow. Why?

Many would-be demand creators assume that a magnetic product is all you need. It's not. One of the most valuable lessons to be learned from talking to customers is just how much our buying decisions are ruled by inertia, skepticism, sloth, habit, and indifference. That's why months, even years often pass between the time we hear about a great new product and the moment a purchase is made—if it ever happens at all. While magnetism may get our attention, it almost always takes a specific, action-inducing trigger to move us to buy.

For Netflix in 2001, the issue was an urgent one. The Netflix team knew that the time frame of their opportunity to create and control a stream of demand from online DVD rental was severely limited. The whole world, including thousands of entrepreneurs, was focused on the revolutionary power of the Internet. Hastings was well aware that he wasn't the *only* person in the world smart enough to think of the concept of video rental via the Internet. If he didn't grow Netflix *fast*, there was every likelihood that someone else would swoop in with another version of the same service— but 10 percent better—and take the market by storm. (In fact, rival online movie rental sites had already begun to pop up, with names ranging from DVDovernight, GreenCine, and DVDAvenue to Rent DVD Here, RentAnime, and Clean Flicks.)

What's more, Hastings was convinced that eventually one of the big, rich, experienced companies with a powerful brand name linked to entertainment, retailing, or online merchandising would see the same opportunity he saw. Every day he expected to see a headline announcing that Blockbuster was investing $500 million in an online movie rental business designed to blow Netflix out of the water. Or, if not Blockbuster, then Amazon. Or Walmart. Or Apple. Or maybe Disney . . .

Hastings's only hope was to grow—quietly, under the radar, but *fast*—so that, by the time one of the big players decided that online video rental was worth bothering about, Netflix would already have a discouraging head start. Slow but steady growth was *not* an acceptable option.

So the question nagged at Hastings and his team: Why weren't more people signing up?

Applying their intensely analytic orientation, Netflix's seven key leaders (many of them still helping to run the company today) started their search for an answer by focusing on data about their existing customer base. One hopeful anomaly jumped out at them. Netflix's penetration rate in the San Francisco Bay area (2.6 percent of households) was twice as great as anywhere else in the country. If they could sign up subscribers throughout the United States at the same rate, they'd quintuple their membership to more than 2.7 million.

What, then, was different about the Bay area? Why was the Netflix product seemingly more magnetic there than in Boston or Chicago or Miami?

Everybody on the executive team had a theory.

"The Bay area is where our headquarters is located," one person suggested. "Maybe our employees have been talking about Netflix and getting friends and neighbors to sign up." (That seemed implausible, since the number of people working at Netflix then was too small to have a big impact.)

"The Bay area is filled with high-tech people. They're Internet savvy and comfortable with online shopping," offered another. (Of course, there were plenty of other communities with lots of technologically sophisticated people—and they weren't flocking to join Netflix.)

"It's a relatively affluent community," suggested a third. "Let's face it, Netflix is a luxury, not a necessity. Maybe people with more disposable cash are more willing to spend it on movies." (This was true—but then again, there were lots of affluent people in New York,

Boston, and a bunch of other American cities who were staying away from Netflix in droves.)

"Maybe it's because the Bay area is in California," proposed yet another executive. "It's the home of the movie industry! I'll bet there are a lot of film buffs in the area." (Based on this logic, Los Angeles should have been the number one market for Netflix—but it trailed San Francisco badly.)

Eventually, Reed Hastings put an end to the debate.

"No more theories," he declared. "Let's do some more research." And so an intensive survey was launched to examine the attitudes of both Netflix customers and noncustomers in cities around the United States, with the specific goal of finding out *why* the company's product was more powerfully magnetic in the Bay area than anywhere else.

And when the results came in, lightbulbs lit up in the Netflix offices.

There was one, and only one, consistent difference in the survey responses from Netflix customers in the Bay area—and it was big enough to explain the difference in subscription rates all by itself. Virtually every Netflix subscriber in the Bay area raved about how *fast* they got their movies. Practically no one in the rest of the country felt that way.

The revelation produced much head slapping at Netflix headquarters. The reason for the difference was now so obvious. The distribution center from which all the DVDs were mailed was in the Bay area! So when a customer in Oakland or San Rafael or Palo Alto dropped a movie in the mail for return to Netflix on Monday morning, it probably arrived at the warehouse on Tuesday. The *next* movie on that customer's queue would be mailed out the same day and arrive on Wednesday—a forty-eight-hour turnaround.

By contrast, a customer in New Haven or Baltimore or Seattle might have to wait four, five, or even six days to get a new movie— just long enough to forget about Netflix and make planning a regular

"movie night" around the next picture in your queue feel imprac-
tical.

Netflix customers who received next-day delivery were excited
about its efficiency and convenience. They began looking forward
to their next movie the minute they dropped the last one into the
mailbox, and they bragged to friends, family, and neighbors about
the incredible speed and reliability of Netflix.

Whereas with five- or six-day turnaround, the reaction was more,
"Meh!"

It was a bit ironic. Netflix relied on two remarkable technological breakthroughs—the Internet and the DVD laser disc—and
the incredible software created by a team of brilliant programmers.
The company was a quintessential artifact of the high-tech world.
Yet now its leaders had discovered—to their shock and, perhaps,
their chagrin—that the secret weapon behind the company's success
was a low-tech delivery system founded more than two centuries
earlier by Benjamin Franklin and run by government workers: the
U.S. Postal Service.

And what happened next illustrates another trait that makes
Reed Hastings such a successful demand creator. The minute he discovered this rather startling truth, he acted on it.

On January 21, 2002, Netflix opened its *second* distribution
center. It was in Santa Ana, California, just south of Los Angeles. The
following month, the third center followed—in Worcester, Massachusetts, just west of Boston. During the subsequent weeks, Hastings and his team closely watched the subscription rates in Los
Angeles and Boston—and found that they began a steady climb,
until they matched the double-the-normal rates of the Bay area. Netflix members in those communities, stunned to discover that they
were suddenly receiving new movies within forty-eight hours, were
telling their friends and neighbors—and those friends and neighbors were joining Netflix. That was the only possible explanation,
since Netflix, in the spirit of scientific inquiry, had deliberately re-

frained from doing any local advertising or promotion that could skew the results.

Nine more distribution centers were opened before the year was out. During 2003, twelve more were opened. And in every area where a new distribution center was opened, subscription rates swiftly doubled.

It was as if a switch was being thrown, in one city after another, that was triggering demand for Netflix like the ignition key of a car generating power.

As of late 2010, Netflix was operating fifty-six distribution centers, making next-day movie delivery available to the vast majority of Americans. The Netflix subscriber rolls now number more than 20 million. Which tells us that Reed Hastings's demand-creating engine still has plenty of room for growth.

Even before 2001, Reed Hastings and his team had created a magnetic product, which is the first essential ingredient for the creation of new demand. But a magnetic product is not enough. What was missing back in 2001 was a *demand trigger*—a critical element in the business design that would make it easy for lukewarm fence-sitters to get truly *excited* about the magnetic product and transform themselves into customers.

Actually, we've already seen this effect at work. Remember how *density* turned out to be the key to Zipcar's popularity, and *instant access to books* made the crucial difference for Kindle? These were triggers that opened the spigots of demand. In the same way, *delivery speed* was the crucial trigger that supercharged demand for Netflix.

You've experienced the power of demand triggers yourself. Think about the last really great new product you bought. Now consider: How much time elapsed between the day when you first heard about the product and the day when you finally plunked down the cash or credit card to take it home?

The difference between hearing about a product and actually

buying it is the demand trigger. Triggers work by overcoming customer inertia and by strengthening the magnetism of an offer. Some
triggers do this by enhancing the functional aspects of magnetism:
For example, they may improve the product's price, make it more
convenient, or make it more customizable. Other triggers increase
a product's emotional resonance: Brilliant advertising, promotion,
marketing, or word-of-mouth campaigns can help make this happen.
And some triggers get the customer to move by providing an occasion to test and purchase the product, as when samples, free trials,
or discount memberships are offered. Triggers that have a lasting
impact on a product's magnetism will be more powerful than those
whose effect is fleeting. (Netflix's ultrarapid movie delivery is a brilliant example of the former.)

A magnetic product is a rare and wonderful thing. But without
a trigger, even a magnetic product may generate little or no demand.
Which is why the search for a trigger—or, better yet, two or three
triggers—is a prominent feature in practically every story of demand
creation.

❑   ❑   ❑

BY THE TIME Reed Hastings and the Netflix team had their epiphany
about next-day delivery in 2001, they'd already invested three
years of incredibly hard work in getting their company to the point
where a great demand trigger could produce liftoff. The Netflix
saga, like the stories of Zipcar, Kindle, and Tetra Pak, illustrates
precisely how difficult it is to create demand, and how many smart
moves lie hidden in the history of every great demand-producing
team.

Reed Hastings had learned a lot from his experiences in founding and nurturing Pure Software. "I had the great fortune," he likes
to say, "of doing a mediocre job at my first company." As it grew
from ten to 640 employees, "I found I was definitely underwater and
over my head." Losing self-confidence, he even *asked* the board to

fire him and was frankly relieved when the company sale went through in 1996. He used the subsequent downtime to ponder his experiences and draw lessons to apply to his next start-up.

One of the lessons Hastings had learned was the importance of using resources available in the outside world to create the backstory needed to support your product, rather than trying to create it all from scratch. When you're in the hunt for elusive new demand, there's never enough time, money, talent, or emotional energy to master all the thousand-and-one backstory details that you *have* to get right. Investing resources in reinventing the wheel is a recipe for failure.

So rather than trying to invent a delivery infrastructure (as retailers do when they invest in real estate and physical plants in hundreds or thousands of locations), Hastings and his team devoted themselves to figuring out how to take advantage of a preexisting delivery infrastructure. It was, of course, the same infrastructure that would eventually provide the essential demand trigger—the U.S. Postal Service.

But piggybacking on the neighborhood mailman turned out to be far from easy. Reed Hastings's quick-and-dirty experiment sending a batch of CDs through the mail had demonstrated only that *one* local post office, under *one* set of conditions, was capable of handling discs safely. Postal Service facilities varied enormously, from tiny rural outposts in Wyoming and Alaska to giant urban centers that sorted millions of letters and packages using a wide range of machines, some ultramodern, others antiquated. A Netflix that served customers anywhere in the country had to work with all of them while keeping the damage rate vanishingly low. (Imagine being an avid movie fan who has just joined Netflix. How many broken discs would it take to sour you on the service? One? Two? Probably not more.)

Jim Cook, one of the early Netflix team members, recalls:

To understand how the post office backend worked, I spent hundreds of hours at a few of the largest regional Postal Centers observing and asking tons of questions.

I noticed letters being sorted by several high-speed spinning circular drums. While these crushing metal drums enabled the separation and processing of over 40,000 standard-size letters per hour, it was obvious a thin plastic DVD would not survive the journey. With a sinking stomach, I felt the business idea slip away. But then I noticed a separate conveyor belt sorting magazines and other larger pieces of "flat mail." How would I ensure the package always used this flat mail machine and not the letter sorter?

Netflix worked on designing a unique, ingenious envelope that would automatically get routed through the flat mail system. It also had to hold a DVD securely, shield it from the canceling device, and provide a postage-paid return envelope that could be quickly and easily opened by Netflix warehouse personnel with minimal risk of scratching or dropping the enclosed disc. And it had to be as light as possible, since every additional ounce would increase the company's postage bill.

They tried and tried and tried again. Some of the early envelopes were made of paper, some of cardboard, some of plastic. (The plastic was soon scrapped—not recyclable.) Some contained a foam insert to cradle and protect the DVD. (That was scrapped, too—weighed too much.) Some were airtight, which meant they inflated and swelled when transported by plane. (A small air vent was added.) Some required the customer to peel off a sticker to reveal Netflix's return address. (Too complicated.) One was printed with user instructions that included eight bullet points and no fewer than seventy-six words. (Arggh.)

It took Netflix scores of iterations to come up with the perfect envelope. They made one odd discovery after another, such as the revelation that printing the inside return address upside down made processing more efficient. In the end, they developed an envelope made of light yet sturdy paper with an inner baffle that safely secured the disc, a slit that permitted the bar code on the DVD sleeve to be read without opening, and even room for paid advertising. The winning design was simple, bold, and eye-catching. Most important, it was capable of navigating the postal service infrastructure with a damage rate far below 1 percent.

You probably know this envelope well, even if you're not a Netflix member. It's an unmistakable bright red and, at many post offices, it constitutes up to one-quarter of the daily mail deliveries. (And at $500 million, Netflix's annual mailing costs represent a significant fraction of the U.S. Postal Service's operating budget.)

One hundred and fifty versions of an envelope may sound excessive. But every detail tweaked by the Netflix design team meant some tiny customer hassle reduced, even if by an infinitesimal amount. Saving the customer three seconds when opening the envelope or reducing the risk of a damaged DVD from .08 percent to .06 percent may seem trivial. But multiply those numbers by millions of customers and hundreds of millions of deliveries, and the net benefit to Netflix members is substantial.

And at the same time, Hastings and his team were tackling the hundreds of other details they had to get right to make the Netflix product truly magnetic. (Such obsessiveness, we've found, is normal among great demand creators.)

They were innovative where they needed to be, imitative wherever they could be. Through months of experimentation, a team of direct-mail fulfillment experts, mechanical engineers, and software developers built an amazing distribution system around unique high-speed optical scanning machines capable of sorting and dispatching millions of DVDs every day, with a vanishingly small error rate. (Like everyone who is lucky enough to visit one of Netflix's facilities, we were left slack-jawed by the vast size and incredible efficiency of the Fremont, California, distribution center we toured.) No one else has a system like it—and its mere existence is likely sufficient to deter other companies from trying to launch rival services.

Rather than wasting precious economic fuel and creative energy in designing a great retail website from scratch, Hastings studied Amazon's and did a 90-percent-plus emulation. Netflix's site mirrored Amazon's navigation system, product and button placement, search tools, inclusion of reviews by customers and professional critics, and even the use of small, low-resolution cover images to allow fast Web page loading.

You might call this strategy "Imitate to be unique." Of course, it must be used appropriately. The *core* of a new business design can't be based on imitation. (In Netflix's case, the core was "Reliable, convenient, affordable movie rental by Internet and mail." A unique website design wasn't part of that definition.) Like great artists and writers, great demand creators shamelessly imitate *minor* things so they can focus their originality on *major* things.

In pursuit of fast, below-the-radar growth, Hastings used viral marketing and word of mouth rather than expensive advertising. He also searched for marketing partners to help Netflix recruit members. Hastings made agreements with Sony, Toshiba, and Panasonic, which sold a combined 85 percent of all DVD players in the United States, to offer a free trial subscription to Netflix with every DVD player shipped.

Under normal circumstances, manufacturers are hesitant to make such deals. "But at the time," Jim Cook explains, "these DVD player manufacturers were actually in fear of becoming another failed Laserdisc or Betamax." So they loved the idea of offering their customers ten free video rentals straight out of the box. Creating a backstory ecosystem that harnessed the marketing power of allied organizations multiplied Netflix's customer reach while freeing up resources for other challenges.

And having honed its product to address one movie-rental hassle after another, Netflix then asked—as great demand innovators
always do—what *else* can we do to connect the dots for our customers? To enhance the product's value, Netflix offered not only video
rental but also a convenient individualized queue for movie selections, movie previews, comments by critics, advance reservations
of upcoming releases, and much more.

But their most powerful product enhancement was the Cinematch recommendations engine. (Here, again, Hastings drew inspiration from the world's leading online retailer, Amazon, which had
pioneered the concept of algorithmically generated product recommendations. Japan's Tsutaya was developing its own media recommendation system along parallel lines.) Cinematch predicts how
an individual customer will rate a particular movie based on his or
her pattern of past ratings (the average Netflix member has rated
more than two hundred movies). The system has become so popular that 60 percent of Netflix customers pick movies based on the
hundreds of millions of recommendations that Cinematch offers
each day.

Combined with the queue system, the recommendation engine
goes a long way toward eliminating one of the most frustrating hassles of traditional movie rental—the fruitless Friday night ramble
through the video store aisles. Once you've created your Netflix
queue—aided by Cinematch's personalized recommendations—you
have a standing list of ten, twenty, or more preselected movies you're
likely to enjoy, the next one ready to land in your mailbox the
moment you request it.

Over time, Hastings and his team honed and refined their product, continually learning from mistakes and searching for opportunities to improve the customer's hassle map even more.

For example, Netflix once employed staffers to watch a dozen
video monitors as DVDs returned by members were played back at

high speed, in search of scratches and other imperfections that might spoil viewing. Eventually they discovered an electronic scanning device that performed the same task automatically with much greater accuracy, making the monitor system obsolete.

As circumstances change, the product may need to be modified to meet ever-rising expectations. Reed Hastings and his team have developed a deep, instinctive understanding of this reality. Combined with their analytic mind-set, it drives them to study the ever-changing customer with manic intensity. On any given day, Netflix conducts, on average, around two hundred separate surveys—online, by phone, through the mail, and via in-home research by live interviewers. (Taking on the role of "media anthropologists," Netflix employees actually sit with customers as they watch movies and TV shows, observing their behaviors—how and when they hit the pause button, where they put the remote control, when and why they stop watching altogether.) And then there are the customer focus groups constantly being held at Netflix facilities around the country, attended not just by marketing specialists but by the engineers who will later write the software code to address the customer issues they learn about, along with such purely routine inquiries as the e-mails asking members how long it took to receive their last movie (Netflix sends out hundreds of thousands of those every day). When an urgent issue demands it, Netflix can run a survey in twenty-four hours, yielding an instant snapshot of the mood of its members.

People at Netflix like to draw a connection between Reed Hastings's engineering background and his company's obsessive attention to tiny details. "Pure Software's product was software that found bugs in other people's software," one of them reminded us. "That's Reed's whole orientation—to find something wrong where other people think everything's fine." This is the mind-set that helps a company drive error rates—like deliveries of scratched or inaccurately labeled DVDs—below 1 percent and then below one-tenth

of 1 percent and ultimately below one-hundredth of 1 percent . . .
each downward tick representing a customer hassle eliminated.

❏   ❏   ❏

MEANWHILE, AS HASTINGS and his team were launching, building, and
improving their business, what were their potential rivals doing?

The answer, shockingly, was nothing. Months went by. Then
years. Netflix kept growing—slowly at first, then, especially after the
discovery of the delivery-speed trigger, faster and faster. Blockbuster
didn't respond. Neither did Walmart, Apple, the movie studios, or
any other big media player. The new demand Netflix had discovered
was seemingly invisible to the most likely competitors.

Neither Blockbuster nor any other major incumbent responded
until 2003, four years after Netflix's launch, when Walmart finally
launched its own Web-based movie rental service. Netflix's stock
price tumbled: A mere press release from the world's largest corporation was enough to send shivers down competitive spines. But by
2005, Walmart was out of the online movie rental business, having
sold its modest subscriber list to Netflix.

That same year, after a fifty-eight-month delay, Blockbuster entered the fray, and in a big way. Blockbuster by Mail boasted lower
prices and many more movie titles than Netflix (25,000 versus
20,000). Again, Netflix's stock fell sharply. Surely David was in big
trouble now that the sleeping Goliath had finally wakened.

But Netflix responded swiftly and decisively, as if it had been
preparing to do so for years. It cut prices to match Blockbuster's.
It rapidly expanded its movie catalog. By the end of 2005, Netflix
boasted a far larger library than Blockbuster, an advantage it has
maintained ever since. It accelerated the improvement of its recommendations engine. David kept loading and reloading his slingshot
and firing in the direction of a bewildered Goliath.

Nevertheless, Blockbuster fought back. The company invested
some $500 million into developing and promoting the online

business. At first Blockbuster kept its two services completely separate—a slightly odd strategy, since it failed to capitalize on the company's biggest potential advantage, its vast chain of physical stores. But in early 2007, Blockbuster shifted gears. It announced a new program called Total Access, which powerfully linked its on-line service with its physical outlets. Blockbuster by Mail customers would now be permitted to return discs to any Blockbuster store, exchange them for a *free* movie, and also get their next regular movie delivery by mail.

It was an attractive package—the first magnetic new product Blockbuster had offered in years. The second quarter of 2007 was the only period in Netflix's history when its subscriber base actually *shrank*. Defections to Blockbuster were the reason. For a moment, it appeared that Reed Hastings's worst nightmare—an aroused and effective Blockbuster—was coming true.

But Total Access created two big headaches for Blockbuster. One was that many of the chain's franchised store owners refused to par-ticipate in the program. The other was that Total Access involved so many free giveaways that Blockbuster actually *lost* money with each membership.

Hastings and his team studied the numbers and quickly realized that Blockbuster's gambit was unsustainable. They resolved to stay the course, continue to ratchet up the quality of their own product, and hope (fingers crossed) that Blockbuster would throw in the towel sooner rather than later.

Within a few months, the other shoe dropped.

By mid-2007, Blockbuster yielded to financial pressure and com-plaints from its franchisees by dramatically altering the Total Access plan. It raised prices, sharply limited the number of free disc ex-changes, and instituted charges for in-store movie returns thereafter. The new Total Access presented a cacophony of choices, ranging from a one-DVD-at-a-time, $8.99-per-month, through-the-mail-only plan to a $17.99 mail-and-store plan that included three DVDs at a time and up to five in-store exchanges per month—with several other options in between. Many customers found the new program more confusing than empowering.

The consumer review website Gizmodo analyzed the changes and concluded, "Thanks, Blockbuster, for making it that much easier to recommend Netflix."

When the dust cleared, Netflix's lead over Blockbuster in online movie rental had only grown. The upward march of Netflix's subscriber numbers resumed. By the end of 2008, Netflix's corporate value (as measured by the total value of outstanding shares of stock) was ten times greater than Blockbuster's. By 2010, Blockbuster was in bankruptcy, and in 2011, Blockbuster's business assets were up for auction.

◻   ◻   ◻

TODAY'S NETFLIX BUSINESS DESIGN is magnificent—a well-oiled machine that supplies more than 20 million members with a hypermagnetic product they can't stop telling their friends about.

But the attention of Reed Hastings and his team is already focused on the next issue.

DVD technology, like VHS before it, has a limited shelf life. Movie downloads and streaming video are the key to the next generation of movie distribution. Over time, Netflix's incredibly efficient delivery machine that piggybacks on the U.S. postal system will become increasingly irrelevant. As the rules of the game change, will Netflix be agile enough to stay one step ahead of its customers and two steps ahead of the competition?

The answer is taking shape today.

As early as 2008, Netflix quietly began infiltrating the infrastructure of the streaming video revolution. By mid-2009, streaming video from Netflix had already been made available in 3 million homes via PCs, Xbox 360 and Sony PlayStation 3 game players, Blu-ray disc players from Samsung and LG, and dedicated video gadgets like TiVo and Roku (the last-named a Netflix spin-off). In 2010, many more devices were added to the list, including the Nintendo Wii, Apple's iPhone, iPod touch, and iPad, and Apple TV. By the end of 2010, Netflix anticipated serving more than 10 million members through more than 200 devices.

Hastings and his team aren't ready to abandon the DVD or mail deliveries. Instead they are negotiating a gradual transition that they expect to take several years. "Netflix is a three-act play," says company spokesman Steve Swasey:

> Act one was strictly DVDs by mail. In 2010, we're in act two, which is DVDs by mail and streaming service to your TV and your computer. And act three, which will be streaming only, no DVDs, is coming faster than any of us imagined. In fact, we launched a pure streaming service in Canada in September 2010—no DVDs!
>
> We'll continue to send DVDs to Netflix members in the U.S. for several more years. But as Netflix expands internationally, with a second region anticipated in 2011, it will be pure streaming.

The precise timing of the transition is unpredictable, though it appears to be moving more quickly than most experts anticipated. (A streaming-only plan was introduced in the U.S. in November 2010.) But whenever it happens, Netflix will be ready.

Streaming video requires a new business model. Under the copyright law's "first sale" doctrine, anyone who buys a DVD can sell or rent it with virtually no restrictions. (For the same reason, you can sell a used book without paying royalties to author or publisher.) But selling streaming content demands a contract with the owner/creator that provides for long-term revenue sharing.

Will this change gum up the financial works of Netflix's finely tuned business model? Not necessarily. As DVD mailing decreases, a growing fraction of Netflix's annual $500 million postage bill will be freed up to pay for the new streaming business. "Once we cut our physical distribution costs in half," Swasey observes, "we'll have $250 million extra to spend with the movie studios—and those are Walmart numbers, big enough to make us one of their biggest customers."

Thinking ahead, Hastings and his team have been working that side of the field for years, cultivating relationships with the movie studios, TV networks, production companies, and other content suppliers. "Our strategy," Hastings has observed with a wry smile, "is to write them big checks." Today Netflix has deals with dozens of them, from the Disney Channel, NBC Universal, Warner Bros., MGM, and CBS to Twentieth Century Fox, Lionsgate, New Line Cinema, and Epix, yielding a catalog with thousands of movies and TV programs available for instant streaming.

This new world means new competitors for Netflix—ad-supported video streaming companies like Hulu and YouTube, pay-per-view download companies like Apple and Amazon, and pay-per-view services offered by cable companies like Comcast On Demand. Netflix represents a different business model—subscription-based streaming. At the moment, all these models are growing, and Hastings expects this to continue as video streaming penetrates more and more American households.

Netflix is in a leading position as the next phase of this multi-player chess game begins. But what will the consumer's new hassle map look like, and what will be the key demand trigger? Will it be ubiquity of access? (If so, Netflix has a huge head start with its presence on hundreds of devices from almost every major electronics manufacturer.) Will it be highly prized exclusive content? Will it be some technological leap that brilliantly enhances the viewing experience, like in-home 3-D? Will it be a blend of entertainment and social networking, with world-spanning groups of people sharing live events featuring beloved performers?

No one today knows the answer—not even Reed Hastings. But we wouldn't bet against him being among the first to discover it.

NESPRESSO AND THE DEMAND
THAT ALMOST WASN'T

No two demand creation stories are the same. Netflix is a classic David-and-Goliath tale: Entrepreneur Reed Hastings and his team of upstarts created a vast new stream of demand under the very noses of a giant industry leader.

Now we look through the other end of the telescope, at the tale of a huge, very successful company struggling to nurture the tiny flame of a new demand creation idea that didn't fit comfortably into its existing business model. It's a story with very different challenges, but with even more surprising twists and turns.

Our story begins in the early 1970s at the Battelle Research Institute in Geneva, Switzerland, where scientists had developed the basic design for a new kind of single-serve espresso brewing system. In 1974, the right to commercialize this design was purchased by Nestlé, the Swiss-based corporation that is the world's largest marketer of consumer packaged goods. Nestlé then invested more than a decade in further technical development under a team led by engineer Eric Favre.

By the mid-eighties, the new system—dubbed Nespresso—was perfected. Through a three-step prewetting, aeration, and extraction process, the Nespresso brewer expanded, irrigated, and drew flavor from coffee pods at optimal pressure and heat, thereby producing delicious coffee with greater ease and cleanliness than any other system. Unlike traditional espresso makers, which were bulky, breakdown-prone, and demanded the practiced touch of a skilled barista, it was compact, reliable, and simple to operate. The unique technology was protected by thirty separate collections of patents.

The Nespresso system offered coffee lovers a host of advantages. Its one-cup-at-a-time brewing capacity made espresso an easily *personalizable* treat. Nespresso developed a selection of different flavor varieties, each available in a different-hued gleaming aluminum pod. Thus a hostess and her dinner guests could enjoy several different coffees—Ristretto for one ("Composed of pure Arabica beans from Latin America for its finesse and a touch of Robusta for its intensity"), Capriccio for a second ("A satisfying smooth espresso"), and Volluto for a third ("The mellow richness of early Latin American beans gives this blend a distinct elegant, subtle bouquet"). Responding to the varied demands of individual customers can be a powerful demand multiplier: Make the product perfect *for me,* and I will want it that much more.

Thanks to features like these, even the most demanding espresso aficionados found the Nespresso system impressive, making comments like "It's the first time I've been exposed to such a range of espresso tastes. . . . You can produce good espresso every time. . . . It's such a neat, intuitive way of producing coffee of professional quality."

Here, then, was a seemingly magnificent demand creation opportunity for Nestlé: a convenient new technology for preparing the world's most popular beverage, boasting innovative features that millions of consumers were likely to enjoy. Yet in the early years of Nespresso, demand lagged. On more than one occasion, the business came close to extinction.

What was the problem? It was the lack of a trigger—or, better still, a series of triggers—that could overcome consumer inertia and convert *potential* demand into *real* demand. The quest for those triggers turned out to be the central drama in the saga of Nespresso.

❏   ❏   ❏

ONE KEY TO UNDERSTANDING the Nespresso story is the special challenges involved in building a groundbreaking new business inside a very large, successful organization.

When the Nespresso opportunity came its way, Nestlé was already one of the world's great companies, with revenues in the tens of billions and hundreds of thousands of workers in eighty countries producing profits "year after year like a Swiss clock," as one observer has put it. For this giant corporation, the opportunity to commercialize the Nespresso brewing system offered a portal into the world of roast and ground (R&G) coffee, where Nestlé lagged in fourth place. (Nestlé already dominated *instant* coffee through its Nescafé brand.) Since R&G made up fully 70 percent of the world's coffee business, the leaders of Nestlé had long wondered how they could profitably serve those hundreds of millions of customers. Nespresso seemed to be the answer.

But there was a complication. The idea of building a brand around a *machine* rather than around packaged food ran contrary to the instincts of most executives at Nestlé—a company with no experience in the appliance industry. And when it came to launching a brand-new product that didn't fit neatly into its existing business model, Nestlé's size and its enviable track record were a two-edged sword. The company's rigorous management systems and its conservative style were better suited to protecting and expanding its existing businesses than to experimenting in a radically different market.

Helmut Maucher, Nestlé's CEO, had long understood the difficulties of demand innovation at big companies like his. An out-of-the-box thinker, Maucher had been among the first to see the enormous potential of bottled water and pushed the company to acquire brands like Perrier and Vittel at the start of that trend. He'd come to believe that creating new streams of demand in mature markets was *the* key competitive challenge Nestlé faced, and he understood that Nestlé's size, history, and culture might prove to be both assets and obstacles in this quest.

New additions to Nestlé's packaged goods lineup, like bottled water, fit comfortably within its traditional way of doing business. But the Nespresso brewing technology was an outlier. So in 1986, when the Nespresso system was finally ready for the marketplace, Maucher took steps to insulate the start-up from the rest of Nestlé.

He created a separate affiliate wholly owned by Nestlé yet protected from the skeptical challenges and profit-now pressures of
the button-down world of the corporation. Then he housed it in a
building of its own across the street from company headquarters—a
symbolic gesture that spoke volumes. Camillo Pagano, the executive then shepherding Nespresso, explained:

> The business was physically moved out of Nestlé so that it could
> establish credibility and so that it didn't have to fight against all
> the company's rules. . . . Any innovation immediately hits resis-
> tance in an organization. Small satellites like this can help people
> gain insight into how a business could be developed differently.
> These offshoots provide an opportunity to train and test people. If
> they make a mistake there, it's not so costly.

Ensconced in their new "skunkworks," the eight-person Nespresso team led by Pagano and engineer Favre got to work on
commercializing the coffee pod technology. We can imagine their
feelings—a blend of exultation and anxiety over being pioneers
in a new industry worlds away from Nestlé's traditional market
strongholds.

Unfortunately, results for their pilot programs weren't encouraging. The team experimented with marketing Nespresso machines
to cafés, restaurants, and offices, where most espresso is made and
served. But the two chief advantages of the machines—their compact size and their ease of use—meant little in those markets. Most
offices and restaurant kitchens were not particularly short on counter
space, and most baristas regarded a quick-and-easy espresso maker
as a threat to their livelihood. By 1987, only half the machines built
had been sold.

In most big companies, the natural response would have been
to shut down or sell the nascent business. Why should a successful

packaged goods company be distracted by the unproven potential of a failed kitchen appliance? We can guess that many inside Nestlé must have been beginning to ask that question; some may have been growing irritated over the special treatment the Nespresso team enjoyed.

But Camillo Pagano insisted that the new technology deserved another chance. He convinced Maucher to make another unconventional move, recruiting Jean-Paul Gaillard to take over Nespresso in 1988.

Nestlé rarely hires executives from the outside. But Gaillard's previous assignment had been to launch a clothing line, Marlboro Classics, within the Philip Morris tobacco empire. Pagano sensed that Nespresso fit the same mold—"a stab in the dark" for a big, traditional business.

Gaillard wasn't merely an outsider; he also had an outsider's mentality—in spades. Brash, talkative, even boastful, he was the opposite of the reserved, politically and socially conservative team players Nestlé would normally hire. He was also demanding, inflexible, willful, and impatient with structures and systems not of his own devising. Pagano recalls, "We needed to find somebody who wouldn't react like a Nestlé manager." Gaillard certainly fit the bill.

Soon after arriving, Gaillard decided that the future of Nespresso lay with the home market. Addressing Nestlé's board, he declared that well-heeled, sophisticated homemakers with a taste for gourmet coffees could be won over by a great home brewing system. This called for a dramatic shift away from the middle price range implied by a restaurant-and-office strategy and toward the high-end luxury consumer market—another arena in which Nestlé had little experience.

Unfortunately for Gaillard, the evidence supporting his proposed strategy was scanty. Survey data and market trials suggested that the potential demand for home espresso machines was modest, and that a price higher than 25 Swiss centimes (about 16 cents) for a single coffee pod would kill demand. (Gaillard's target price was 40 centimes.) A test in which five upscale appliance stores were provided with one hundred Nespresso machines and asked to promote them aggressively had been a complete failure: Fewer than thirty machines were sold.

But Gaillard had no intention of quitting. He spent days buttonholing his fellow Nestlé executives and plying them with bold (if not always supported) forecasts of the vast new demand stream Nespresso would soon uncork. Addressing the board, Gaillard put the best possible face on the test-market data, gliding quickly over the discouraging numbers and burnishing the few bright spots as best he could. Then he pointed out, perhaps with fingers crossed, that fax machines and mobile phones had received similar bad results in *their* early market testing.

It would have been understandable for Nestlé board members to regard Nespresso as an irrelevant distraction from the company's packaged goods business. But CEO Maucher backed the maverick Gaillard. The board members swallowed whatever doubts they had and agreed to support Gaillard's continued experimentation with Nespresso.

Gaillard would have one more opportunity to prove that demand for Nespresso was out there, waiting to be tapped. But the pressure for results was mounting.

❐ ❐ ❐

HAVING FAILED with Nespresso in the café, restaurant, and office markets, Gaillard and his team had fallen back on the home market, more by default than by design. And they quickly learned the same lesson many others have learned—that an innovative product alone is not enough to generate large demand.

Sales of the new coffeemakers to the home market started slow, leading to a cascade of negative effects. Most appliance stores were reluctant to stock the unfamiliar machines, and those that did were unwilling to carry a large assortment of coffee pods. With the pods selling slowly, supplies eventually grew stale, leading to unhappy customers and even weaker demand for the Nespresso concept. The downward spiral threatened to destroy Nespresso in its cradle.

It was the kind of crisis many an ambitious manager in a large corporation has faced. To this point, Gaillard had handled very effectively the inherent tension between the need to experiment with brand-new demand creation approaches and Nestlé's conservative culture. But if he couldn't find a demand trigger to jump-start sales of Nespresso machines—and pull coffee pods through the sales pipeline before they turned stale—it would all add up to nothing.

Desperate, Gaillard proposed to his Nestlé colleagues an unorthodox solution: marketing directly to consumers.

"We'll let customers order coffee pods over the phone for quick shipment by mail," he declared hopefully. "How convenient—coffee on your doorstep within a couple of days! We'll call our service the Nespresso Club, and we'll automatically enroll everyone who buys a Nespresso maker."

Direct selling would guarantee the freshness of Nespresso coffee pods. But it posed huge problems of its own. For one thing, the independent retailers who'd been selling Nespresso machines—or at least *trying* to sell them—hated the idea of having Nespresso do an end run around them. They also feared their customers would balk if they couldn't get a supply of pods from the same store.

What's worse, in its entire corporate history, Nestlé had never sold anything direct to consumers before. Proposing a wholly new business model to a large company with a long track record of remarkable success is virtually certain to provoke pushback. (Under similar circumstances, executives in most corporations might well have reacted to Gaillard's proposal with consternation: "He can't sell his coffee in stores like everybody else, so he wants to start a *club*?")

But cajoled by Gaillard and prodded by CEO Maucher, Nestlé's board approved direct selling. It was a high-wire moment for Nespresso and its champion. If they lost this bet, Nespresso would surely tumble to its doom.

Gaillard took a deep breath and declared the Nespresso Club open for business. On the first day, three people signed up.

On the second day, eleven more.

On the third day, not a single one.

Even the supremely self-confident Jean-Paul Gaillard must have had second thoughts.

But as the days turned into weeks and months, the numbers slowly began to swell—into the teens, then the hundreds. Each new member became a steady customer for Nespresso coffee pods, ordering between $300 and $400 worth every year. By 1990, two years after its founding, the Nespresso Club had 2,700 members in Switzerland, France, Japan, and the United States. By 1992, outposts were established in Germany, Belgium, the Netherlands, and Luxembourg; in 1996, Spain, Austria, and the United Kingdom were added. By the end of that year, the Nespresso Club had more than 220,000 members worldwide. A year later, the number was 300,000, generating revenues for Nestlé in the range of $140 million.

It was enough to keep Nespresso alive. And it turned out to be a triple play: a move with three distinct sets of benefits—for Nespresso customers, for Nespresso's management, and for Nespresso's bottom line.

For the customers, direct selling guaranteed fresh supplies of coffee capsules and consistently high service standards. The Nespresso Club delivered coffee and accessories within forty-eight hours and offered information and advice around the clock via phone and later online. The superb service increased the odds that Nespresso drinkers would not only enjoy their machines and the coffee they made but also recommend them to their friends—helping to stimulate the next round of sales. (In a similar vein, remember how Netflix sub-scriptions soared every time a new distribution center cut delivery times, sparking enthusiastic word of mouth among local members.)

In the years to come, the customer benefits offered by the Nes-presso Club steadily multiplied. Members began receiving special Limited Edition coffee offerings, the biannual *Nespresso* magazine—a glossy "coffee pleasure guide" distributed in eight languages across fifteen countries—and access to a beautiful array of coffee-drinking accessories: china and silverware cups, plates, and bowls, milk froth-ers and heaters, cleaning and descaling kits, ice crushers, and much more. Free machine pickups and loans were provided in case a coffeemaker broke down, and the company even mailed out a clean-ing kit when its records indicated that a customer's filter was due for a scrub.

Almost by accident, Nespresso had created its first great demand trigger. Thanks to the Nespresso Club, word of mouth became a powerful demand creation tool for Nespresso. In a survey of French Nespresso customers, 71 percent agreed with the statement "I love this product!"—double the percentage among users of rival coffee-makers—and 60 percent reported praising Nespresso in conversa-tions at least once a month.

At the same time, the club provided Nespresso's management with direct access to customers for marketing messages as well as a valuable stream of customer data that their marketers could use to enhance their demand creation efforts. Which customers buy the most coffees, accessories, confectionery goods, and other products? How do their patterns of consumption change over time? What sea-sonal buying habits do they develop? What kinds of special offers will excite them? Nestlé's marketers could answer such questions by sifting through the flows of data the Nespresso Club provided. And the club produced a huge boost for Nespresso's profit margins by enabling it to sell directly, without additional markups by retailers. The higher margins fell right to Nespresso's bottom line.

Perhaps most remarkably, with its direct-selling model, Nespresso had even begun to revolutionize the half-a-millennium-old coffee business. Just as Apple's iPod is a portal to the "music world" of the iTunes Store, and Amazon's Kindle is a portal to the "reading world" of the Amazon bookstore, a Nespresso machine had become a portal to the "coffee world" that club members are privileged to enjoy. As John Gapper, a columnist for the *Financial Times,* wrote: "It did not occur to me before Nespresso came along that I ever needed such a thing. Now that I have it, however, I am attached to it."

◻   ◻   ◻

BY THE MID-NINETIES, more than twenty years after the invention of the new brewing technology, demand was finally beginning to flow. And then Nespresso discovered its second, even more powerful demand trigger.

In 1994, seeking new markets, Nespresso introduced a coffeemaker designed for first-class aircraft galleys. This proved to be a catalytic move, and not so much because of the value of direct sales to airlines, which are a relatively small market, but because it helped the Nespresso team to recognize the extraordinary impact that *tasting* their coffee could have on potential customers.

Swissair was the first airline to serve Nespresso. Others followed, and sales of Nespresso machines began a modest climb. The connection was apparent. First-class airline passengers—wealthy, well-traveled, sophisticated—turned out to be the perfect customer set for sales of Nespresso machines. Soon first-class aircraft cabins weren't the only venue where Nespresso tastings were being offered. High-end restaurants in France, Belgium, and other European countries were sold the machines. Selected opinion leaders, including politicians and journalists, were given *free* machines with which to serve VIP guests in their offices. The growth of Nespresso sales began to improve.

Gaillard and the Nespresso team had stumbled upon what would

prove to be their product's single most powerful demand trigger—
the chance for consumers to *try* Nespresso for themselves. Over the
next several years, in various forms and venues, trial would gradually convert thousands, then millions of coffee lovers into Nespresso
customers.

In August 1997, the feisty Jean-Paul Gaillard left Nespresso, first
moving to another assignment within Nestlé, then leaving the corporation altogether. His place at Nespresso was taken by the
Dutch-born Henk Kwakman, a lifelong Nestlé executive. Though
a "very structured manager" in the classic Nestlé mold rather than
a headstrong cowboy like Gaillard, Kwakman scaled back none
of the innovations Gaillard had pioneered. Instead he pushed them
further.

Unlike Gaillard, however, Kwakman emphasized the value of intensive customer research as a basis for shaping demand creation
strategy. Within the first few months of starting his new assignment,
he commissioned a study to investigate more fully the *meaning* of
espresso for consumers. The goal: to identify the steps needed to
make Nespresso the natural choice for coffee lovers, so that its steady
but slow growth could be dramatically accelerated.

Nespresso's survey of coffee drinkers in five European countries yielded several crucial insights. The first was that espresso has
an intensely *emotional* meaning for consumers. The emotion begins with the taste, which ideally should be a short, powerful burst
of flavor—"a tango for the tongue," in Kwakman's colorful phrase.
But it doesn't stop there. Those who love espresso also associate it
with a host of less tangible qualities: the good life, as represented
by a delightful meal in a sophisticated restaurant, as well as high
style, trendiness, connoisseurship, and "Italian-ness." Fundamentally,
espresso is a *sexy* drink—worlds away from the utilitarian pick-me-up
represented by the standard morning cup of joe.

Kwakman and his team began to realize that, for all the brilliant technical work that had been done to perfect the Nespresso machine, they might have stopped just short of the final, crucial development step—emotionalizing the product to capture and express the unspoken expectations and longings of espresso aficionados.

The research team delved still deeper. Some 15 percent of respondents said they'd bought espresso machines, but most were disappointed with them. Most had purchased conventional, pre-Nespresso devices whose output fell short because of insufficient water pressure, no frothy *crema* atop the coffee, lack of body, and too few flavor options. Half of those with espresso machines at home had stopped using them.

Finally, the researchers found that only 1 percent of espresso lovers had even heard of Nespresso. Those who'd bought a Nespresso brewer were mostly pleased with the product—though their comments were fairly lukewarm, reflecting a feeling that the coffeemaker, while well made, had no real magnetism. Its relatively high cost was a further enthusiasm damper. And many mentioned a small but irritating hassle: the drop of coffee invariably left on the kitchen counter or floor when removing the used capsule after brewing.

All in all, the research painted a discouraging picture of how far Nespresso still had to go to achieve a major demand breakthrough. But Henk Kwakman was delighted—even with the complaint about the spilled drop of coffee. "When you discover a problem, you discover a business," he declared, deftly summarizing the philosophy that drives all of the world's great hassle-fixers.

Kwakman and his team set about redesigning Nespresso based on their new insights into the mind and heart of the coffee lover. It started with a redesign of the Nespresso machine itself—a process that ended up taking nearly two years.

Fixing the problem of the spilled drop was the least of the challenges. (Adding a compartment into which empty coffee capsules were automatically ejected after brewing solved that one.) More challenging was working closely with appliance manufacturers to transform the brewer from a conventional squarish black box into a stylish, sexy-looking device—"the Armani of coffee," as Kwakman put it. After months of experiments, they came up with a series of designs ranging from a streamlined Art Deco look to an ultra-modernist style accented with brushed stainless steel and vivid color panels—in the words of *New York* magazine, "race-car-sleek machines designed to seduce the gadget-happy and modernize the fustiest Park Avenue kitchen."

To further enhance the product's magnetic appeal, Kwakman and his team worked with designers to create a new, more elegant logo for the budding brand. "I was a crazy fan of Nike," Kwakman recalls. "I loved the way they put their symbol on a cap, a T-shirt, a trouser, a shoe—constantly reinforcing the Nike image without having to say 'Nike' over and over." The new stylized *N* logo, subtly suggestive of a pair of high-heeled shoes one atop the other, quickly found its way onto the machines, the coffee packaging, even the cups and spoons, capturing a bit of the premium sheen imparted by the Chanel monogram on a handbag or the Mercedes-Benz symbol on the hood of a sedan.

These design innovations were a huge step toward intensifying the appeal of the product. Nespresso had found its missing emotional energy.

At the same time, Kwakman wanted to make his machines accessible to a wider market, which meant significantly reducing their price. He negotiated deals with Nespresso's manufacturing partners, assuming a portion of the financial risk from reduced retail prices. In effect, Kwakman was betting a bit of Nestlé's money that the stylish new machines would sell well, leading to a rapid increase in volume and a sharp consequent drop in manufacturing costs. In the end, the new lineup of machines ranged in price from a modest $199 to more than $2,000 for a multifeatured machine connected to an in-home water supply.

Nespresso was now affordable for the vast majority of coffee gourmets. Demand soon began to respond.

But Kwakman was far from finished. "Our awareness remains low in priority markets," he complained. "Word-of-mouth is a slow process. We have to find other means of making the Nespresso concept known."

A logical solution was advertising. But Nespresso's print ads in magazines had produced little impact on demand. In rethinking the advertising strategy, Kwakman and his team focused on the power of trial. Could advertising somehow *simulate* the opportunity to try the Nespresso machine, thereby triggering action rather than mere brand awareness?

The solution: shift from print ads to television commercials. More expensive, yes—but this medium allowed the beauty, simplicity, speed, and elegance of the Nespresso machine to be vividly *demonstrated* rather than merely described. The impact was remarkable. When the first commercials debuted in time for the 2000 Christmas season, demand responded with a severalfold increase.

Even in the indirect form of a televised demonstration, trial was once again revealing its power to trigger demand.

◘   ◘   ◘

KWAKMAN'S APPRECIATION for the power of trial kept growing—and so did the ingenuity with which he and his team made it available to potential customers.

They induced more airlines to offer Nespresso to their first-class passengers. By 2000, some 1,100 planes flown by twenty different airlines were using the machines, and 3.5 million travelers had the chance to experience the aroma and flavor of Nespresso each year.

But even better than sipping espresso prepared by a flight attendant was the opportunity to test the machine oneself. Nespresso began working intensively with retailers, encouraging them to do much more than simply display their handsome machines. By 2000, retailers throughout Europe as well as in the United States were being provided with extensive training in demonstrating the devices. Nespresso developed target lists of stores by asking customers, "If you were thinking of buying an espresso machine, where would you go to buy it?" Then they made sure the stores consumers named were signed up as distributors. Soon hundreds of retailers were showing off Nespresso machines, offering trials that demonstrated the fun and ease of using the devices.

Kwakman and his team also discovered a crucial new element that could make the trial trigger even more effective. It was simple, really. Many retailers demonstrated the Nespresso machines. Others went one step further: They actually *served coffee* brewed from Nespresso coffee pods.

The results were staggering. Retailer surveys revealed that stores providing customer trials of *both* the machines and the coffee generated *six times as many sales* as those that merely demonstrated the machines.

It might seem obvious that tasting Nespresso and trying the machine is crucial to triggering demand. It is—in hindsight. Consider: Between 2007 and 2010, hundreds of thousands of customers bought Kindles *without ever seeing one*. (Until their arrival at Target stores in mid-2010, Kindles were not available in retail outlets.)

For the would-be demand creator, figuring out what kind of trigger will convert fence-sitters into customers is *not* about reasoning from a priori logic or even from the evidence of other businesses. It's about seeing what happens when you try. Some products don't require trial. Others, like Nespresso, depend upon it. Give customers a chance to love it, and many will. But without trial, "nothing happens"—the two most dreaded words in the universe of demand.

The six-to-one multiplying power of trial opened the demand floodgates for Nespresso. Taking a page from the playbook of high-end cosmetics manufacturers like Yves Rocher, company executives approached department stores with a proposition: "Give us twenty square meters of your valuable floor space. We will create a Nespresso store-within-a-store, with our own host and hostess trained in offering product demonstrations and sample cups of coffee. We'll do the staffing and sell the machines, and the revenues will flow to you."

The famous Galeries Lafayette in Paris was the first department store to accept the offer. Sales of Nespresso machines at the store rose from around fifty per year to around seven hundred. Soon every major retail chain in Europe was asking for its own Nespresso shops.

This success led directly to the development of an even more unconventional and audacious demand creation strategy, being played out today on the leading commercial boulevards in two hundred of the world's most stylish cities—the launch of a chain of Nespresso retail stores. It was yet another unprecedented move for the conservative Nestlé organization.

Once again, the Nestlé board must have had some qualms—and once again, they accepted the dare. A single Nespresso boutique was commissioned on an experimental basis and opened in the heart of Paris in 2001. When sales far outstripped expectations, Kwakman got the green light to replicate the concept. Designed by leading architects in gleaming polished woods, metals, and glass panels, the Nespresso boutiques—now two hundred in number—are located on the grandest avenues in many of the world's most glamorous cities, from Zurich, Milan, and London to Tokyo, Rio de Janeiro, and New York. Staffed by specialists who advise customers on machine purchases, help them sample coffee varieties, and even serve snacks and pastries that complement the coffees, Nespresso boutiques provide the single most compelling way for people to test the machines and taste the product.

On busy mornings, the original Nespresso store on the Champs-Elysées has lines around the block—just as many of the gorgeous

Apple stores do when a hot new device is available for a test drive. And the Nespresso sales curve took a sharp upward tilt after the launch of the boutiques—28 percent annual growth in 2001, then 34 percent, then 37, then 42—that bears an uncanny resemblance to the sales spike enjoyed by Apple products when the first of more than two hundred Apple stores opened later that same year.

Today, with a steadily expanding network of well-staffed boutiques, fully 80 percent of Nespresso employees work in direct contact with consumers, providing an invaluable stream of voice-of-the-customer feedback that can help the company stay ahead of the changing shape of demand.

Many casual observers today attribute Nespresso's success to its current advertising program, featuring the debonair actor George Clooney, and its high-glamour sponsorships of events like the America's Cup yacht race and the Cannes Film Festival. But the Clooney ad campaign, launched in 2006, is not the central driver of Nespresso's growth. Advertising has helped to build awareness of Nespresso, but the trial-generating machine—from airline galleys to department stores to freestanding boutiques—is what really creates the customer.

Converting fence-sitters to customers remains a challenge for Nespresso, as it does for many companies. Fifty-seven percent of customers we surveyed reported a time lag of a year or more between hearing about Nespresso and finally buying a machine. Without a couple of powerful triggers, the emergence of real demand might never happen. Today, about half of new Nespresso purchases are triggered by word of mouth, while the other half come through free trial, whether in an appliance store or a Nespresso boutique.

Like density for Zipcar and delivery speed for Netflix, *trial* has become the crucial trigger that supercharges demand for Nespresso.

Triggers are not mutually exclusive—they can often reinforce one another. This is particularly true of word of mouth, which is one of the most effective triggers, yet also one of the most difficult to create. Fortunately, since magnetic products have strong story elements that spark great customer conversations, the same triggers that increase a product's magnetism can stimulate word of mouth and increased sales, setting off a self-reinforcing spiral of positive effects. Nespresso exemplifies this dynamic. Today, 50 percent of Nespresso's new customers come from referrals. After all, what's more natural than sharing a delicious cup of coffee with friends and family? The inevitable result is curiosity about the great coffeemaker—and, often, another sale.

In his understated way, Henk Kwakman demonstrated even more creativity and courage than the iconoclastic Gaillard. He discovered the crucial importance of emotionalizing the product, and he invested the time and effort in transforming the look of the Nespresso machine to make it stylish and sexy as well as efficient. He spearheaded the creation of an advertising and design program that reinforced that glamorous image. Above all, he leveraged the power of trial through the creation of Nespresso stores-within-stores, and convinced his colleagues to invest in freestanding Nespresso boutiques. It was a huge bet that none of Nespresso's rivals dared to try—and one that has proven to be a huge winner.

❐   ❐   ❐

THE NESPRESSO DRAMA hinged on the discovery of triggers that made potential demand real. But of course demand is multifaceted, and an important element in the continuing success of Nespresso is the growing array of backstory features that combine to make the customer experience remarkable.

We've already touched on many of these features—the technical ingenuity behind the brewing system, the high-quality service provided by the Nespresso Club staffers, the training of retail hosts and hostesses to make product trials fun and accessible, and so on. But yet another, which reflects the long-term orientation that is one of Nestlé's great gifts, is the commitment to building a world-class dedicated supply chain for Nespresso products.

Henk Kwakman gives much of the credit to Nestlé executive

Rupert Gasser, whom he describes as "an old coffee man" and a longtime internal supporter of the Nespresso project. By 2000, with Nespresso entering its period of intensive growth, Gasser decided the time had come for Nespresso to stop relying on its corporate parent for its coffee supply. "If you're going to run an art gallery," he told Kwakman, "eventually you have to learn something about art. If you're going to run coffee boutiques, you will have to learn about coffee."

With Gasser's encouragement—and a significant investment from Nestlé—Nespresso began building its own supply infrastructure. Coffee experts were added to the company staff to monitor product quality and pass on their knowledge to Nespresso's marketers and service people. A dedicated factory to produce Nespresso coffee pods was opened in Orbe, Switzerland, in 2002. And today, Nespresso has a network of field experts visiting coffee plantations from Brazil and Colombia to West Africa, meeting with brokers and farmers, selecting fields, and choosing coffee crops—all with the goal of maintaining ultrahigh product standards even as demand for Nespresso continues to expand.

No one at Nespresso wants to see the day when their customers can no longer get the intense "tango on the tongue" they've come to expect from their products. They're investing in backstory infrastructure today to make sure it never happens.

Kwakman moved on to fresh assignments within Nestlé in 2002. His successors at the Nespresso helm have pushed the growth of the business still further. By 2007, Nespresso's CEO Richard Girardot was talking about more than doubling the number of boutiques into the five hundred range.

When we asked Girardot how Nespresso tries to track how the customer is changing, he paused for a minute. "Our number one job is to *listen*," he explained. "We have ten million customers. They communicate to us all the time, telling us what they like, what they don't, and they are constantly generating ideas. You have to remember that our customer is our number one salesperson. They really *care* about this product."

He pointed to his iPhone and said, "I received three letters from customers just today. That's what we have to focus on. Most of the answers are there. We just have to listen.

"One message that always keeps coming through from them is their fanatical love of the quality. That's why my teams and I spend so much of our time traveling the world in search of the very best coffee farms, today and tomorrow. We have built relationships with forty thousand farmers, but we're always looking for new ones and helping set them up if necessary. Finding the absolute best sources of coffee is where the magic of Nespresso begins, and, like our customers, we are quite fanatical about it."

Today, Nespresso is Nestlé's fastest-growing brand, with annual growth greater than 30 percent from 2005 to 2010 (right through the Great Recession). In 2009, its growth accounted for fully one-fifth of the overall growth (excluding acquisitions) of its giant corporate parent. With more than 10 million Nespresso Club members, Nespresso is the European market leader in single-serve coffee; in April 2010, the company proudly announced it had surpassed sales of rival Lavazza in Italy, "the cradle of espresso." Nespresso's annual revenues are nearing $3 billion, and though this does not yet rival Starbucks' $10 billion, Nespresso actually sells more servings of coffee every year than the Seattle-based chain.

Nespresso now faces challenges on several fronts. One is a legal battle to keep the demand stream it has created from being diverted. Despite the patents that are supposed to protect the exclusivity of the Nespresso design, at least two companies intend to sell coffee pods designed to fit Nespresso machines—one of them is the Ethical Coffee Company, a start-up headed by none other than Jean-Paul Gaillard himself.

The stakes are high. The price of a Nespresso capsule is fairly modest, currently ranging from fifty-five to sixty-two cents a shot, but multiply that by the daily consumption of 10 million Nespresso drinkers and you have a very nice revenue stream that is well worth protecting—and fighting over.

Nespresso is prepared for the challenge, aware that its decades of experimentation and the triggers it painstakingly developed have given it a unique set of advantages. "If a competitor wants to enter this market," Girardot declares, "I say good luck to them. I do not want to sound pretentious, but the work done by the Nespresso team over twenty years is not easy to imitate.

"Our response," he adds with a smile, "is not to respond."

A second ongoing challenge for Nespresso is the quest to expand its success beyond Europe—in particular, to grow beyond a mere toehold in the North American market. While other competitors, including Keurig (owned by Green Mountain Coffee), Flavia (part of the Mars candy empire), and Italy's Lavazza and Illy, have a head start in penetrating the U.S. market, none have Nespresso's upscale image or a comparably magnetic product.

However, an even bigger challenge for Nespresso may be the nature of that market itself. Unlike Europeans, most Americans aren't espresso fanciers—at least not yet. According to the National Coffee Association, while 68 percent of American adults drink coffee at least once a week, the corresponding figure for espresso is just 8 percent. But the U.S. market is evolving rapidly, and Nespresso may turn out to be well positioned to both drive and ride the future growth of espresso in the States. In the last five years, U.S. sales have grown from $15 million to $150 million.

Nespresso's history has been a remarkable one—a tale of exploration in uncharted territories. Demand creation is largely about respecting, discovering, and then reshaping the unknowable. Nespresso has had to do that repeatedly, and is looking ahead to doing so in the future. As Henk Kwakman puts it: "If you pioneer something new into a market, there is no example, there is no roadmap, so that the key thing is that you have to try. Nobody knows what will happen, so the more you try, the more you discover, the faster you learn, the faster you go."

One gets the distinct sense that despite its enormous success, Nespresso's commitment to discovery remains undiminished.

5.

Trajectory

(truh-JEK-tuh-ree) *noun* 1. the rate at which the magnetic characteristics of a product are enhanced over time 2. rapid performance improvement (technical, emotional, affordable, content) as the key that unlocks new layers of demand

GETTING SMARTER FASTER: TEACH FOR AMERICA'S DRIVE TO RESHAPE EDUCATIONAL DEMAND

Novelist and social critic Aldous Huxley, author of *Brave New World*, had a favorite motto: "Nothing short of everything is ever really enough." We've seen this principle at work repeatedly in the world of demand. For the demand creator, building a magnetic product is essential, but it isn't enough—you also need to understand the customer's hassle map and figure out how to connect the dots in ways that reduce those hassles or eliminate them altogether. Making an emotional connection with the customer is crucial, but it isn't enough—you also need to make certain that all the backstory elements are in place, so that you can be sure to avoid the Curse of the Incomplete Product. And even *that* isn't enough—you also need to find the most powerful triggers and deploy them effectively if you hope to overcome consumer inertia and transform potential demand energy into real demand.

What's more, great demand creators instinctively understand that even creating a powerful stream of demand isn't enough—not unless you make a commitment to intense, ongoing improvement so as to meet, and exceed, the ever-rising expectations of your ever-changing customers. Like Olympic athletes who work year-round to shave another tenth of a second off their best time—and occasionally invent the dramatically new technique that revolutionizes their sport and catapults performance to a startlingly higher level—demand creators are always in training, constantly seeking ways to get better faster.

The rate at which a product gets better after its first release is its *trajectory.* The steeper the trajectory, the better for customers. Some products improve at a shallow, 5-degree angle, others at a more formidable 45-degree slope. A steep trajectory makes current customers happier, and gets new customers to join. It also sends a daunting signal to would-be competitors: *If you want to tap into the demand we've created, it's not good enough to produce a product that* matches ours—*because by the time you reach the market, we'll be two miles further up the mountain.*

Trajectory thinking often separates demand creation winners from also-rans. Not so long ago, Facebook was the second-ranked social networking site, while MySpace led the pack. But News Corporation failed to invest in innovation after it acquired MySpace in 2005, while Facebook charged ahead. By 2009, Facebook had overtaken MySpace; today, it's hard to remember when the race was even competitive.

☐   ☐   ☐

REED HASTINGS'S COMMITMENT to building a steep trajectory catalyzed one of the most curious—and celebrated—scientific challenges of recent years: the $1 million Netflix Prize, offered to anyone who could improve the accuracy of the company's Cinematch movie recommendation system by a mere 10 percent.

Launched in October 2006, this unique competition attracted no fewer than thirty-five thousand participants from 180 countries, ranging from expert teams based in universities, think tanks, and corporate research labs to lone tinkerers like psychologist Gavin Potter, who based his approach on insights from behavioral economics and enlisted his daughter Emily, a high school senior, to help with the math. (Potter's quest may sound quixotic, but at one point, his entry climbed as high as sixth on the leaderboard.)

After a spirited scientific race followed like a sporting contest by observers around the world, the Netflix Prize was claimed in September 2009 by a team of seven mathematicians, engineers, and computer scientists known as BellKor's Pragmatic Chaos.

A 10 percent improvement in movie choices sounds modest. But offering brilliant, spot-on movie recommendations is one of the crucial hassle-reducing tools that make Netflix powerfully magnetic. The contest yielded an impressive array of new insights into the tastes and preferences of movie fans. For example, customer ratings for some specific movies tend to shift in particular ways over time. People usually give the schmaltzy Robin Williams flick *Patch Adams* a high rating immediately after viewing it; after taking time to reflect, they assign it a noticeably lower grade. The opposite pattern applies to the complex psychological thriller *Memento*, which appears to grow on people during the days and weeks after they watch it (as they gradually disentangle the convoluted plot).

Another finding: Most movies draw reactions that appear logical based on categories like genre, style, period, and performer: If you like one John Wayne oater, you'll probably like the next. But a few pictures seem to defy such classifications. Two examples are the quirky indie films *I ♥ Huckabees* and *Napoleon Dynamite*. Both tend to draw wildly disparate, love-it-or-hate-it reactions and fall into no logical grouping. (Liking *Huckabees* doesn't seem to correlate with liking *Napoleon*, for example—or with anything else in particular.)

And still another finding: The winning BellKor team discovered that Netflix users' ratings of pictures are dependent, in part, on their mood at the time they enter the rating. Sounds obvious, maybe, but the insight has a specific resonance that's both subtle and useful.

When a Netflix patron visits the company website to pen a negative critique of a picture he has watched, and then lingers on the site to rate other movies, those ratings are likely to be lower than they would otherwise be—a form of temporary bias that the team learned how to anticipate and correct for in their system.

Netflix has good reason to keep advancing the science of movie selection. Each time a Netflix customer receives a recommendation that's misguided, he or she may be disappointed, maybe even angry or insulted. So the company figures that a 10 percent improvement is worth more than a million dollars in customer retention—probably a lot more. (And indeed Netflix reports that customer satisfaction and retention rates have already begun to climb.)

The Netflix Prize illustrates one of the qualities that make Reed Hastings a premier demand creator. Having labored for years to create a magnetic product, he didn't quit once he was ahead. He and his team kept going, experimenting with ways to get better on the dimensions that matter most to customers. The steep slope helps Netflix remain magnetic and sparks continuing conversation about the product among millions of consumers.

❐   ❐   ❐

RATHER AMAZINGLY, there's a remarkable example of a steep trajectory in an arena where most Americans, and many experts, have concluded that *any* improvement is next to impossible: the world of public education, long dominated by discouraging statistics, financial headaches, and political disagreements.

Into that world parachuted a twenty-two-year-old woman armed with $2.5 million in start-up donations and an idea she'd developed for her senior thesis at Princeton. Wendy Kopp's key insight: What American education needed was a way to lift its flatline trajectory. Her vehicle: the nonprofit organization she founded and leads—Teach For America (TFA)—which today is at the forefront of a powerful and growing education reform movement. TFA is climbing a steep trajectory on several dimensions that are crucial to the future of American education.

Kopp's journey began in 1988, during her senior year at Princeton, when she encountered the hassle map for aspiring teachers who hope to improve America's educational system:

> I was still trying to figure out a practical answer to my own uninspired job search. Teaching might just be it, I thought. I went to the career services office. They referred me to the teacher preparation office, which helped ten to twenty Princeton students attain teacher licensure each year. It was too late for me to enter this program, but the office pointed me to a file cabinet stuffed with job applications and certification requirements from school districts across the country. The files were a mess of mismatched, multicolored, jargon-filled papers.

Most young people would just roll their eyes and cross teaching off their list of potential careers. But Kopp—like Reed Hastings, Michael Bloomberg, and other demand creators—understood that the hassle map could be an opportunity map. She understood, too, that a huge gap existed between the kinds of careers that many talented students at America's top colleges really wanted and the work toward which they'd traditionally been channeled. There was an equally huge gap between the kind of education that at-risk public school students received and the kind they needed.

Pondering these cases of mismatched demand, Kopp came up with an idea. Why not create a teachers' corps modeled on the Peace Corps? She could sidestep bureaucratic hiring hurdles and recruit college graduates who were willing to commit to two-year teaching assignments. They'd receive intensive, hands-on training by experienced teachers, job assignments from school districts in poor rural or urban communities that were desperate for young talent, and year-round feedback, mentoring, and assistance to help them achieve meaningful results with their students.

Kopp was convinced that her young peers—many of them seeking fulfilling career options, just as she was—would find this a powerfully magnetic alternative, one that provided the opportunity to make a real difference in the world. And if her teachers' corps could stimulate, and satisfy, demand for teaching jobs among bright, talented young people, why couldn't those idealistic young teachers stimulate new demand for high-quality education among students in some of America's most neglected school districts?

Kopp got to work. She raised seed money from corporations that had earmarked funds for educational causes and hired a staff of five people—socially conscious recent college graduates like herself—who traveled the country making campus connections. Within a year, they managed to recruit TFA's first class of teachers—five hundred in all. After an intensive summer of training, they applied for jobs in local school districts identified by TFA as needing an infusion of new talent. They started teaching in classrooms across the country in the fall of 1990. Teach For America was up and running.

It was an impressive start—the first evidence supporting Kopp's conviction that there was real hidden demand for the challenge of teaching among America's young college graduates. But it was just a start, and even before the founding of TFA, Kopp was practicing trajectory thinking. "Only a monumental launch," she has written, "would convey the urgency and national importance of our efforts."

By 1999, Kopp's teacher recruitment team had ten staffers. By 2010, it numbered 142 recruiters, who worked, in turn, with paid student representatives on more than 350 campuses around the country. Today, TFA recruiters are as familiar a presence on elite campuses as their counterparts from the big consulting firms and investment banks. They're also fixtures at state universities, historically black

colleges, and scores of other institutions. They're in constant contact with faculty members, career counselors, and deans who can
identify the most accomplished students on campus; there's scarcely
a student government officer, black or Latino caucus leader, or fra-
ternity president they don't meet.

You might imagine that TFA attracts applicants by downplay-
ing the hardships of inner-city teaching—the long hours, the scanty
resources, the often dreary surroundings, the discouraging two-
steps-forward-one-step-back pace of progress. But just the opposite
is true. Elissa Clapp, TFA's director of recruitment, says:

> The work we're offering is incredibly challenging, and we work
> aggressively to get people to understand that. We need people
> who are able to push forward despite the barriers, who are will-
> ing to put in the hours of unglamorous effort it takes to make
> magic happen in the classroom. Actually, we have a saying around
> here: "There's nothing magical in what we do—hard work is the
> magic." So we bring current corps members and recent alumni to
> campuses to tell their true stories to students who are thinking of
> applying. The type of person who finds a really tough challenge
> appealing is the type of person we want.

Hungry for just such a meaningful challenge, thousands of the
country's brightest college students now clamor for places on the
teacher corps waiting list. In 2011, 48,000 graduates applied for around
5,000 Teach For America slots—an increase of 2,000 over 2010's then-
record applicant pool. The staggering numbers are a direct result of
TFA's aggressive recruiting methods—only one applicant in six had
considered becoming a teacher *before* hearing about TFA. At nearly
forty colleges and universities, TFA is the top employer of graduating seniors. Twelve percent of all Ivy League graduates applied for
TFA positions in 2010, including 13 percent at Harvard. Seniors at
historically black Spelman College applied at a 20 percent rate.

Back in 1996, just six years after founding TFA, Wendy Kopp rather brashly declared that she hoped a stint as a teaching corps member would one day be considered as prestigious as a Rhodes fellowship. Today, it is. The demand that no one believed existed— no one but Wendy Kopp, that is—has turned out to be a gusher.

Perhaps Kopp was so confident in her ability to get young people excited about the challenge of teaching because she shared that excitement herself. "I'm glad that I somehow landed on this thing that I became so passionate about," Kopp has said, "because I've spent not one bit of energy for twenty years trying to figure out what I really want to be doing." Like most demand creators, Kopp is very smart—but even more important, she has a powerful heart that is fully invested in her vision.

And even as the sheer numbers of TFA applicants grow, their *quality* also continues to rise. Corps members in 2010 boasted an average GPA of 3.6 on the 4.0 scale—the highest in TFA history. The steady expansion of TFA recruiting efforts belies the widespread assumption that bright young Americans "just don't want to teach." It also represents the first of three crucial dimensions along which TFA has established a steep slope of improvement.

The second dimension is even more important: a steady increase in the classroom effectiveness of Kopp's young teacher corps. It isn't enough to send bright, well-intentioned young college grads into troubled schools around the country. They need to achieve results— improved grades, higher test scores, and enhanced skills in reading, math, science, and history.

In pursuit of these goals, Kopp has built a system that develops ever-increasing information, insight, and knowledge about the educational methods that *actually work* in the classroom. For all its importance, teaching has traditionally been regarded as a kind of "art," ineffable and practically impossible to describe. Today that is beginning to change.

TFA corps members don't step into the classroom until they've benefited from an intensive five-week Summer Institute. The graduates receive training and support that extends throughout their two-year teaching assignment.

The results have been impressive. TFA teachers have been among the most thoroughly scrutinized in the history of education. And while research studies since 2002 have showed varied results, the most recent have credited TFA corps members with being more effective than other new teachers and equally effective as experienced teachers in such core subjects as math, science, and reading, despite their lack of traditional credentials—teaching certificates, education courses, master's degrees.

What's even more impressive is the way in which Kopp and her leadership team are pushing the organization and its members up a steep slope toward improved performance, year by year. Journalist Amanda Ripley has tracked TFA's largely unprecedented research into teacher effectiveness:

> For years, [TFA] has been whittling away at its own assumptions, testing its hypotheses, and refining its hiring and training. Over time, it has built an unusual laboratory: almost half a million American children are being taught by Teach For America teachers this year [2009–2010], and the organization tracks test-score data, linked to each teacher, for 85 percent to 90 percent of those kids. Almost all of those students are poor and African American or Latino. And Teach For America keeps an unusual amount of data about its 7,300 teachers—a pool almost twice the size of the D.C. system's teacher corps.

We described Netflix as "an entertainment company run by a computer scientist." Wendy Kopp is no computer scientist—she majored in public and international affairs—but she has instilled the same kind of show-me-the-numbers culture throughout Teach For America. "We're so data-driven," Amanda Craft, TFA's director of strategy for human assets, told us, "that we literally change our models and processes every year based on what's working and what's not. The tweaks are constant."

Applying this mentality to TFA's enormous pool of information about teachers and classrooms from Memphis to New Mexico, Phoenix to Charlotte, East Los Angeles to the Twin Cities, has produced one of the first large-scale efforts to objectively define the qualities of exceptional teachers. TFA researchers have been studying what happens in the classroom through teacher observation sessions, surveys and interviews, "reflection sessions" between teachers and support teams, and studies of student learning data designed to isolate the most effective teaching techniques.

TFA's analytics have identified the specific behavioral traits shared by highly effective teachers. Steven Farr, TFA's director of learning, has described and analyzed these six traits in his book *Teaching as Leadership*. Now the specialists in TFA's Teacher Preparation, Support, and Development division are translating these traits into specific teaching strategies and tactics for inclusion in the Summer Institute. The methods are also illustrated via annotated "rubric-norming" video clips of real-life classroom interactions, enabling TFA corps members to see what works, compare their own methods, and make rapid, concrete improvements, not through trial and error but by learning from the best.

The findings have been revelatory. As Farr puts it, "When we look at what our most effective teachers are doing, it is so clearly replicable. It is not magic. We can describe it, and that means that many teachers who are good can become much, much better. It's just a matter of turning the light on what our most effective teachers are doing differently from our moderately effective teachers."

TFA is also using its research findings to develop better systems for identifying high-potential teachers. For example, when Angela Lee Duckworth, a psychology professor at the University of Pennsylvania, studied the work of 390 TFA corps members, she discovered that those applicants who scored high on a "perseverance" scale, as measured by a multiple-choice test, ended up producing learning results 31 percent better than those of otherwise matched applicants. More surprising, applicants who scored high on "life satisfaction" outperformed their colleagues by 43 percent. Duckworth's study suggested that such teachers may exhibit extra zest, enthusiasm, and energy in the classroom, which gets communicated to students. Now TFA deliberately tests for perseverance and other key personality traits when evaluating new applicants—just a few of the more than thirty data inputs considered in TFA's unique selection model.

"Life satisfaction" as a defining trait of a great teacher—who'd have guessed? And that's the point, of course. Demand creators don't rely on assumptions, intuition, or "common sense." They dig for evidence and follow wherever it leads—often to the unexpected places where demand is hiding.

Developing objective standards and techniques for measuring and increasing teacher effectiveness is a huge and complex challenge. But TFA's efforts are already beginning to bear fruit in the form of rising standards of student achievement. Internal studies appear to show that the performance of students taught by corps members has improved year by year, suggesting that the enhanced teacher selection and training methods are achieving real traction. That upward slope of improvement represents thousands of children with improved skills in math and reading, better equipped to meet the challenges of higher education and twenty-first-century careers.

Yet the ground-level stories of TFA teachers and the lives they've touched are even more impressive than the statistics. Yale graduate Yoona Kim is now in her third year of teaching special education students in New York's Spanish Harlem—the kinds of children for whom expectations have traditionally been very modest. Not so in Kim's classroom. "If there is one thing I really admire about Teach For America," she says, "it is the organization's emphasis on *continuously* increasing your effectiveness as an educator. It requires constant assessment and reflection on learning data to inform what you will teach and how you will teach it." The trajectory thinking that helps make TFA a uniquely effective organization has been adopted by individual corps members like Kim.

Tools created by TFA help Kim and her students as they climb their individual trajectories:

> In math and reading, I keep a spreadsheet of every single New York State standard for the grade level I'm teaching. Standards may be tiered or ranked from the absolutely essential to the less important. If a student has not demonstrated mastery of a standard—80 percent or higher—that cell is coded yellow, for 70 to 79 percent mastery, or red, for 69 percent and lower. It is easy to scroll down a column for a particular standard and say, "The majority of cells are yellow or red. I have to reteach this standard. Why did the kids perform poorly on that standard? I may not have taught it effectively, or maybe the kids need more repetition. Perhaps I'll incorporate manipulatives, the interactive SMART Board, or review remedial skills." By analyzing the data across standards or students, you start to notice patterns that help you differentiate your instruction. It is a great reflection tool that TFA provides for its corps members.

From her TFA mentors and fellow corps members, Kim has also picked up a host of simple yet powerful methods for engaging students in the challenge and fun of learning. She starts by setting high standards, "Higher maybe than they think is possible. But you know it's possible. And how do you know? Because you map it out, and you show them that it's possible."

Visit Kim's classroom and you immediately see how she applies these principles every day. Whether working with individual students on a writing challenge or presenting a new math concept to the entire class, Kim is continually interacting with students on an

individual level, her eyes quietly scanning the room for signs of confusion, uncertainty, disengagement, excitement, and understanding.
Based on the subtle, often nonverbal feedback she receives from
each of her seventeen students, she repeatedly adjusts the tempo,
style, and structure of her instruction. She senses when an example
needs further discussion and when a small joke, a reminder, a gen-
tle prodding, or a friendly cajoling will work best to keep the class
focused and learning.

It so happens that the ability to make these kinds of artful adaptations is one of the six traits of highly effective teachers identified
by TFA researchers. These teachers understand that "great implementation" in the classroom isn't a matter of simply following a well-
made lesson plan. As Steven Farr explains, "Great implementation
means I'm making smart adjustments to my plan when I'm on my feet,
because no classroom I've ever taught is exactly the way I thought
it would be when I wrote my plan out on paper."

Kim considers such adjustments crucial to her classroom effectiveness. "I think ninety-five percent of my effort in teaching is about
adapting to the needs of individual students," she reports. Over the
course of a school year, she learns which students absorb information best through words, which through images, which through
hands-on activities; she gets to know the family situation of each
student and uses her understanding to help her determine how best
to connect with a particular child. These are techniques that gifted
teachers have always employed, often instinctively; TFA helps its
corps members to learn and use them more quickly, consciously,
and effectively.

As her students grow in skill, knowledge, and confidence, Kim
makes a point of rewarding small victories along the way. Her "Club
80" honors any student who earns a score of eighty or higher on a
weekly assessment; Club 80 students see their names posted in the
classroom and earn Club 80 certificates in a small Friday ceremony.

Kim's kids also publish their essays on an online e-zine and create their own poetry podcasts, discovering the thrill of seeing their names in print and of having their peers listening to and appreciating their creative work. The ripples spread outward from there. "So much of teaching is investing students, families, or guardians in the learning process," Kim says, "and then just celebrating like crazy when you get there."

Kim's TFA colleague, Parker Rider-Longmaid, taught math and science to seventh and eighth graders in Philadelphia. He describes the experience as "emotionally draining." Yet he too was obsessed with how to keep *improving* his own effectiveness and the classroom experience. He attended the monthly workshops TFA program directors organized to enable TFA teachers to share techniques and learn better ways to teach. He also constantly exchanged notes and modules with his peers. "I prepared great notes for math, they did the same for science, and we swapped. Saved us both a lot of time."

Seeking a motivational tool for his eighth-grade class, Rider-Longmaid wrote to eighty different colleges and universities, asking them to send a school pennant. Twelve responded. He hung those pennants in his classroom, along with drawings of the colleges. What had been a distant idea to most of Rider-Longmaid's students began to look very tangible, very concrete.

"We then used preparation for high school entrance tests to some of the city's best schools as a sort of 'dry run' for preparation for college entrance exams," Rider-Longmaid recalls. In the process, more and more students started thinking differently about college.

Consider the impact of TFA on the mind of the customer. Parents' initial perspective is often "School didn't do much for me. It won't do much for my children. They're not going to college anyway, so what difference does it make?" And many students, their enthusiasm for learning dampened by peer pressure and low societal expectations, share the same feelings.

But after a few weeks with a teacher like Kim or Rider-Longmaid, some things begin to change. Students start to say, "The teacher cares about me, talks to me, goes to my games, talks to my parents." And parents begin to say, "This is not a standard classroom experience. I read my child's essay online, I hear a podcast of his poetry readings. I can see how my child is picking up computer skills, and I know that will be useful to him."

At some point, both student and parent cross an invisible line. The expectation changes. It becomes "Maybe I *can* go to college," and then, "I *will* go to college."

Once those words are uttered, the *demand* for "education that really works" begins to materialize among more and more students. For some it becomes intense.

That shift from "I don't care" to "I really want to" is the moment when the demand happens. And it is as hard-edged and tangible as the moment when a consumer shifts from "I don't care" to "I want a Zipcar," "I want Netflix," or any other product.

That little miracle is now happening in classrooms hundreds of times a day.

We need it to be millions. But the secret code for creating that demand has been cracked. Now what's needed is to scale up.

❐   ❐   ❐

BY CREATING A SYSTEM to help school districts identify skilled teachers and train them in proven methods of motivating and inspiring kids, TFA is working to improve on the third and most challenging dimension of all—changing American attitudes about education.

No one has been more deeply discouraged by the current state of teaching in America than educators themselves. Some have given up on at-risk kids, competing instead for the handful of jobs in high-prestige suburban school districts. Others, feeling beaten down by the lack of support they receive in lackluster school systems, have quietly resigned themselves to waiting for retirement while making as few waves as possible. And still others have become incapacitated by living in the miasma of what Steven Farr calls "the smog of low expectations":

> Sometimes we breathe that smog through personal interactions, like when a stranger stops [TFA teacher] Crystal Brakke in Walmart as she buys school supplies to say how sorry she is that Ms. Brakke has to work with "those kids at that school." Or when a cynical school administrator suggests that second-grade teacher Alaina Moonves stick to "finger painting and puppets" with her students with special needs.

TFA's research provides hope that teachers, principals, and school administrators can finally stop breathing smog and start building effective programs that serve all kids—not just in the schools directly served by TFA, but all across America.

Many of the TFA tools for helping teachers improve their effectiveness are publicly available through published materials and on-line sources, and anecdotal evidence reveals that growing numbers of teachers around the country are taking advantage of them to enhance their skills. Steven Farr reports that more and more school districts around the country are asking TFA for help in designing their own teacher recruiting, evaluation, and training programs. Researchers at the Bill & Melinda Gates Foundation, which has made school reform a priority, are supporting TFA's research program and spreading its findings throughout the educational community. And the U.S. Department of Education's "Race to the Top" educational initiative is providing extra funding to school districts that implement effective new tools for recruiting, training, and retaining the best teachers. It's a subtle broadening of the traditional emphasis on school accountability (in other words, testing) to include TFA's focus on finding and developing great teachers. Educators who believe in this approach were galvanized by the change. Timothy Daly, president of the nonprofit New Teacher Project, called it "the big bang of teacher-effectiveness reform . . . It's huge."

TFA has its critics. Some consider TFA's model a mere Band-Aid that supplies bright young teachers for a few thousand classrooms while failing to address the systemic problems, including under-funding, that plague our nation's school systems. Others say that TFA's standard two-year teacher enlistment produces mere dilettantes rather than the dedicated career educators our kids need. The expanding impact of TFA's methodology on American education suggests one response to the critics. Not every classroom can be led by a TFA corps member, nor should it. Yet in time, the most powerful lessons from TFA's research into teacher effectiveness can become part of every teacher's toolkit.

Even more important, Kopp and her supporters stress the value of having TFA alumni in influential posts throughout society; many are already serving in state and local governments, for example, where some are spearheading education reform movements. In fact, Steven Farr suggests that one of Kopp's key insights has been that TFA should *not* be viewed as "in the teacher-production business," but rather "in the leader-production business," creating thousands of young people in many walks of life—including teaching—who are transforming the demand for education throughout American society.

❑   ❑   ❑

ALTHOUGH ONLINE MOVIE RENTAL and education reform may not have a lot in common, the stories of Netflix and Teach For America have converged in some remarkable ways. Both organizations were founded by insightful leaders who glimpsed potential demand lurking in hassle maps that millions of other people ignored or resignedly accepted. Both have grown rapidly by dramatically improving a local service through a national system designed with close attention to detail and an unrelenting focus on what people *really* want as opposed to what they have traditionally settled for. And both are now creating steep improvement trajectories based on unprecedented research that is enabling them to serve customer needs with greater precision and effectiveness with every passing year.

Armed with these powerful demand-creating tools, Wendy Kopp and TFA aim at nothing less than a transformation of the United States, their goal a country in which educational inequalities no longer doom half our citizens to lives that are unproductive and unfulfilled. And while this process still has a long way to go, the progress attained so far has been remarkable, as she explains in this interview from April 2010:

> We have made extraordinary progress in the twenty years I've been at this. Twenty years ago there were a very small handful of visible examples that it is possible for students in low-income communities to excel academically when given the opportunities they deserve. Today, there is overwhelming evidence—in the form of hundreds of visible examples of teachers and schools that are attaining extraordinary results. Today, dozens of communities have at least one and in many cases growing numbers of schools that are effecting not just incremental progress but transformational change in students' trajectories. So, the conversation has changed. Now the question isn't whether we can put students facing socioeconomic pressures on a level playing field, but rather whether it is possible to accomplish this at the level of the whole system.

The fact that the organization at the forefront of this nationwide revolution sprang from the dream of a twenty-two-year-old college student speaks volumes about the incredible power of long-suppressed demand, once unleashed, to transform society.

THE BEST LUNCH EVER: PRET A MANGER AND THE QUEST FOR THE PERFECT SANDWICH

Demand creation never happens "once and for all"—with the triumphant launch of a product, for example. If it happens at all, it happens day after day, in a prolonged and complex process that unfolds in hundreds or thousands of often unlikely places.

Consider, for example, the surprising demand-creation role played by Tracy Gingell, general manager of the Pret A Manger sandwich shop at 60 Broad Street in New York's financial district.

When Gingell took over the job in 2009, he quickly made a discovery concerning his store's chief obstacle to successful demand generation. It wasn't competition from the many other food vendors in the neighborhood. It wasn't the difficulty of getting enough super-fresh tomatoes, lettuce, and avocados to make a new batch of crisp and flavorful sandwiches every morning, or the high price of the free-range organic chicken he ordered for the shop's most popular sandwiches. It wasn't even the economic woes that had forced many regular Pret customers to start brown-bagging to save a few dollars.

Tracy Gingell's biggest enemy was none of these. It was entropy.

He figured that out the first time he climbed a ladder to inspect the crystal chandelier that was one of the most striking decorative features of his shop.

It was dusty.

If you've ever been in a Pret store, you know that they are all remarkably clean. (People tend to use words like *sparkly* and *dazzling* to describe the typical Pret.) And Gingell admits that his Broad

Street store was perfectly clean as far as any customer was likely to see. But when he got within a few inches of the chandelier, he realized that the crystals bore a thin layer of dust and that a few burned-out bulbs had gone unchanged.

As a Pret A Manger veteran, Gingell was horrified—and energized. He got right to work. "I spent two hours taking all those crystals off and polishing them, four at a time. I replaced all the lightbulbs with big, bright new ones. It ended up looking great. I felt so good!"

The dusty chandelier turned out to be only the most obvious symptom of a bigger problem. Talking with the store's staffers, Gingell gradually pieced together the story. During the previous year, as the economy worsened and sales slumped, the previous store manager had cut back on workers' hours, causing Pret's sky-high standards of cleanliness to slip just a bit. Employee morale suffered, and the perpetually cheery service for which Pret stores are famous became inconsistent. Sales declined further. Downward spirals start small, but they tend to keep going. After a while, they are very hard to reverse.

The shop at 60 Broad was succumbing to entropy—the gradual dissipation of energy and loss of order that is the natural tendency of any system that is not constantly reinvigorated from outside.

Gingell got on the phone to his boss. "I'm not going to make any money here for a while," he explained. "I've got to fix the store, and I'm going to do it according to the Pret recipe—the right people, amazing service, delicious food and drink. Then the shop can grow and get profitable."

Over the next six months, Gingell carried out his plan. He recruited new employees, including some he'd personally trained at other Pret locations. He organized a storewide cleanup and freshening campaign. For several weeks he deliberately *overstaffed* the shop and stocked the stainless steel display shelves with *too much* fresh and appealing food. The idea was to combat entropy, and start the flow of demand, through an unmistakable infusion of energy.

It worked. Within a few months, the shop at 60 Broad had been transformed into a gleaming store plentifully stocked with delicious-looking sandwiches, soups, sweets, and other treats and staffed with smiling workers who serve a steady stream of customers with efficiency and charm. It's "the best Pret in the city," according to a friend who has visited them all, and Tracy Gingell is "the quintessential Pret person." And Gingell's team has continued to push the shop up a steep improvement slope: "We have three people who spend two hours a day doing nothing but organizing the food displays. We want our food to look sexy at all times. The avocados have to be placed at *just* this angle in the salads—for aesthetics, but also to make sure that every item in the salad is visible so you can see what you're purchasing. We have a bin here in the back where food that the chef doesn't think is picture-perfect gets rejected and thrown away."*

Entropy is a persistent danger in business—and never more so than in fast food, where thousands of stores in far-flung locations must serve millions of meals both quickly and affordably, all while maintaining consistently high standards of quality, flavor, nutrition, and service.

Fast-food industry behemoths fend off entropy through rigid standardization, the creation of vast centrally managed supply chains (starting with industrial-style factories for "manufacturing" foodstuffs from beef and chicken to apples and potatoes), and the breakdown of labor into its smallest possible components, so that employees with minimal skills and training can be shuttled in and out of jobs interchangeably at a moment's notice. The standards are strict—but also low.

That isn't Pret's model. Like other fast-food companies, Pret wants to grow, eventually providing fresh, wholesome, and delicious

---

* By spring 2011, a few months after we met him in New York, Tracy Gingell had moved on to manage a Pret store in Chicago.

sandwiches in cities around the world. Yet even as it expands, a few stores at a time, Pret is also working to create a steep trajectory of improvement—one that rival chains will be hard-pressed to match.

The sheer energy required to pull this off is difficult to overstate. Much of it radiates from Julian Metcalfe, one of today's most high-energy, high-intensity business leaders. When Tracy Gingell climbed that ladder at 60 Broad Street and set about polishing each of the crystals on the neglected chandelier, he was channeling the soul of Julian Metcalfe.

❑   ❑   ❑

BACK IN 1986, Metcalfe was not a restaurateur, chef, or small businessman, but a twenty-three-year-old former art student and a chartered surveyor who had dabbled in several fields and formed an attachment to none. He was also highly opinionated and demanding, with a tendency to become obsessed over hassles that other people preferred to ignore or merely accept. One he found most irritating was the abysmal quality of lunches available in the busy heart of London. All the choices were bad. You could reserve a table at an overpriced white-tablecloth restaurant and invest a couple of hours and quite a few pounds for a meal of unpredictable quality served by a snooty and perhaps hostile waiter. Or you could duck into a storefront sandwich place and wait in line for the privilege of choosing from a narrow selection of unappetizing foods—soggy lettuce, day-old eggs, stringy meat, flavorless tomatoes—served by a surly clerk in a smelly apron.

"Why should people put up with this crap?" Metcalfe wondered.

It was a classic *eureka!* moment of demand creation. Metcalfe looked at the hassles most people shrug at and accept, and saw opportunity. As Metcalfe puts it, "We developed Pret . . . not by being caterers but by going through a long list of things that annoyed customers and getting rid of them."

Metcalfe teamed up with Sinclair Beecham, a friend he'd met at

Central London's polytechnic college. They lost eighty thousand pounds in their first twelve months and labored through several "miserable" years of trial and error. Metcalfe spent countless hours in the kitchen behind their first shop on Victoria Street, cooking chickens, baking breads, tinkering with sauces, trying different varieties of tomatoes, avocados, and eggplants in search of the perfect combination of texture, flavor, and color for a mouthwatering sandwich or salad—a veritable mad scientist in his own laboratory of lunch.

By 1990, Metcalfe and Beecham finally had a menu that worked. The Victoria Street shop turned its first profit. They tried opening a second shop, plowing money from the first shop into equipment, décor, staffing, and supplies. The second shop paid for itself within fifteen months.

Pret A Manger was on its way.

Studying Pret today, it's not terribly hard to list the magnetic ingredients that make it unique. It starts with the look of the stores. No two Pret outlets are precisely the same, but all share a certain sophisticated aesthetic, well captured by one New Yorker: "There's a real ambience to the place, like a neighborhood coffee shop in Brooklyn's Park Slope. The industrial chic décor adds to the ambience— the cold sterility of the stainless steel display racks (which Pret people call 'langers') and the roughness of the exposed ductwork in the ceiling are tempered by the warm wood tones of the small tables and individual seats and by the rich brown and tan leather upholstery of the banquette seats. The track lighting on the ceiling appears to have purple bulbs, which cast a warm glow into the space."

Then there's the welcoming attitude of the staff. Customers invariably notice the Pret people, who are uniformly young, attractive, smart, and friendly. They behave as if they *like* working at Pret— and in fact they do. As a result, they give service that's both pleasant and extremely efficient.

The other day, our friend James made his first visit to Pret, hoping to grab a quick sandwich prior to a series of business meetings. The fellow who sold James his chicken and avocado sandwich seemed concerned that he had no drink to go along with it. After James finished his sandwich, the clerk came to the table, cleared the wrapping, and asked, "Anything else I can get you? Maybe a glass of water?"

James shook his head when he told us the story. "He didn't *have* to do that!" he marveled. James made a mental note to stop at Pret the next time he needed a quick bite served with a genuine smile.

Of course, it's the food that matters most. And the food at Pret is strikingly different from what you'll get at other fast-food places, delis, or diners.

For one thing, it's fresh—really fresh. Every sandwich is made on the premises the same day it's sold. (Leftovers are donated daily to charities like New York's City Harvest, which feeds the poor—more than 120,000 pounds of food in 2009 alone.) You notice the difference after just a bite or two: the creaminess of the mayonnaise, the crispness of the lettuce, the firmness of the chicken or the ham, the juicy tang of the tomatoes. Same-day sale also reduces the need for additives and preservatives, which Pret leans over backward to avoid. "Pret food is real" is the company's mantra. The contrast with the highly processed, often frozen-and-reheated fare served at fast-food places or the grub of dubious freshness offered at many delis and diners is obvious.

The ingredients are also high in quality. Consider some of the "fun facts" about Pret cookery, which fans of the chain swap like trading cards: The avocados are hand-turned regularly to ensure they ripen evenly on all sides, shipped at room temperature, and sliced in each Pret kitchen every morning . . . Pret orders handpicked bunches of basil that are delivered daily and placed in sandwiches one leaf at a time . . . The oats and fruits used in the snack bars are stirred by hand with a four-foot paddle . . . Every Pret espresso is in fact a double (since they put fourteen grams of coffee into each one) . . . and so on and so on.

Or consider some of the hundred-odd items currently on the Pret menu. The sandwiches include Balsamic Chicken & Avocado; Egg Salad, Spinach & Parmesan; Slow Roasted Beef & Blue Cheese; Smoked Ham & Egg; and Summer Herb & Hummus. There's the Chicken Jalapeno Hot Wrap, the Salmon & Brown Rice Salad, the Tuna Nicoise, and the Slim Brie & Tomato Baguette. And then there are the soups—Carrot Ginger, Italian Wedding, Moroccan Lentil, and several more—each served with a fresh-baked seven-grain roll. From the standpoint of a typical customer—a busy office worker or downtown shopper looking for a quick, affordable, and enjoyable midday bite—it's a brilliant selection: nothing that would strike the average Brit or American as "weird" or off-putting, but with a note of sophistication and cosmopolitan flair that clearly distinguishes Pret from run-of-the-mill lunchtime options.

To keep the menu interesting, even surprising, Pret rotates items in and out of the shops while continually testing new choices. When a new sandwich or soup appears on the shelf, it gets highlighted with a sticker that announces, "I made it through the auditions." And when customer requests (reviewed store by store in a daily staff meeting) induce Pret to reintroduce an item, it bears a sticker that reads, "I'm back!"

"I compare Pret to the inside of a beautifully made Swiss watch," Julian Metcalfe says. "If all 10,000 cogs are turning, it works . . . [but] you only need a few dozen of those cogs not to turn for the whole thing to start suffering. I'll tell you that." And when all the cogs are turning—the stylish décor, the charming and efficient staff, the clever marketing, and above all the fresh, delicious foods—the magnetic appeal of Pret is difficult to resist.

❐   ❐   ❐

BUT AS WE'VE SEEN, building a magnetic product is never a one-shot deal. If you hope to attract *enduring* demand, you need to begin a trajectory of improvement the same day your product goes on sale.

This imperative is especially urgent in the fast-food world, with its multitude of rival firms and its low barriers to entry. In the fast-food world, you face competition literally every day. As Metcalfe himself observes, "Customers do shop around, of course. If they go to Pret every day, they are spending £20–30 per week, so it's no wonder they will look at alternatives."

In response, Pret is creating a fast rate of improvement on three distinct dimensions. One involves steadily improving the quality, taste, affordability, and overall appeal of its food offerings. Another centers on maintaining and elevating the already high standards of customer service. And the third focuses on expanding store outlets so that Pret becomes a convenient option for more and more people around the world.

The first two challenges—maintaining and improving the quality of the food and the service—are in the hands of founder Julian Metcalfe, now in the role of "creative director," an appropriate job for someone with a natural flair for trajectory thinking. ("I'm never satisfied," Metcalfe says. "Things could always be slightly better. I really don't like praising my work. I tend to see the faults in it rather than the joy.")

Metcalfe's obsession with improvement is quite real and even a source of some exasperation to Metcalfe himself. As he says (the words coming out in a rush), "That's the difference between mediocre and great and it's extremely elusive and some of our sandwiches are bloody great, they really work. It takes years—years—of relationships with the suppliers to get the right cheese, to get the right seasoning mix in the mayo. You can't just go and buy Hellman's mix and bung it together. It looks so simple but it isn't."

Pret constantly reinvents its offerings, even those that are popular and successful. Thus Pret's pickle recipe has been revised fifteen times, the chocolate brownie thirty-six times, and the carrot cake fifty times—in fact, restaurateur Sally Clarke, the "grande dame" of English cooking, reportedly worked with Metcalfe for nine months to perfect this single confection.

Metcalfe also keeps pushing to improve the quality of Pret's foods in other ways. One of the lunchtime hassles that first motivated him was his disgust with the unhealthful qualities of most fast-food lunches—loaded with salt, sugar, chemicals, and ingredients from ecologically disastrous factory farms. Now as more and more consumers go green, Pret is under ever-increasing pressure to raise its wholesomeness bar still higher.

So in June 2009, after Julian Metcalfe saw the documentary film *The End of the Line,* about the dangers of overfishing, he promptly banned the use of endangered bluefish tuna in sandwiches and sushi served in Pret stores. Similarly, in 2010, after fielding complaints about the saturated fats in some of its sandwiches, Pret began posting basic nutritional information, including calorie counts and fat content, in every store, and providing additional detail online. Most food chains do this only when mandated by law.

Like other great demand creators, Pret has the courage to listen to customers. In every Pret store you'll find a box with cards that read something like this:

My name is Tamir. I'm the General Manager at this Pret Shop.

My team and I meet every morning.

We discuss the comments you've made, the good, the bad and the ugly. If we can deal with it ourselves, we will.

If we can't, I'll forward this card to Julian Metcalfe back at the office. I know he'll do what he can.

If you have a minute, please do ask to speak to me or one of my team right now.

The bit about "Julian Metcalfe back at the office" is quite sincere: Metcalfe's phone number appears on each food package. (He says he gets a couple of customer calls every day—but only a couple, since most people assume the number is a joke.)

Pret store managers review the latest customer comments with the entire staff each morning before the front doors are opened. Good ideas for improving the store, the food, and the service are quickly acted upon. In the New York stores, for example, the mix of products is continually adjusted based on customer feedback and requests. (The Seventh Avenue store, in the heart of the fashion district, stocks lots of vegetable wraps and Caesar salads; customers in the Wall Street shops prefer hearty meat sandwiches like chicken bacon.) Based on customer requests, one manager suggested providing baby-changing facilities in the stores. They're now being installed throughout the chain.

Thanks to Metcalfe's obsession with continually raising his team's already high standards, Pret remains several steps ahead of even its closest competitors. Here's how one critic compared Pret with the Eat chain in Britain, which has sought to rival Pret by opening superficially similar stores:

> The principal difference between the two concerns is that old chestnut, service. Eat never seems to make enough of anything; most of the nice stuff has gone by 2 p.m. They put up a silly sign saying something like, "Oops, we'll try to make more tomorrow," but they never do. They also always seem to have an endless queue. Compare this with the speedy service at Pret, even during the lunchtime crush, and the well-stocked shelves. (I once expressed my disappointment at the lack of tuna sandwiches, and the manager simply made me one.) Eat is full of good intentions, plastering its walls with fun signs and a jovial tone of voice, but its staff seem less trained, less friendly and less motivated than their counterparts in the maroon overalls.

Such customer-centricity has to start at the top—and at Pret, Julian Metcalfe carries the principle to an extreme.

In August 2009, Metcalfe received a tongue-in-cheek letter from customer Paul McCrudden, complaining about the time he'd "wasted" waiting in line in Pret stores and demanding reimbursement. Rather than consigning it to the circular file or fobbing off the correspondent with a canned missive, Julian Metcalfe sent the following personal response:

Dear Mr. McCrudden,

Thank you so much for the invoice for the time spent in our Cafes. I understand your time on the planet is valuable and I am indeed sorry you were not able to spend more time in my competitors' establishments.

You are of course, absolutely right. The time you spent in my Cafes will greatly help the profitability of our company.

I'd like to take this opportunity to thank you for the generous discount you have applied to your bill.

I believe there is an error with this invoice as you've forgotten to add the £22 spent with our company, no doubt also an inconvenience. I've taken the liberty of adding this sum to what we owe you and what's more, I have added a nominal sum to cover interest.

I hope you will appreciate prompt payment. I've asked our accounts department to issue a cheque today as I see no reason why you should be kept waiting.

I'm sorry to have to pay you by cheque as I am aware of the effort and time it will take you to pay this into the bank.

I have therefore taken the additional liberty of increasing the amount by £1 to cover your walk to the post box.

I'm so sorry that we have put you to all this inconvenience

and thank you for taking the time to read this correspondence.

> Best wishes,
> Julian Metcalfe
> Founder

A check for £62 was enclosed.

The amount of positive coverage this story is still receiving—just Google "McCrudden" and "Pret" and see how many links pop up—was worth much more than £62. Especially when contrasted with the *negative* publicity received by some of the other companies McCrudden billed at the same time as Pret. The managing director of Cranberry, a chain of franchised fruit-and-nut shops, responded with an invoice for £18.75 for the "12 minutes of my valuable time" that it took him to read McCrudden's letter.

Metcalfe's response to McCrudden was impressive. But more impressive is his determination to transmit his own obsession with quality to the employees who are Pret's direct interface with customers. Such determination is rare in business—except among the demand creators. They know that creating a steep trajectory is virtually impossible unless the entire organization—right down to every local manager at Zipcar, every classroom instructor from Teach For America, and every cashier at Pret A Manger—is an enthusiastic participant in the ascent and a cocreator of demand.

CEO Clive Schlee is an experienced executive who'd spent seventeen years working in Hong Kong for the multinational corporation Jardine Matheson, including helping to run their fast-food brands (Pizza Hut, Sizzler, Taco Bell), before Metcalfe brought him to Pret in 2003. Schlee has been working to devise managerial, organizational, and training systems to replicate Metcalfe's cheery obsessiveness and replant it in store locations around the world.

The process starts with a unique personnel system. Rather than following the usual fast-food practice of hiring most any youngster who asks for an application—and then living with the exceptionally rapid turnover that inevitably results—Pret invests significant resources in selecting, training, and rewarding its entry-level staff members. Prospective recruits are asked to spend a day working, for pay, in a typical Pret shop. Then their fellow workers *vote* on whether they should be hired.

When was the last time you heard about a company that treats hiring decisions as a matter for democratic input rather than autocratic fiat? Pret really does it. Clive Schlee talks proudly about the fact that his nephew applied for a job at Pret and was *voted down* by the store staff. Another time, a prominent business executive in line for a board directorship was asked to spend a day working in a Pret shop. When his fellow sandwich makers found him insufferably arrogant and lazy, the directorship offer promptly vanished. Like Wegmans, Pret A Manger has created a rare company culture in which social norms—relationship-centered and built on respect, caring, and community—play as great a role as market norms.

To maintain a living connection between the front lines and the back office, every Pret manager is required to spend four days a year on the shop floor. And frontline employees are empowered to resolve problems based on their own best judgment—offering a free meal to a disgruntled patron, for example—without waiting for a manager's permission.

Pret rewards its employees generously. Pay for frontline U.K. workers starts at seven pounds per hour, about a pound above industry average. Any employee singled out for customer praise receives a specially designed sterling silver star from Tiffany; weekly bonuses are disbursed based on ratings by a mystery shopper. And all employees are eligible for more substantial awards. For example, the manager of the store that wins "top shop" designation based on quarterly sales results receives a check in the $20,000 to $30,000 range.

Pret summarizes its personnel policies this way: "We hire happy people and teach them to make sandwiches." Based on the reactions of customers, this simple system works remarkably well.

◻   ◻   ◻

THE THIRD DIMENSION of Pret's trajectory—making the product conveniently accessible to more people around the world—involves expanding the store network. (A friend in London tells us, "I always assume there's a Pret nearby whenever I want one," which is *not* the case in any other city in the world—not yet.) But rapid expansion while maintaining the improvement in food and service quality might well put a strain on even the most brilliantly organized company. And Pret is no exception.

Flush with its early success in Britain, Pret entered the U.S. market in 2000. Soon more outposts were established in Japan, Hong Kong, and Singapore, and plans were drawn up to open shops in Holland and then elsewhere on the Continent. Pret appeared to be on track to go global within a decade. But then some of the cogs became jammed. In Japan, a Pret franchisee expanded too quickly. Quality suffered, and the Japanese Pret stores were soon shuttered. Spotty international results contributed to a company loss of £20 million for 2002.

In 2003, Metcalfe and new CEO Clive Schlee announced that henceforward Pret would eschew franchising, the better to maintain control of its most valuable assets—its magnetic product and its steep trajectory. "We could have spread rapidly all over the place by franchising," Metcalfe says. "I would rather do less and try and do it well."

Store manager Tracy Gingell is happy to explain Pret's patience-makes-perfect expansion model. "When you begin to franchise out," he volunteers, "what's to stop a store manager from buying the five-dollar case of chicken instead of the thirty-five-dollar case that's organic? No one's going to know the difference. That's why we don't franchise. We have one vendor, and when we order chicken it's the organic farm-raised. There's no way to cut corners."

Pret's expansion now continues at a deliberate pace. By 2010, Pret had more than 250 stores worldwide—213 throughout Britain, 26 in New York, 2 in Washington, D.C., 1 in Chicago, and 8 in Hong Kong. To help ensure that the expansion serves *customer* needs, Pret actively seeks out feedback from the public as to the location of future shops. (A message on the company's website states, "If you have an opportunity in one of the towns, cities, schemes or streets listed below that you think we should consider please contact [us].")

The strategy seems to be working. In 2010, Pret's global revenues were projected to be around £320 million. Perhaps most significant, annual revenue per store hovered around £1.2 million—more than 50 percent higher than Eat, the most direct competitor, with other rivals, such as Greggs, much further behind. In 2009, the chain enjoyed same-store sales increases of 11 percent, which it believes are the highest in the food business. The intensity of the demand that Julian Metcalfe discovered more than two decades ago is as strong as ever.

Yet the pressure to keep improving is equally intense. Potential rivals to Pret are numerous, with more appearing every year. Consumer preferences are continually evolving, driving Metcalfe and his team to keep inventing exciting new menu items that will attract new customers while retaining the loyalty of old ones. The stagnant global economy has forced Pret to find ways to reduce prices (a £1.99 ham sandwich is now on the U.K. menu). And every new city where Pret opens a store requires creative analysis of and adaptation to local tastes and customs.

And, of course, constantly looming overhead is the risk of entropy—the slow, subtle, yet ultimately fatal decline in quality and excitement that could kill Pret from the extremities inward if the company fails to develop thousands of employees to serve as Pret's cocreators of demand.

It all adds up to a daunting trajectory challenge. Thankfully for Pret and its fans, the fertile, obsessive brain of Julian Metcalfe is working on it night and day—augmented by a growing team of thousands of Tracy Gingells, channeling Metcalfe's spirit and energy. The years to come will show whether Pret can manage to stay two, three, or more steps ahead of its many competitors in the race to serve the world's lunch.

6.
Variation

(vary-AY-shun) *noun* 1. the different hassle maps experienced by different types of customers 2. the art of respecting and responding to differences in customer needs, preferences, and behavior 3. the science of developing cost-effective ways to provide individual customers with products that precisely fit their varying needs

SELLING THE SYMPHONY:
IT'S NOT JUST ABOUT THE MUSIC

One of the subtlest, and most important, challenges confronting the would-be demand creator is the Myth of the Average Customer.

Consider, for instance, the work of a marketing manager for one of America's great symphony orchestras. His job is a tough one: to figure out how to attract a stream of customers who are willing to pay high ticket prices and make their way downtown to hear live performances of classical music—all in preference to any of the dozens of other forms of entertainment, many of them free, competing for their time and attention.

This challenge has long been a daunting one. But now it turns out that the secret to unlocking future demand for classical music depends on discarding the Myth of the Average Customer and instead embracing the reality of a world in which people—and their demands—are endlessly, amazingly varied.

Most music marketers have always assumed that convincing potential new subscribers to give the symphony a try is the key to growing demand. "Get people through the doors!" is the mantra practically every orchestra marketer repeats. The assumption is that, once people venture into the local symphony hall to hear a concert, the sheer beauty of the music will draw them back.

There's only one problem with this theory: It just isn't so. Every year thousands of potential new listeners are persuaded to attend their first classical concert. The concert hall is beautiful, the performances stunning, the music ravishing. *Yet most of those one-time visitors never return.* They respond to follow-up solicitations with an indifferent shrug or even outright hostility.

As a result, orchestra marketers have to spend every year scrambling to find yet more thousands of customers who can be persuaded to try a concert, just to make their budgets and keep their orchestras afloat.

The trial trigger may have worked magic for Nespresso. But for the symphony, it simply doesn't.

The problem is something called "customer churn"—demand that is fleeting, inconsistent, unreliable. With its relatively high-paid performers and its costly downtown concert hall to maintain, a symphony orchestra needs to generate a strong and steady level of demand in order to survive. When the churn rate is consistently high, creating demand is like racing to fill a bucket with a large hole in its bottom.

The apparent failure of orchestras to convince one-time attendees to become longtime supporters poses quite a puzzle. Are the renowned artists at great American orchestras not talented enough to please audiences? That seems unlikely. Is classical music simply too "highbrow" or "old-fashioned" for modern listeners? That's a counsel of despair, suggesting that the ultimate demise of the orchestra is probably inevitable.

The real problem is the Myth of the Average Customer. Designing a product offer to appeal to some archetypal customer is always wasteful. It leads to overage (providing features many individuals don't want), underage (omitting features they do want), and sheer

inaccuracy (choosing features based on guesswork and approxima-
tion rather than reality).

Instead demand creators have to constantly focus on *demand
variation*, asking how customers differ from one another and how
they can respond to those differences. Then they can break down
customers into as many subgroups as necessary to get close to
what they really feel, experience, and want as individuals rather
than as members of the mythical average group. This process of
"de-averaging" can be a complex challenge—but it also offers huge
opportunities. That's why great demand creators *love* variation. It
gives them the chance to serve more people, more precisely, and
often more profitably, than traditional average-customer approaches.

In 2007, nine symphony orchestras joined forces, hiring a team
of researchers to analyze symphonies' marketing challenges. The
results from this Audience Growth Initiative—or, as it was informally
called, the "churn project"—were presented in mid-2008 to a gathering in Denver of hundreds of musical professionals from orchestras
around the country.

The study confirmed that churn was a major issue for the nine
orchestras in the consortium. On average, 55 percent of symphony
customers changed from one year to the next—a big, costly problem.
Among first-time concertgoers, the churn rate was even worse—an
almost unimaginable 91 percent. So much for the supposed magic
of "getting them through the doors."

But when the researchers got past the *average* figures and
started focusing on customer variation, a possible solution began
to emerge. The symphony audience, they found, was divided into
several starkly contrasting groups. They included the *core audience*—
subscribers who attend numerous concerts every year for many
years; *trialists*—first-time concertgoers who attend a single performance; the *noncommitted*—people who attend a couple of concerts in a given year; *special-occasion attendees*—people who attend

only one or two concerts a year but return consistently, year after year; *snackers*—people who consistently purchase small concert subscriptions for many years; and *high potentials*—people who attend a lot of concerts but have not yet purchased a subscription.

So there were at least six different customer types—dramatically different from one another. In Boston, for example, members of the core audience were found to represent just 26 percent of the customer base, while buying 56 percent of the tickets sold. By contrast, trialists were 37 percent of the customers but bought only 11 percent of the tickets. Statistics from all nine orchestras found remarkably similar patterns.

The core group held the key to *today's* demand. Though they made up just a quarter of the audience base, they provided the bulk of the revenue flow that made the very existence of live classical music in America possible. (Revenue analysis showed that, between ticket purchases and donations, a single core household yielded an orchestra some $4,896 over a typical five-year period.)

So satisfying the core is essential. And fortunately, it is a skill that the best orchestras have mastered. Subscription data confirm that, once a person becomes a regular supporter of the local orchestra, he tends to renew his subscription year after year, often for decades.

But what about *tomorrow's* demand? How could American orchestras escape the curse of customer churn and the seemingly endless marketing treadmill?

The answer lay with one variant customer set: the trialists—that relatively vast stream of customers (over a third of the ticket buyers in any given year) with their horrifying churn rate of 91 percent. By contrast with the core families, who provided almost five thousand dollars in orchestra revenues apiece, the typical trialist family in the study had a five-year value of just $199.

So the problem wasn't generally "to reduce churn" or to "keep more customers." It was, quite specifically, *to convert trialists into steady customers,* transforming them from one-time samplers of classical music into snackers, high potentials, and, eventually, into members of that ultravaluable core.

But how to do this? To answer this question, the research team had to figure out what the trialists actually cared about, so that a product could be created that was magnetic *for them,* not for the mythical average audience member.

The researchers moved into phase two of their study. They set about to create variant hassle maps of the symphony experience for the different customer types—especially the all-important trialists. Identifying and eliminating the stumbling blocks that were discouraging trialists from returning could be the key to future demand.

The technique the researchers applied was *factor analysis.* With the help of orchestra marketers, they brainstormed an initial list of seventy-eight different attributes of the classical music experience, including everything from the architecture of the auditorium and the service at the bar to the guest conductors leading concerts and the availability of ticket information on the Internet—practically anything they could think of that *might* have an impact, good or bad, on the trialists' experience.

Then, using online surveys and other tested techniques for examining customer behavior, they whittled the list down to sixteen factors with the greatest real impact on the hassle maps of the audience subgroups, especially trialists.

The results were fascinating, and often counterintuitive. It turned out that factors like the relative prestige and quality of the local orchestra were *not* terribly important in attracting return visits by trialists. Neither was the beauty of the concert hall, the opportunity to hear contemporary music, or the selection of refreshments.

And what *did* make a difference? At the top of the list was parking. The simple ability to travel to and from the concert hall with a minimum of fuss was the single most powerful "driver of revisitation," as the researchers put it. It was the key demand trigger for trialists.

Parking was something few orchestra companies had ever focused on. "The subscribers never complained about parking, so why did we really have to worry about it?" as one symphony executive told us. But the silence of the subscribers was deceptive. Veteran members of the core audience had long ago devised their individual travel solutions, eliminating parking from their hassle maps. But for trialists, parking was a significant hassle—big enough to prevent thousands from becoming orchestra subscribers.

For many orchestras, fixing this hassle is as simple as negotiating a special rate at a nearby parking garage and including detailed driving directions in the ticket mailing. Yet this simple step turned out to be a powerful demand trigger.

The study identified a handful of other triggers, some of them equally simple. For example, it turns out that trialists enjoy the performance much more when the conductor takes a few minutes to offer personal comments about the program—the history behind a selection, the life story of the composer. (In retrospect, it seems obvious: Most Americans are unfamiliar with classical music and need some context to give meaning to what they are hearing. But picking this item from the original list of seventy-eight was far from obvious.) Similarly, the ability to quickly and easily exchange tickets makes an enormous difference in the comfort level of trialists, for whom the traditional "No refunds, no exchanges" policy is a potentially deal-breaking hassle.

Finally, the research team tried to determine what kind of follow-up offers would be most likely to entice a typical group of trialists. Would romantic compositions on the program do the trick—or would twentieth-century music prove more magnetic? Would an opportunity to meet and greet the musicians draw a crowd? What about vocal soloists versus instrumentalists?

Orchestra directors and marketing executives could guess at the answers—and in fact that's what most of them had done for decades. Instead, the research team used hundreds of small-scale experiments to develop and test a series of "killer offers" tailored to particular orchestras and the tastes and preferences of local trialists. For instance, for unconverted trialists in Boston, the team recommended a single-ticket offer that included a Saturday night concert; a program that included music by an especially popular composer and both familiar and unfamiliar selections; a "bring a friend for free" and a "free drink at the bar" offer; and free ticket exchanges.

Taken together, all these product enhancements—the tailored concert program, the free ticket for a friend, the convenient parking, and the rest—add up to a hassle-free music experience for trialists.

We sometimes assume that individualizing a product to address demand variation must be prohibitively expensive—after all, a bespoke Savile Row suit costs a lot more than an off-the-rack model from a department store. The orchestra study proves otherwise—as do the experiences of many other demand creating organizations that have found cost-effective ways to vary their product offers while keeping them affordable.

The unveiling of these findings to orchestra managers from around the country has sparked a quiet revolution in the marketing of classical music. One orchestra after another has begun to adopt and test its own responses to demand variation, with initial results that are startlingly hopeful.

When the Boston Symphony Orchestra tested the killer offer designed specially for trialists against a traditional ticket offer, the killer offer drew 34 percent more ticket purchases—the equivalent of 5,100 additional ticket sales over the course of a season. The New York Philharmonic found that the killer offer outperformed a standard offer by five to one. The Cincinnati Symphony offered half of its Summer Pops trialists a traditional subscription, the other half a customized single-concert offer; the latter offer outsold the subscription by twenty to one.

Now more and more orchestras are adopting variation-based programs, with remarkable success. The Pensacola Symphony, which had recently lost a hundred subscribers—one-seventh of the total—in a single year, gained three hundred new subscribers and was oversold for the entire 2008–2009 season. The Stockton (California) Symphony added three hundred subscribers and boosted its ticket sales for the season by four thousand. And the San Antonio Symphony, which had filed for bankruptcy as recently as 2003, enjoyed sales for its "Classics" series that were 27 percent higher than the year before. These across-the-board demand increases are especially notable during a time of slow recovery from the deepest recession in memory.

Some orchestra marketers found that the churn study confirmed insights their own sharply honed instincts had already suggested. For example, Kim Noltemy of the Boston Symphony Orchestra (BSO) had long recognized the importance of demand variation. She'd developed special marketing programs focused on the customer set where demand was weakest—people under the age of forty, the symphony supporters of the future.

To boost demand for classical music among the young, Noltemy and the BSO have developed product offers that addressed their unique needs. For school-age youngsters and their parents, the Boston Pops' Holiday Pops and Spring Pops concerts have long been designed to be family-friendly, with cabaret-style seating and food service so that restless kids can eat during the performance. Noltemy spearheaded the addition of special Kids Matinees with customized menus and streamlined programs that cater to youngsters' shorter attention spans. To engage teenagers, free tickets subsidized by a generous donor are provided for kids up to eighteen years old at daytime concerts at the Tanglewood Music Center, in the Berkshires. For just $10, high school students can hear the symphony at an open dress rehearsal that includes a context-setting talk by a performer (one of the product features, you'll recall, that trialists find most magnetic). College students can attend their choice of dozens of concerts at Symphony Hall every season just by buying a $25 college card (between 200 and 400 show up every night). And yet another donor-subsidized program lets the BSO provide cut-rate $20 tickets to customers under forty years of age.

"We put the college students and thirtysomethings in some of the best seats in the house, right up front," Noltemy says. "Our older subscribers enjoy seeing them there, knowing that the music they love is attracting a new generation of fans." (It's interesting: People *like* it when goods they favor become popular with a larger, younger audience—a social element of demand that's often overlooked but quite powerful.)

Thanks to initiatives like these, the BSO's annual audience now numbers more than 12 percent of the metro area population, a higher penetration rate than that enjoyed by any other major U.S. orchestra. (The figure in San Francisco, for example, is around 6 percent; in New York, just about 3.) On Noltemy's watch, the BSO's list of participating households has grown from around 16,000 to more than 45,000. Perhaps most impressive, the average age of subscribers has actually *fallen* from fifty-eight to forty-eight, defying trends that are troubling other orchestras, and demonstrating that specially tailored offerings can spark fresh demand for classical music among younger audiences.

The lessons of the churn study don't spell an end to the challenges facing American orchestras. Persuading members of the hip-hop generation to give classical music a try remains an uphill battle. But the concept of demand variation offers hope. Tomorrow's customers are out there, waiting to be discovered, if leaders can only put on the right lenses to see them in all their diversity, to decipher what makes them tick, and to know what, how, and at what prices they will buy.

THE SEATTLE OPERA GROWS ITS AUDIENCE
ONE MEMBER AT A TIME

Perhaps the most impressive organization responding to demand variation to grow future customers for classical music is the Seattle Opera, a powerhouse company that manages to hold its own by comparison with bigger, older rivals in much larger cities. (As Rebecca Chawgo, the opera's associate director of individual giving, puts it, "A city the size of Seattle simply *should not have* an opera company like the Seattle Opera.")

Seattle's secret weapon: a set of programs developed by a former high school teacher with an amazing talent for touching hearts and minds. The story of Perry Lorenzo is a case study in how a personal passion can get transformed into a virus that, eventually, infects an entire city—one customer type at a time.

Speight Jenkins, general director of the Seattle Opera, first encountered Lorenzo back in the late 1980s, when the company was not yet a demand-building dynamo. Lorenzo taught humanities and coached the debate team at Kennedy High School, a Catholic school in the Seattle suburb of Burien, and he invited Jenkins to judge an annual contest in which teams of students created sets and costumes for an imaginary opera production. Jenkins was astonished by the quality and sophistication of the student projects. Lorenzo modestly deflected Jenkins's praise, but it was obvious that here was an unusually gifted teacher and communicator.

Jenkins recruited Lorenzo to direct a new education department for the opera. Lorenzo had found his calling, one he would pursue for seventeen years, until his untimely death from lung cancer in December 2009.

One of Lorenzo's role models was Leonard Bernstein, the New York Philharmonic maestro whose legendary Young People's Concerts, broadcast on CBS television from 1958 to 1973, used clever stagecraft, vivid musical examples, and the personal passion of a charismatic performer to introduce a generation of Americans to the wonders of classical music. Guided by instinct and his own boyish spirit, Bernstein had cracked the code for attracting the young to great music, almost as the churn project later did for orchestra trialists. As soon as Bernstein DVDs were available, Lorenzo bought a complete set to study and passed them around to his colleagues on the education team.

Inspired by Bernstein's example, Lorenzo developed a collection of brand-new musical products specifically designed to make opera intensely attractive for high school age kids. His motto was, "Prepare, experience, respond." He carried it out by providing detailed information kits that teachers could use to prepare their students before a trip to the opera—for example, helping a social studies teacher prep a class for a performance of *Tosca* by explaining the story's context in the history of the Italian city-states during the Napoleonic era, or giving an English teacher materials with which to compare Verdi's *Falstaff* with Shakespeare's. Then he worked with teachers to help their students respond to the opera experience by writing reviews (for an English class), sketching or painting their impressions (for an art class), or preparing a report on the social implications of the conflict depicted (for a history class). Many current subscribers to the Seattle Opera—as well as members of the opera company's staff—vividly recall getting hooked on opera as sixteen-year-olds entranced by a Perry Lorenzo talk before a dress rehearsal.

Especially remarkable is the product Lorenzo created for an even younger customer set, elementary school students, under the title of Opera Goes to School. A team of teaching artists—singers, musicians, and other performers—visits a lucky school and takes up residence there for an intense week, during which they work with some sixty fifth graders to mount a full production of a specially crafted one-hour opera. It might be *The Magic Flute: A Hero's Quest,* adapted by Lorenzo and Tony Curry from the Mozart classic; *Theft of the Gold,* adapted from Wagner's *Ring of the Nibelung* by Jonathan Dean, Lorenzo's protégé (and now Seattle Opera's director of public programs and media); or Dean's sequel, *Siegfried and the Ring of Fire.* Young musicians learn the score under a director's tutelage; other students perform in the chorus or as master dancers; still others work on lighting, sets, and costumes.

Getting a chance to attend an opera is a great experience for a schoolchild. But spending a week immersed in actually performing an opera—and a "real" opera at that, not a musical version of "The Three Little Pigs" or some other children's tale—is an amazing opportunity that few fifth graders who experience it will ever forget.

At the end of the week, the opera is performed in front of the entire school as well as family members, friends, and people from the neighborhood. Like other great demand creators, Perry Lorenzo realized that demand variation often includes broadening the definition of the "customer." Opera Goes to School reaches beyond today's ticket buyers to transform an entire community into music lovers—with many of them, ultimately, becoming ticket buyers, too.

The Seattle Opera's education department now has plans to publish complete scores and librettos for its opera adaptations, together with detailed instructions on how they can be used to introduce young people to opera. It's a brilliant and potentially powerful contribution to the cause of nurturing future audiences for opera throughout the nation. Imagine what the nation's fifteen leading opera companies can do if they pool ideas and resources to create collaborative demand-building programs focused on crucial customer types—in this case, school-age kids. What they could accomplish to win converts to their beloved art form! And the same goes for the twenty-five best symphony orchestras, the top ten ballet companies, the fifteen best modern dance troupes . . .

Lorenzo also developed a series of powerful demand-creating programs aimed at specific customer types among adults. Before every new production, his education department team produces a flurry of community events to introduce the opera to groups such as arts lovers, university students, and avid readers. For example, in January 2010, Seattle Opera presented a new production of *Il Trovatore*. In the weeks before its premiere, preview lectures were presented, free of charge, at venues around the city ranging from the Frye Art Museum to Seattle University to public libraries in several neighborhoods. Radio previews were broadcast in several time slots on the major local classical station, and director Speight Jenkins gave a talk about the opera at the city's beloved Elliott Bay Book Company. It's frankly difficult to imagine living in Seattle during this multimedia assault and *not* being aware that *Il Trovatore* was coming to town.

Another crucial customer type is young people in their twenties and thirties (one of the groups, you'll recall, that Kim Noltemy targeted for the Boston Symphony). For many of them, the social aspect of classical music is its most magnetic feature—even twenty-somethings who are lukewarm about opera enjoy a night out with friends, and in the process some get hooked on the music. In response, the Seattle Opera has developed a collection of powerful social tools for attracting demand from this customer set. They range from its active podcast, Facebook, Twitter, and YouTube programs (which provide content to thousands of people daily) to the Bravo Club, a social group for people in their twenties and thirties that numbers over seven hundred members and helps draw them painlessly into the opera experience. When the Seattle Opera staged Bizet's *The Pearl Fishers*, a member hosted a "Pearls and Fishnets" celebration at the local bar he owns; other Bravo Club activities have included a fund-raiser in Seattle's famous Space Needle restaurant and overnight trips to nearby wine-tasting events. These cost-effective enhancements to the Seattle Opera's product attract hundreds of young people, some of whom will become enthusiastic members of tomorrow's core audience for opera.

Speight Jenkins became general director of the Seattle Opera in 1983 after years as a music-loving journalist, critic, and editor of *Opera*

News. Like many other great demand creators, Jenkins brought an outsider's sensibility to an industry that was ready for a shakeup— think of trader Mike Bloomberg revolutionizing the media business, online merchant Jeff Bezos developing a breakthrough electronic device, educational novice Wendy Kopp transforming American schools, or one-time surveyor Julian Metcalfe changing the world's lunch habits. In similar fashion, Jenkins has helped the Seattle Opera embrace audience-friendly change—for example, in 1984, it became one of the first opera companies in the world to use the new technology of "supertitles" to make lyrics and dialogue easier to follow. And Jenkins's passion makes him an untiring salesman for great music; he claims he's never taken a plane flight on which he hasn't convinced at least one fellow passenger to try the opera.

Under Jenkins's leadership, the Seattle Opera has achieved demand growth that is nothing short of spectacular, increasing its budget more than ninefold (from around $3 million in 1983 to almost $28 million in 2009–2010). And having built America's most dynamic opera audience by using Perry Lorenzo's brilliant product variation strategies, Speight Jenkins takes pains to stay in touch with the thousands of varied, ever-evolving individuals who make up his customer base. After every Seattle Opera performance, Jenkins himself appears for a question-and-answer session with the audience. It's a late-night finale to a long day of work, but Jenkins says, "I wouldn't miss it. After all, this is my best opportunity to get feedback and ideas from the audience." Thanks to the success of his company in turning Seattle into one of the most opera-loving cities in the nation, Speight Jenkins has been named one of the twenty-five "most powerful" people in American opera as well as one of the 150 "most influential" people in shaping the character of Seattle.

◻   ◻   ◻

IMPRESSED AND FASCINATED by the stories we'd heard about Opera Goes to School, we asked a member of the Seattle Opera's Young Artists Program to explain its impact on the families she'd met. The young soprano told us about the mom and dad who approached her after one fifth-grade performance.

"We don't know what you people do," the woman said, "but you've done something incredible with our daughter. She came home from school the other day, and she was singing—*singing*! She never sang before. Never!

"I asked her, 'How was your day at school?' Usually she just shrugs, and says, 'Nothing much.' Not this time. She couldn't stop talking about *Siegfried and the Ring of Fire*, how her classmates had worked together to prepare the stage, how the kids in the orchestra had been practicing their parts, how she and her friends in the chorus were learning the score. She went on and on, full of energy. I couldn't believe it!

"I don't know what you people do," the woman said again, "but you changed our daughter's life. It's a little miracle."

Whereupon the young soprano launched into a detailed, engaging explanation of exactly what opera people do. She recognized it as another opportunity to spread the benign virus of musical passion . . . the kind of opportunity that the Seattle Opera people never pass up.

Stories like this tell us that, twenty years from now, the chances are very good that the Seattle Opera will continue to thrive . . . selling tickets, yes, but more important, changing lives. And they illustrate how a genuine understanding of variation can help an organization nurture demand not just for today, but for future generations.

DEMAND VARIATION, FROM THE CORNER STORE TO EUROSTAR, THE EIGHTH WONDER OF THE WORLD

You might think that demand variation is of concern mainly to big companies that serve thousands of customers from many different demographic segments. In fact, small businesses—even mom-and-pop stores—that thrive in the face of competition from huge corporate rivals often do so largely by using the power of variation to create deep connections with individual customers. Three businesses from our own neighborhood of Cambridge, Massachusetts, offer vivid examples of how it works.

Fresh Pond Market was founded in 1922 by Armenian immigrant Nish Semonian. Eighty years and three generations later, it is still going strong—despite the presence of bigger, more convenient, and definitely cheaper big-box food stores within a few minutes' drive.

Fresh Pond Market reminds you of other places you've loved—warm, open, inviting, well organized, but not sterile. It's always busy, but rarely packed or overcrowded. The produce bins are old-fashioned, but the fruits and vegetables always look fresh and beautifully arranged; the variety of canned goods isn't quite as wide as you'd find in a superstore, but it includes enough unusual delicacies to pique your interest; the wine and beer section offers unfamiliar wines from Argentina and Portugal and New Zealand that are worth a try. The total visual package sends a clear message: *This is food on a human scale.* And the proprietors take advantage of that scale to address different needs at the single-customer level. In effect, they've made Fresh Pond Market into a store that enables them to provide goods and services tailored to the specific needs and wishes of the individuals who shop with them.

Marc Najarian, the founder's grandson, shares an example or two:

> What we do here is treat people as if they were members of our family. We know them, we help them. For example, if there's a product they want and can't get elsewhere, I'll say, "Let me see what we can do." Mrs. Wilson's husband likes almond butter. We tracked it down, and now we get it for him. We do that lots of times.

People also love our meat department. Not only is it great product but they can get exactly the cut they want. It's a huge, huge draw for us, and of course once they're in the store to get a steak or some chops they buy other stuff as well.

It's possible that the manager of a grocery chain store might order a specific product for an individual customer—a jar of almond butter, a certain cut of steak—as a one-time service. But it's unlikely he'll remember to keep that product routinely on order as Marc Najarian does; the scale and complexity of the business simply make it impossible. Fresh Pond Market may lack some of the advantages of a chain like Stop & Shop, but it can create offer variation at the individual customer level, an edge that Marc Najarian makes the most of.

We asked Marc about the extensive wine department, a feature most neighborhood grocery stores don't offer:

Ah, that's a funny story. My grandfather Nish didn't really want to sell liquor. But he finally agreed to sell wines and sherries as a favor to Judge Coonahan, who lived in the neighborhood and wanted to buy his wine at our place. It was just a small section in the back.

I got serious about it in the sixties and spent the time to figure it out and build up the department. Our customers love it today. It's not enormous, but it has a terrific selection, and because I'm always talking to the customers I know what adjustments to make—what new varieties to try, what countries and regions are hot. It's like the meat department—it brings them in, and they buy other things, and it's a good contributor to the business.

Every food retailer changes its product mix from time to time. Fresh Pond Market changes in direct response to customer requests:

the wine shop, the new varieties of herbal teas, the heirloom toma-toes in the produce section, the gourmet chocolates near the cash register that you have to know to look for. What doesn't change is the connection to individual customers, which is what keeps people coming back. And both pieces reflect the individual-customer-based approach that has made Fresh Pond Market a community fixture.

Five minutes away is Porter Square Books, which opened in 2005—*after* Amazon and the giant chains had swept the field. How was that even possible? And why is the store doing better today than ever?

Dale Szczeblowski, Carol Stoltz, and Jane Dawson, three of the store's five owners, crowded into their small back office one Tuesday morning to talk with us. Staff members popped into the room from time to time to ask questions or to get a customer issue resolved. The store, as always, was filled with browsers and buyers, busy, but not frenetic—an inviting place to be.

"How do you do it?" was our only question.

Their answer began with the word *service*—a term that's so ge-neric it almost amounts to a nonanswer. But as they spelled out the details, it became clear that the service they provide is all about of-fering varying customer types, down to the individual reader, the book-related products and services they particularly value. Like Fresh Pond Market, their store has become a platform offering a wide array of products that can be organized and configured around custom-ers' varying, ever-changing needs.

"We treat people who come in here as if we were inviting them into our home," Dawson said. "As if they were guests. If someone asks for help finding a book, you *never* just point to the stacks—you get out from behind the counter, walk with them to the shelves, and put the book in their hand."

"If the book's not there, we can get it for them in a couple of days," Szczeblowski added. "In most cases, that's plenty of time."

"Keep in mind, this store doesn't stop at the four walls," Szcze-blowski said. "When there are conferences in town, we'll often do the bookselling table at the conference, and we work with local schools when they do book sales for fund-raising." Szczeblowski was describing a service provided to meet the unique needs of two customer types who might otherwise buy their books elsewhere, or not at all—conference attendees and families of local schoolkids.

"Don't forget the readings," said Stoltz. "Every Wednesday morning, we have a reading hour for toddlers, one and a half to four years old. Doria [a Porter Square staff member] loves to read for the kids, and of course the kids love it, too."

"We have readings for adults, too," said Dawson. "We can't always get the big names that the big stores get, but we do okay. We've had Annie Lamott, Tracy Kidder, David Sedaris, and Alexander McCall Smith. In fact, it was our buyers who discovered McCall Smith and introduced him to America. He's loved us ever since."

"We've got twenty-five people working here, full- and part-time," Szczeblowski said. "They love to talk books with the customers. What did the reviewers say about that novel? What's hot in nonfiction? Who's the best new mystery writer? What will my six-year-old nephew like? They always have tips, ideas, and recommendations, and they enjoy talking about them. And many of our best customers enjoy it, too. For them, it's not just 'Come in, find the book, buy the book, and leave.' It's a conversation that never really ends."

That notion of a never-ending conversation is a thread that links Fresh Pond Market and Porter Square Books. They're businesses in which social norms operate alongside market norms, fostering human connections and the offer variations these connections encourage: Mr. Wilson's almond butter, the toddler who fell in love with *Amelia Bedelia* at a Wednesday reading. If anything separates small-business survivors like these from the chain stores they're up against, that's it.

A third example is Skenderian Apothecary, which has done business on Cambridge Street for decades. Today Joe Skenderian and his brother Bob run it.

The Skenderians tackle the variation challenge somewhat differently than Fresh Pond Market and Porter Square Books. The brothers' strategy emphasizes two variation tools: the use of proprietary information to tailor product offers for individual customers, and the creation of organizational solutions to meet specific needs. Of course, as the down-to-earth people they are, the brothers don't really think of it as a "strategy," just as a way of caring for customers as human beings who deserve respect and consideration. Joe Skenderian told us about it:

> Look, there are two ways to run this business. One way is where the patient calls in, they pick up their prescription, they pay, and they walk away. That's what most people experience at the pharmacy today.
>
> The second way is a lot different. You might call it talking to the customer. Asking them questions. What are their concerns? What's their situation? What do they want to know about their medication? And making them comfortable enough to ask the questions they really want to ask.

Our ears pricked up. Proprietary information—the gathering of data about the customer, not as a marketing tool but as a way of helping people demand what they really need and want rather than settling for something else. Skenderian provided a simple example:

> You know, when you talk to customers, you just can't help finding things out. There's a family here in Cambridge that are our customers, a blue-collar family, hard-working people. I didn't know there were more than eighty of them, here in this area, all under different names. I only figured it out a little while ago, and it's a funny thing how it happened. A while ago, some kids came

in—leather jackets, nose rings, colored hair. We treated them with respect, listened to them, answered their questions. Like we do with everybody. Turns out they're part of this family, and they aren't always treated well at other establishments.

Well, word got around, and the way they were treated at our pharmacy was really appreciated by other members of the family. They had always been good customers, but now they became incredibly loyal to us. They recommend other customers to us all the time.

At a large corporation, "proprietary information" may mean files stored in a vast database and analyzed using complex software. But at a small business like Skenderian Apothecary, it means knowing people's faces and treating them the way they like to be treated.

Skenderian went on to explain the organizational arrangements their system requires:

You have to set up your business to be able to operate this way. My brother and I take turns in the store, and we have three pharmacists working for us. So we have the flexibility to take the time for the patient.

You know, if you really know the patient, it always makes a difference. Things you learn today make a big difference down the line, when the patient comes in five years later with a different condition. And your chances of avoiding a bad drug interaction are really lousy if you're not familiar with all the medications they're taking.

Sometimes paying attention pays off in the long term, but sometimes it happens much sooner. Last summer, for instance. A young woman walked in here with her two young children. She was wearing shorts, and I noticed one leg seemed bigger than the other. I pointed to her swollen leg and asked if she was in pain.

"It's killing me," she answered.

We talked for a few minutes, and I asked her to go to the emergency room to have it examined right away. Cambridge City Hospital is just three blocks away.

Two hours later, she was back. She'd been treated for a blood clot and came back with a prescription for blood thinners. Of course, if the clot had broken off in her leg and traveled to her lungs, she could have had a pulmonary embolism, and the kids would have been without a mom.

Now you don't get a chance to help a patient like that every day, but if you don't know them and you aren't constantly asking, you don't even get a chance to try in the first place.

As the stories of Fresh Pond Market, Porter Square Books, and Skenderian Apothecary illustrate, the scale and scope of small businesses give them a unique advantage over their larger, richer corporate rivals when it comes to responding to very different types of customers. It's actually possible for the staff at a corner store to know every customer who walks in the door and to tailor product offerings to their particular needs and wants.

It's the ultimate in demand variation—one customer at a time.

❐   ❐   ❐

DEMAND VARIATION can happen almost naturally in a small-scale, human-faced business like a local grocery store. (*Almost* naturally— because there are plenty of small businesses where customers *don't* get the kind of personalized treatment they receive at stores like the three we just described.) It plays a powerful role in other kinds of organizations where one-on-one human interactions are vital in creating demand—consider, for example, the way Teach For America's Yoona Kim devotes 95 percent of her effort to adjusting her teaching style to the varying needs of individual students. But variation can also be a powerful demand-creating tool even for a gigantic international business operating the technological marvel that has been called the eighth wonder of the world.

People had been talking about the idea of linking Britain and

France by a tunnel since as far back as 1802. Those nineteenth-century tunnel plans were scuttled by political and military worries—there were always Britons fretting over the idea that some new Napoleon might march a French army through the tunnel and so conquer England.*

The pacification and unification of Western Europe following World War II improved the prospects for a Channel tunnel, and finally in 1986 a joint British-French corporation known as Groupe Eurotunnel S.A. was founded to make the idea a reality. Eight years later, the project was completed. It cost some £9.5 billion (three-quarters of it borrowed), about double the original estimate. On May 6, 1994, Queen Elizabeth II and French president François Mitterrand presided over opening ceremonies for the "Chunnel."

It was an impressive technical achievement—the second-longest railroad tunnel in the world and the longest undersea link anywhere.[†] More important, with the launch of Eurostar train service via the Chunnel, a new era of convenient rail travel between two of the world's great capitals—London and Paris—had begun. The engineers, construction crews, and business visionaries had successfully realized a nearly two-century-old dream.

They had built it—but then nobody came.

"Nobody" is an exaggeration, of course. But not much of one. Prior to the start of Eurostar service, experts had predicted that 15 million travelers would use the line annually. But in the first full year of service (1995), only 3 million tickets were sold.

---

* British paranoia on this theme actually persisted well beyond the Victorian era. The late business historian Robert Sobel liked to tell the story of the job created by the British government in 1803, under which a man was hired to stand on the white cliffs of Dover with a spyglass and ring a bell if he saw Napoleon coming. The job was finally abolished in 1945.

† The world's longest railroad tunnel, the Seikan Tunnel in Japan, connects the islands of Honshu and Hokkaido; it is almost 54 kilometers long, about 3 kilometers longer than the Chunnel. Planning for the Seikan Tunnel began in 1955, a year after five ferries sank in the strait during a typhoon, killing 1,430 passengers. It opened in 1988 after almost two decades of work that claimed the lives of thirty-four construction workers.

The architects of Eurostar had placed a very large, very costly bet on future demand—and lost, big-time. Eurostar's management team had no choice but to rethink their business and develop a new strategy for finding the missing demand.

One problem, they realized, was the "black box" forecasting model they'd used to forecast demand. A set of macroeconomic projections and a set of assumptions about factors like competition from air travel were fed into a single complicated mathematical formula. A monolithic ridership number emerged at the other end. It was a complex, sophisticated system, and no doubt a great deal of intelligence and labor was devoted to creating it—but the results it produced were wildly inaccurate.

Eurostar realized it needed to start over again—to create a system for analyzing and forecasting demand that acknowledged the sheer heterogeneity of demand for Eurostar. The new forecasting approach replaced the black box with a "glass box." Through extensive interviewing of Eurostar passengers and potential passengers, they constructed a list of various customer types, each with its own characteristics, history, expectations, preferences, and values. The process involved science, math, and a bit of intuition as well as hard data.

For each customer type, new ridership forecasts were developed, factoring in macroeconomic and competitive information. Then all these separate forecasts were built up into a total while remaining easily accessible, segment by segment, for updating, rethinking, and revision. Hence the "glass box" moniker.

Applying variation principles to Eurostar's customer base gave the company a fighting chance. Like wiping the greasy lenses of a pair of eyeglasses, it replaced Eurostar's previously blurry, indistinct image of the Average Customer with a clear, realistic picture that revealed the line's potential ridership in all its complex diversity.

The first realization was that some categories of possible Eurostar travelers held far greater potential for demand growth than others. (Great demand creators understand that all customers are important—but, like the symphony trialists, some customer types are particularly crucial to growth.)

There was, for example, a group called Silver Set Anniversary Night travelers—older couples who used Eurostar for quick overnight getaways to celebrate special days in romantic style. (As you might guess, this segment includes more Londoners who travel to Paris for their anniversaries than the reverse: "Paris" goes with "romance" a bit more naturally than "London" does.) This was a relatively affluent group, which might make them an appealing audience for Eurostar's marketing efforts—except for the fact that anniversaries come only once a year, creating a natural ceiling on these couples' travel frequency.

Another customer type was Overseas Travelers—tourists from North America and elsewhere who might use Eurostar to tack a few days of Continental travel onto a holiday in Britain. This might seem a likely source of big potential growth, but a bit of research into the marketing practicalities largely dashed that hope. Cost-effectively targeting a relative handful of American tourists who are scattered over a nation of continental scale and share no single, affordable communications medium is difficult. The conclusion: Overseas Travelers would likely be a source of future demand for Eurostar, but a modest one that would be hard to reach and develop. The company's search for growth needed to focus elsewhere.

The more the Eurostar team analyzed the numbers, the more they found themselves circling around the same group of potential customers: businesspeople for whom a trip from London to Paris—or vice versa—was an opportunity to meet with clients, woo customers, canvass suppliers, or scout out the competition. These business travelers had money to spend, had frequent reasons to travel, and put the highest priority on exactly what Eurostar could do best: saving time.

Just as studying variation in the symphony audience had thrown a spotlight on the critical importance of trialists, a similar analysis had revealed that business travelers held the key to the growth of cross-Channel train travel.

The Eurostar team immediately put these findings to work. The original two-level Eurostar ticket plan—a standard one-way seat for £95, a first-class seat with meal for £195—was replaced with a more diverse system that catered to varying passenger types. For those wanting simply a fast trip at the most affordable price, a standard ticket at £99 was available. Someone willing to pay a bit more for a quieter car and the opportunity to earn frequent traveler points—a budget-conscious business person, for example—could buy an economy plus ticket at £110. Business first class at £175 offered perks designed to make the life of an executive faster and more comfortable—ten-minute check-in, taxi service, and a dedicated lounge. And luxury leisure travelers could spend £196 for a premiere first-class seat that included, among other benefits, a meal with champagne.

The new system paid immediate dividends. After Eurostar's sputtering debut with just 3 million riders in 1995, passenger totals rose steadily for five years: to 4.9 million in 1996, 6 million in 1997, and eventually to 7.1 million in 2000. People obviously liked having the opportunity to buy a travel experience that more closely matched what they really wanted from their trip.

The numbers were hopeful. But the line was still far from the break-even point. Could customer variation enable Eurostar to climb all the way to the seemingly unscalable peak of profitability?

◻   ◻   ◻

DESPITE THE EXCITING potential revealed by the de-averaging study, Eurostar continued to struggle through its first decade of operation. Service breakdowns and delays earned the line a spotty reputation. Richard Edgley, Eurostar's first managing director, spent much of his time making damage-control statements to the press and giving out more than £2 million worth of free tickets to customers whose trains had arrived more than half an hour late during the line's first year alone.

Edgley's successor, Hamish Taylor, described the situation he inherited as "simply suicidal." He pushed for service improvements, including—most crucially—the building of a new high-speed rail link between London and the Chunnel, which would bring the English portion of the journey closer in speed to the Continental leg and cut precious minutes off the overall travel time. Taylor managed to improve the revenue picture slightly, though when he departed in 1999 Eurostar was still losing more than ten pounds for every passenger it carried.

New managing director Gordon Bye ran into his own string of problems—a global recession, an already aging fleet of trains, and more service breakdowns. Low-cost airlines, led by easyJet and Ryanair, had aggressively pursued vacation travelers and by 2001 had grabbed a significant share of demand on the London-to-Paris route. In September of that same year, the terror attacks in New York and Washington devastated worldwide business travel and further depressed revenue growth. Ridership, which had peaked at 7.1 million in 2000, fell in each of the next two years.

Eurostar's awkward and fractious ownership arrangement, linking the French and Belgian governments with an array of public and private British interests, complicated these problems further: During 2003 alone, no fewer than fourteen different entities, each with its own agenda, claimed partial ownership of Eurostar.

This was the situation when a new executive named Richard Brown took the helm in August 2002. Thirty years earlier, straight from university, Brown had turned down more lucrative offers from Shell and Mobil to join British Rail—a career move his father had warned him against. Even then, railroading was seen as a dying business. ("People were talking about 'The Rail Problem,'" Brown recalls. "There was even a book with that name.") But Brown found rail travel "interesting" and ended up sticking with it.

Highly regarded in the industry, Brown was widely seen as the ideal person to bring sound, savvy leadership to the struggling Eurostar. A profile in the London *Times* described him this way: "Short, balding, courteous, with a great slab of a face and a Desperate Dan chin, Brown is by reputation one of the best man-managers and strategists left in the rail business." Desperate Dan is a wild-west character from an old British comic strip, known for both his oversize chin and his extraordinary toughness—he can lift a cow with one hand and shaves his beard with a blowtorch. Brown would need a bit of that same toughness in his new assignment at Eurostar.

Corporate change is rarely easy. In an organization as complex as Eurostar, it's especially challenging. "We've got three nationalities in the work force, three main operating bases in Brussels, Paris, and London, and four hundred staff who deliver the service onboard," Brown notes. "So redesigning even the smallest process means getting a substantial number of people to change their behavior. Something like changing the rolls on the breakfast tray—finding a new supplier, retraining staff—can be surprisingly complicated."

Brown rolled up his sleeves. He started by dropping the defensive rhetoric of his predecessors. He acknowledged the desperate need for service improvements and promised that these would be a top priority for his new administration. Brown also admitted that demand creation was his other major challenge. "We are working in a very competitive consumer market," he declared, using customer-oriented language that previous Eurostar chiefs had rarely employed.

Most important, Brown set about courting business travelers, who were the single biggest key to Eurostar's growth. This wasn't just a matter of advertising or marketing. The existing Eurostar product did a relatively poor job of addressing the hassles that mattered to this crucial customer type. New product features had to be designed and implemented. In September 2002, just one month after his arrival, Brown launched a £35 million "Eurostar for Business" program, which

included the creation of speedy fifteen-minute check-in lines exclusively for business travelers—a direct assault on his key customers'
hassle map.

To learn more about the needs and wishes of this customer
type, Brown and his team employed traditional business tools, such
as surveys and focus groups. But Brown also personally befriended
the lawyers, bankers, and financial managers who traveled between
London and Paris dozens of times a year. (Brown stresses that both
formal and informal ways of talking with customers are critically
important, "and either one is poorer without the other.") A number
of Eurostar regulars had banded together to form Club 180, named
after the number of minutes it took to make the trip via Eurostar.
Brown spent extra time learning from these club members, whom
he described as "gold dust" because of the value of their feedback—
especially their complaints about travel hassles, many of which ended
up on Brown's to-do list.

If Brown was particularly interested in listening to customer
complaints, he would soon have all he could want.

Breakdowns continued to plague Eurostar. In October 2002, after
Eurostar travel was canceled for a third straight day due to weather-
related system malfunctions, fifty stranded customers—many of
whom had spent the night sleeping in empty train cars or on the
floors of terminals—gathered outside Eurostar's offices at London's
Waterloo station. Police were called to control the stamping, clapping
crowd as they chanted, "We want to see the manager!"

Displaying the courage to talk to customers that all great demand
creators share, Brown soon emerged with several other Eurostar
directors in tow. He spent an hour absorbing the blistering complaints. Then, as a goodwill gesture, Brown offered every stranded
passenger a free trip on Eurostar's new high-speed line.

Singed by the experience, Brown redoubled his efforts to better
serve the all-important business travelers. In June 2003, he unveiled
plans for new Premier First cars created by Philippe Starck, famous

for designing interiors for Ian Schrager's legendary boutique hotels and even for the private apartments of French president François Mitterrand. A conventional two-plus-one seating layout would be replaced with individual egg-shaped swivel seats. "Premium First will be better than a private jet," Starck proclaimed. "There is no plane in the world that will have the same level of comfort." Meanwhile, all seats in first and standard class would be upgraded to include headrests with wings for better comfort; power sockets for laptop computers would be provided; and the two bar cars in each train would be refitted.

By 2004, Brown's efforts were finally beginning to pay off. Ridership increased for the first time in four years. And even as business travelers began to gravitate toward Eurostar, some of the other passenger types identified in the variation study began to yield increased demand as well.

Somewhat surprisingly, one of the best sources of sustained growth for Eurostar proved to be a customer type labeled VFR, which stands for "people visiting friends and relatives." A significant number of Eurostar passengers were expats—Britishers who'd moved to Paris, or French men and women who'd moved to London. The VFR segment had been growing steadily, thanks in part to the increasing economic and cultural unification of Europe (one observer remarks that London is now "the sixth largest French city").

As soon as this customer type appeared on the radar screen, Brown and his Eurostar team began experimenting with offer variations to make it grow, including low-fare midweek tickets and specially tailored frequent-traveler reward programs. Based on interviews, the VFR set was further broken down, identifying, for example, one subgroup of retirees and another made up of young people who had moved for school or work, each with distinctive hassle maps and travel preferences. Magnetic product add-ons were devised for these groups. Retirees often have children and grandchildren in tow, so Eurostar packaged tickets with discount deals on kid-friendly activities like trips to Disneyland Paris. Students and young professionals were offered discount tickets to cultural activities like concerts. Eurostar ridership continued to grow.

❑   ❑   ❑

BUT THE BIGGEST LEAP forward for Eurostar was just around the corner—a demand creation breakthrough that harked back to the company's origin in a remarkable feat of infrastructure engineering.

Eurostar's tenacious and meticulous customer research had shown that seemingly small improvements in service—especially reduction in travel times—could have a huge impact on demand, in particular among business travelers. Fast as Eurostar was, an almost three-hour one-way trip still took a significant chunk out of a traveler's day.

With its famous TGV (for "Train à grande vitesse," or very high speed train), France had long experience with building and maintaining tracks for superfast rail travel. Not so Britain. When Eurostar was launched, the slowest link was the trip from London through the county of Kent to the British end of the Chunnel. Upgrading this section of rail to improve the overall travel time would be a huge hassle reducer for the business traveler. Add an extra forty minutes to your workday in Paris and suddenly a leisurely lunch becomes a possibility; if the afternoon meeting runs a little late, you can still get home in time to tuck the kids into bed and have dinner with your spouse.

A major investment in the track upgrade was made by Eurostar's U.K. shareholders. The first stage of the project was completed in 2003, but its impact on service was modest. In November 2007, the rest of the project was finally completed. The new High Speed 1 (HS1) line brought the entire British portion of the trip up to the standard of the existing French and Belgian lines, reducing the one-way trip from London to Paris from three hours to just two hours and fifteen minutes.

The psychological jolt for travelers was enormous. Journalist Andrew Martin experienced the first celebratory run and exulted,

"We were at the Channel Tunnel within half an hour. It was like being teleported. . . . This is the most civilised form of transport available."

Perhaps even more remarkable, given Eurostar's checkered history of service problems, the transition was virtually trouble-free. "It all went so smoothly, that a couple of weeks after the opening, one of the staff said: 'Is that it?'" Richard Brown recalls with a smile.

Shaving forty minutes off the trans-Channel journey provided business travelers with the benefit they considered most precious—time. Brown proudly declared, "A few years ago, you wouldn't have thought about going to Paris on a day trip. . . . We're expanding people's horizons about what they can use Eurostar for."

The advent of HS1 boosted the magnetism quotient of Eurostar more significantly than any other development in its history. It also marked a major shift in the corporate culture within Eurostar—from pessimistic and defensive to confident and proud. This notable technical achievement gave the Eurostar team members an enormous energy boost, helping them to see future challenges, as Brown says, "less as threats than as opportunities."

The infrastructure upgrade produced an important secondary benefit. At the same time that the HS1 line was put into service, the main London terminal for Eurostar service was shifted from Waterloo station in the city's southwest corner to a refurbished St. Pancras International station in northern London. A small difference, seemingly—but a potentially enormous one, for reasons the managers at Eurostar were just beginning to sort out.

Yet another discovery from the customer variation study had been the realization that rail transport was "microgeographic" in its reach. British travelers who selected Eurostar for trips to France were overwhelmingly from London rather than from outlying cities; in fact, specific London neighborhoods close to the Waterloo International train terminal drew far better numbers than London suburbs that might require a thirty- to sixty-minute commute.

Recall the problem Zipcar faced early in its history, when customers shied away from Zipcar's product because of the lengthy walks that were often required to reach the nearest available car. Zipcar addressed the problem by increasing its density in specific urban neighborhoods, reducing access time to its cars from twenty minutes to ten and ultimately to five.

The 2007 shift from Waterloo to St. Pancras had a similar impact on Eurostar. Located at the intersection of six underground lines and seven domestic rail lines, the St. Pancras terminal expanded the "catchment area" from which Eurostar attracted customers, making the train to Paris a more attractive option for residents of London's suburbs as well as northern counties like Hertfordshire, Bedfordshire, and Buckinghamshire.

The move to St. Pancras had redefined, and vastly enlarged, Eurostar's potential customer base. And demand continued to grow.

❑   ❑   ❑

IN THE YEARS SINCE the HS1 breakthrough, Eurostar has maintained its primary focus on the business traveler. One of the most successful strategies has been offering tickets with "optionality"—that is, refundability of ticket purchases and flexibility of travel times. It's another illustration of the power of a carefully tailored product to attract demand among a specific customer type.

Unrestricted ticket changing is especially important to business travelers, who often have to change their plans at the last minute. And since the tickets purchased by business travelers are paid for by their companies (and are a tax-deductible business expense as well), they'll pay a significant premium for that flexibility. Leisure travelers, by contrast, have much more control over their own itineraries and therefore are much less likely to need optionality—or to want to pay for it.

The economic impact of this variation in what different customers want is striking. Whereas the lowest-priced round-trip ticket be-

tween London and Paris *without* optionality can be purchased for
as little as 75 euros, Business Premier tickets for the same route
with optionality start at 339 euros—and provide Eurostar with a
much larger profit margin.

Optionality isn't the only extra product feature that Eurostar is
offering its prized business travelers. It is also promoting lounges
and fully equipped meeting rooms in its terminals and working to
make them easy to reserve online at the same time tickets are purchased. These facilities will shave more precious minutes off the
in-city travel time of businesspeople. And Business Premier travelers can also enjoy an array of other amenities, including chauffeur
service at either end of the trip, complimentary Wi-Fi access in the
business lounges, power sockets for phones and laptops, and meals
and drinks served at their seats. They can even book a cab ride
while on board, thereby avoiding long queues at the taxi stand on
arrival.

As a result of these type-driven product variations, Eurostar has
decisively won the competitive battle with its chief rival—the airlines.* Three-quarters of the coveted business travelers now use
Eurostar rather than flying between London and Paris—a marked
improvement from 2003, when the majority still preferred the plane.
(More than 90 percent of Eurostar trains arrive on time, compared
to fewer than 70 percent of flights into Heathrow.) What's more,
the shift of demand to Eurostar has now begun to turn into a self-
reinforcing spiral: As more business travelers shift to Eurostar, airlines are offering fewer business seats; the fewer business seats
available, the more business passengers turn to Eurostar.

Even more remarkably, the laser focus on business travelers has
also increased Eurostar's appeal to *other* categories of travelers.

---

* Ferry service across the Channel is also available, but the number of travelers who
use it is relatively minuscule.

Customer surveys and Brown's continual buttonholing of individual riders have long made it clear that businesspeople prefer having separate accommodations. People catching up on e-mails or trying to plan or rehearse a presentation while en route to a meeting don't appreciate sitting cheek-by-jowl with toddlers en route to Disneyland or honeymoon couples behaving, well, like honeymooners.

But the less-obvious insight that Brown and his team have uncovered is that leisure travelers feel the same. They find their holiday mood gets spoiled when they have to sit next to a group of pinstriped businessmen and businesswomen clicking away on laptops or negotiating deals on their cell phones.

"It was a huge surprise," Brown recalls, "yet so blindingly clear after the fact—one of those things that make you wonder, 'Why on earth didn't I think of that before?'"

Eurostar has enhanced the travel experience for *both* types of passengers by separating them and catering to both—for instance, by creating, in 2005, the Leisure Select ticket designed especially for well-heeled vacationers in a self-indulgent mood. Like business travelers, they get their own carriages and an attractive set of perks, including onboard newspapers and magazines, and drinks and meals served at their seats. "When we introduced that change," Brown says, "ticket sales in *both* Business Premier and Leisure Select went up significantly." Similar growth has been experienced in Eurostar's other passenger segments. For example, fully 91 percent of cross-Channel travelers in the VFR (visiting friends and relatives) category now use Eurostar.

❐   ❐   ❐

THERE'S A RANGE of techniques organizations can use to address demand variation. Eurostar uses at least two: product variation (with its special services tailored specifically to business travelers and other customer types) and product platforms that can be personalized (for example, with its tickets that provide "optionality," allowing customers who value the right to make last-minute changes to purchase that right).

Like other great demand creators, Eurostar has also developed systems to address the needs of customer types beyond its own end users. For example, it has a dedicated staff of about fifteen representatives who devote their time to meeting with corporate travel managers, a rarity in the industry. Eurostar has also enhanced its outreach to foreign travel agents, who play a big role in shaping demand among tourists visiting England and the Continent. For the first decade, those agents could book clients on Eurostar only through a multistep process that Richard Brown has described as "wading through treacle." In 2004, Eurostar made its way into the same computerized Global Distribution Systems (GDS) that travel agents use to book airline tickets. Thanks to this hassle-reducing breakthrough, those Overseas Travelers that Eurostar found too difficult to reach directly are now being drawn into the web of demand, with annual growth rates exceeding 50 percent in Eurostar ridership among U.S. visitors to Britain.

Just as Brown stresses the importance of both formal and informal methods of talking with customers, he also emphasizes the need to harness both traditional marketing methods (advertising, promotions, public relations) and customer-driven word of mouth. "If you've only got the advertising without the word of mouth, or vice versa, you're not going to achieve the breakthrough. There's a lot of habit about the way people travel, and people don't change quickly. It took us the best part of five years to move from a situation where most business travelers flew between Paris and London to a situation now where very few of them fly. It takes time and a lot of hard work to entice people to make that kind of change."

Yet the change is happening. Overall annual passenger figures, which had risen from just 3 million in 1995 to 7.1 million in 2000, only to stagnate and drop below 7 million for three years thereafter, have now enjoyed six straight years of growth. In 2010, 9.5 million travelers rode Eurostar. By 2012, it's likely the 10 million mark will finally be surpassed—and with it, the corporation is expected to attain overall profitability for the first time.

Of course, Richard Brown and his colleagues at Eurostar are very happy about this. But so are the British taxpayers, who now have real hope of getting out from under the burden of economic loss they've shouldered year after year since the 1994 ribbon cutting at the entrance to the Chunnel. And so are environmentalists, who know that travel by train produces one-tenth the pollution and greenhouse gas emissions as equivalent travel by jet.

Other, less obvious benefits from Eurostar's revival have begun to turn up. Thanks to Eurostar's growing leadership of cross-Channel travel, Richard Brown has been urging British government officials to scale back plans to expand regional airports. (Eurostar, they estimate, now replaces some 250,000 short-haul airline trips every year.) "We are not saying the country doesn't need any new runways at all," Brown says, "but one or two fewer is not trivial." In an era of growing resistance to airport growth because of financial, environmental, and noise pollution concerns, that's not trivial at all.

Today, thanks to the focused leadership of Richard Brown and the cumulative, long-term effects of more than a decade of effort to capitalize on the insights yielded by demand variation, Eurostar is finally showing signs of fulfilling its demand-creating potential.

It's a good thing—since a whole new wave of business challenges is already confronting the company.

One is the reappearance of the old nightmare of service breakdowns. In December 2009, just days before Christmas, five Eurostar trains became disabled, stranding more than 2,500 passengers and disrupting the travel plans of one hundred thousand more. The fiasco delayed Brown's planned promotion to the job of chairman of the newly consolidated Eurostar International Limited.

At the same time, a brand-new competitive threat is emerging. In June 2010, the European Commission's watchdog agency charged with ensuring competitive markets gave its approval to the long-planned conversion of Eurostar into a single, unified business entity—on condition that the Chunnel line between London and Europe be made available to competing companies. Interest in competing with Eurostar was immediately expressed by NedRailways of the Netherlands, Air France, and Germany's Deutsche Bahn.

It will take time for competing railroads to launch cross-Channel service; commercial runs probably won't begin until 2012. But Brown is already pushing back aggressively. He has spearheaded a series of new initiatives to push Eurostar up a steep trajectory of improvement, hoping to get several steps ahead of the growing expectations of customers as well as the capabilities of the new competitors. New marketing and sales initiatives designed to connect the dots for a wider array of traveler types have been announced, including "dynamic packaging" of tickets in partnership with Virgin Atlantic Airways and one-purchase connecting fares to Switzerland.

Brown has also been urging the British government to begin mapping plans for a High Speed 2 connection between London and Birmingham, England's major business center in the north. And in October 2010, Eurostar announced its intention to spend $1.1 billion on ten new high-capacity, higher-speed trains from Siemens and to expand service into a wide array of Continental locations.

The work of the demand creator is never done. But the best ones recognize that a de-averaging of the market is a demand explosion waiting to happen. One wonders what Eurostar's *next* de-averaging move will be.

PEOPLE ACCUSTOMED to "supply-side thinking"—which is the way most of us think—tend to *hate* customer variation. It makes their lives more complicated—all those many differing needs to address, each requiring special thought and attention.

Demand creators are different. They love variation because it gives them many opportunities to serve more customers even better, matching products to wants and needs with even greater precision and finesse.

But they also know that addressing variation isn't easy. It can be complex, tricky, and expensive. So over time, they've invented several differing strategies for cost-effective variation:

1. Create product variations, preferably with a high ratio of common components to keep costs down, as Apple has done with the iPod (available in versions ranging from the $49 iPod shuffle to $399 for a high-end iPod touch).

2. Create a platform with add-ons that fit individuals' particular needs, as CareMore has done with its common service infrastructure and multiple "plug-in services" for conditions from diabetes to congestive heart failure.

3. Provide organizational solutions—dedicated personnel capable of tailoring the product to particular needs and ensuring it works, as Bloomberg and Tetra Pak have done with their thousands of global experts who work closely with clients to customize their services.

4. Use proprietary information to personalize the product offer, as Amazon and Netflix have done with their recom-

mendation engines, driven by previous customer purchases
and ratings.

5. Launch a new division or business, when necessary, to serve
a different kind of customer, as Nestlé did when diving into
the espresso market with Nespresso.

Five different strategies for meeting five different kinds of customer variation challenges—what else would you expect from demand creators who have evolved so very far beyond one-size-fits-all?

7.

Launch

The Achilles' Heel of Demand

TODAY, HYBRID CARS and their all-electric descendants are at the forefront of automotive innovation. Thanks to their fuel efficiency and eco-friendly image, a growing array of these alternative vehicles have sparked steadily growing demand from drivers around the world.

Yet very few of today's hybrid enthusiasts would be able to name the first mass-produced hybrid automobile sold in the United States or correctly guess the date of its launch.

The car was the Honda Insight; it was launched way back in 1999, and from day one it boasted, according to the Environmental Protection Agency, an amazing highway fuel efficiency rating of seventy miles per gallon.

The Insight was a remarkable breakthrough by any measure. So whatever happened to it? And why didn't the Insight trigger the demand revolution that later hybrid vehicles produced?

As for the first question, the first-generation Insight sold a mere 17,000 units *worldwide* before production was stopped in 2006. A redesigned Insight, introduced in 2009, has done reasonably well in Japan, ranking fifth in sales in that country during its first twelve months, but enjoys only tepid demand in the United States (fewer than 21,000 units in the year 2010).

As for the question *why*, there are several answers. To begin with, the first-generation Insight looked like a science project that wasn't ready to leave the lab; the two-door hatchback didn't even have a backseat. The *New York Times* said its styling "suggested Popeye's friend Olive Oyl in her ankle-length dress. The rear fender skirts seemed frumpy." Other reviewers, even those, like the auto analysts at Edmunds, who appeared eager to find reasons to praise the innovative vehicle, offered a host of additional complaints: "Downsides include rear wheel skirts that must be removed before running the Insight through a car wash or when a flat tire needs to be changed, and aluminum body panels that are expensive to repair and replace, which boosts insurance premiums. Mountain dwellers will lament the rapid pace at which the battery pack's charge depletes, leaving them with a low powered gas engine to labor up grades." Edmunds's road test editor warned, "Passing is not something to be attempted much; even a Toyota Corolla is a speed demon next to the Insight," and its features editor reported, "With gusts over 40 mph, the Insight felt like a kite on wheels. . . . Large gusts would literally send the super-light Insight careening into other lanes. Not a fun time to say the least."

Although the Edmunds reviewers claimed, "We're impressed with Honda's technological tour de force," their write-up ended up pleading for mercy for the little car: "Look at it this way. Insight . . . is about conserving resources, not blazing trails." Honda later said the car was "experimental," which doesn't explain why it was ever moved beyond the car-show circuit into the real-world marketplace.

Honda is an outstanding company with an impressive track record of innovation. Yet the Insight, which could have been one of Honda's greatest triumphs, has been at best a disappointment. It's a story that is all too typical of the unpredictable world of demand, in which new product launches result in failure many times more often than success.

This painful reality of launch failure must have been in the minds of the members of the board of Toyota when they were asked, in 1993, to green-light their own proposed hybrid vehicle project.

In a world of unpredictable and steadily depleting petroleum supplies, the idea of an ultra-efficient hybrid vehicle was enormously appealing. But it would also be extraordinarily expensive to develop, especially given the fact that the Toyota engineers were hoping to achieve an even greater level of fuel economy than the Insight claimed; the estimated development cost would be at least a billion dollars. And as the fate of the Insight would demonstrate, the odds of commercial success for a car using this unfamiliar new technology were low—in the case of the Toyota hybrid, they were no better than 5 percent.

When asked why he would take a billion-dollar bet on such a long-shot product, Toyota's Takeshi Uchiyamada, the leader of the project task force, replied by comparing it to one of the most audacious engineering feats of the past century: "If the Americans succeeded in going to the moon, we can succeed with this car."

Going to the moon was a long shot embraced by a bold young president in response to a global challenge by a determined adversary (the Soviet Union)—the kind of organization-risking bet few team leaders are willing to take. Would Uchiyamada be able to make it work? Would Toyota be able to avoid the fate that befell Honda?

❏   ❏   ❏

LAUNCH IS the Achilles' heel of demand. It could be the launch of a new product, a nonprofit organization, a government program, or an educational initiative. All project launches are attempts to disturb and change reality. Yet the vast majority fail, leaving reality untouched. The new product goes unbought; the idealistic nonprofit falls short of its goals; the government program doesn't reach the people it was intended to help; the educational initiative falls on deaf ears. And the demand that the launch team hoped to elicit and satisfy never materializes.

Even the best-managed, most successful organizations in the world often fail at launch. Consider the U.S. launch of Fresh & Easy

Neighborhood Markets by the British food retailer Tesco, which is rightly considered one of the smartest companies in the world. Tesco spent three years painstakingly preparing to launch its new store format in the southwestern United States, even building a separate warehouse with a complete model store inside to test different design variations. Tesco observed customer behavior exhaustively, watching shoppers as they navigated grocery aisles and filled their carts. Tesco ended up creating stores that offered fresh and healthy products, everyday low prices, fast and convenient self-service checkout, and a relatively small (ten-thousand-square-foot), easy-to-shop format.

Observers and commentators predicted a great success. When Tesco launched the new chain in California, Arizona, and Nevada in November 2007, the plan called for 200 stores within two years. Targeted sales were $200,000 per week. Yet actual sales averaged just $50,000 per week, and only 115 stores were opened before Tesco halted the program for further study.

What went wrong?

Despite all of Tesco's intense research and analysis, there was a fundamental misreading of the American consumer. In addition to everyday low prices, consumers wanted coupons. They also wanted cashiers to talk to (rather than automated checkout machines), they wanted to use their credit cards (which Fresh & Easy didn't allow), and they wanted a host of other features that Fresh & Easy didn't provide. What Tesco believed customers wanted and what customers actually wanted turned out to be two very different things.

Tesco's experience is not the exception—it is the rule. Alongside Fresh & Easy in the annals of failed launches by great organizations, we can list Walmart's entry into Germany, IKEA's entry into Japan, Nokia's N-Gage game system, Apple's first MacBook Air, the Sony Librié e-reader, and literally hundreds of others—as well as, of course, the Honda Insight.

Actual failure statistics for project launches are hard to verify, although the estimates provided by knowledgeable industry professionals are distressing enough. Experts say that 60 percent of Hollywood movies fail to earn back their costs. Sixty percent of company mergers and acquisitions end up losing money rather than making it. Information technology projects such as computer system upgrades fail at an estimated 70 percent rate; venture capital investments fail at 80 percent. New food products die on the vine at 78 percent; new prescription drugs at more than 90 percent.

Is there a way to change these long odds? If you're a would-be demand creator, whether you work with a for-profit or nonprofit organization, a government agency or charitable group, can you change the odds of success on your next project launch from 20 percent to 80 percent—or even better?

Perhaps. But success requires changing the genetic thought-code that controls and dooms the typical launch. It requires moving far beyond business as usual, and applying a unique organizational structure, an unusual mix of resources, and a healthy dose of fear. It requires the single-mindedness, toughness, and daring that enabled the team behind the Apollo program to achieve John Kennedy's goal "of landing a man on the moon and returning him safely to the earth."

Most important—and most difficult of all—success requires overcoming some of the innate characteristics that make us what we are. It requires conquering human nature.

❏   ❏   ❏

WHEN WE EMBARK on a launch, we believe, deep down, that the odds are pretty good. That's why we begin the project in the first place. But we're wrong; the odds are unknown and, in all likelihood, terrible. As managers, we generally have great confidence (otherwise we wouldn't even try)—but often that confidence turns out to be an illusion and a liability.

In their 2003 article "Delusions of Success," Dan Lovallo and

Daniel Kahneman describe why people overestimate the odds of success on any project. "When forecasting the outcomes of risky projects," they write, "executives all too easily fall victim to what psychologists call the planning fallacy. In its grip, managers make decisions based on delusional optimism rather than on a rational weighing of gains, losses, and probabilities."

In other words, when the true odds of success are 10 percent, we think they're 40 percent. When the true odds are 5 percent, we think . . . well, we just refuse to believe it.

Lovallo and Kahneman offer a useful prescription to repair this cognitive bias: *Get the data.* Track down actual figures on launch failure rates for your company, your industry, other industries, or projects similar to yours. The numbers will be fascinating—and sobering.

As an example, Lovallo and Kahneman describe the time one of them worked on a major new curriculum project for high schools in Israel. A team of respected academics and subject experts was recruited. Early in the project, the team members were asked to independently estimate the amount of time they'd need to complete the project successfully. When their sealed estimates were revealed, they ranged from eighteen to thirty months.

One of the team members had his doubts. Rather than simply accepting the group's projections, he decided to get the data. He researched the histories of similar curriculum projects and discovered that—when they were completed at all—they invariably required between seven and ten years of work. The consensus prediction of around twenty-four months was off by at least 250 percent.

The point of getting the data isn't to create an atmosphere of negativity or despair. It's to encourage members of the launch team to take a realistic look at the obstacles they face. The point is to turn an Achilles' heel into a secret weapon through a systematic approach to improving the odds at every step of the process. The point is to cultivate the "imagination of disaster" (in critic Susan Sontag's words), then create a whole range of highly effective antidisaster initiatives.

Data alone won't fix the situation. Chances are good no one will believe you—or the data. It's called the Semmelweis Reflex. Ignaz Semmelweis was a Hungarian doctor perplexed at the high incidence of infant deaths from puerperal (or childbed) fever in Vienna in the 1840s. An innovative controlled experiment yielded the solution: If doctors washed their hands with a chlorine disinfectant before interacting with patients, the incidence of death was reduced dramatically.

Unfortunately for Semmelweis, and for generations of families, his work preceded Louis Pasteur's studies of germ theory. Because Semmelweis's idea clashed with their assumptions, few doctors believed him. Semmelweis died in an asylum at age forty-seven, his insights wasted.

The doctors Semmelweis failed to convince were reacting much as people from every way of life generally respond to a challenge to their assumptions. It seems to be human nature to reject new knowledge that contradicts long-accepted norms. In any contest between strongly held beliefs and the data, the data loses.

You know the expression, "I'll believe it when I see it." The Semmelweis Reflex inverts that: "I'll see it when I believe it."

When it comes to improving the odds at launch, the implications of the Semmelweis Reflex are enormous. People find it remarkably easy to dismiss or ignore the data that demonstrate how fragile and risky launches are. As if intoxicated by their own sense of self-confidence, they plunge ahead, often committing many of the same mistakes that have doomed countless launches before them. They end up adding to the dismal failure statistics.

So how do you get people to see something they don't want to see? One technique that can be helpful when organizing a launch effort is this one: Rather than performing the traditional postmortem on a failed project, try a *premortem* before the project starts. Here's how it works.

If you gather a team of experienced leaders and ask them why past projects failed, the explanations flow readily: *The project was bigger than we realized . . . we were too slow . . . our design was flawed . . . we were operating from faulty assumptions . . . the market changed . . . we had the wrong people . . . our technology didn't work . . . our strategy was unclear . . . our costs were too high . . . our organization sabotaged us . . . the competition was tougher than we thought . . . we reorganized ourselves to death . . . we fought among ourselves . . . our strategy was flawed . . . our strategy was good but our execution was lousy . . . we ran into unexpected bottlenecks . . . we misunderstood our customers . . . we were short on resources . . . the economics didn't work . . . we got killed by internal politics . . .*

Unfortunately, most teams never create such a list at the *start* of any project. That's not in the genetic code of most innovators, who are (and who need to be) gung-ho optimists. But what if you ask your team to imagine a failure in advance, and explain why it happened? Research by Deborah Mitchell of the Wharton School, J. Edward Russo of Cornell, and Nancy Pennington of the University of Colorado found that "prospective hindsight"—imagining that an event has already occurred—increases the ability to correctly identify reasons for future outcomes by 30 percent.

Gary Klein, author of *Sources of Power: How People Make Decisions* and *The Power of Intuition*, builds on this "prospective hindsight" theory. He suggests that a premortem exercise frees people to express worries that they might otherwise suppress for fear of appearing disloyal or undermining the team's confidence. Klein says the process reduces the kind of "damn-the-torpedoes attitude often assumed by people who are overinvested in a project." People participating in a premortem might raise red flags before, rather than after, failure.

So try this nightmare exercise: Imagine disaster. Ask why you failed; list all the possible reasons. Then do your best to counter those mistakes before they have a chance to occur. Most launches die from self-inflicted wounds. It means that if you're willing to take a clear-eyed look at the forces seemingly conspiring to derail your next launch, you'll probably find that the most powerful factors are actually under your control.

❐   ❐   ❐

AMONG THE BEST at confronting and dealing with the realities of launch have been the leaders of the Toyota Prius project—Takeshi Uchiyamada, Takehisa Yaegashi, and the other members of their team. They *knew* the odds of success were less than 5 percent. They didn't avert their gaze from this dispiriting fact. But then they asked the critical question: How can we change those odds?

To begin, they created a dramatically different organizational system—almost a company within a company—to design the new vehicle.

The system started with a physical space. A room at Toyota head-quarters was set aside for the project. They called it *obeya,* the big room. It was equipped with some personal computers and two computer-assisted design workstations. Team members assembled in this room daily to collaborate on the Prius project—the first time this had been done at Toyota. The idea was to raise the odds of success by getting all the relevant talent working together, sending off creative sparks and generating an intense sense of focus.

A virtual space was also created as a powerful supplement for the physical space of the *obeya.* Uchiyamada had an electronic mailing list compiled to encourage the team members to quickly and broadly disseminate key issues and problems as they arose. Rather than channeling issues through the usual hierarchical, command-and-control communications model, the innovative e-mail system encouraged everyone, no matter their job title or departmental assignment, to offer a solution to any problem they heard about. The clear message: The best minds throughout Toyota were to be intensely focused on any and every problem related to the new-product development process.

As the project grew, more and more of the company's most brilliant thinkers got drawn into the increasingly fascinating and important set of challenges it posed for engineering, design, manufacturing, distribution, and marketing. In the end, a phenomenal *two-thirds* of Toyota's entire prototyping resources were devoted to the Prius.

Uchiyamada also introduced other organizational innovations designed to intensify the company's intellectual focus on the Prius project. For example, when a new vehicle is ready to go on line, Toyota usually sends resident engineers (REs) to work at the manufacturing plants so they'll be available to handle any problems that arise during the early months of production. For the Prius project, they assigned *reverse* REs from the manufacturing plants to take part in the design development process. This was a form of premortem, a way of identifying possible manufacturing glitches even *before* the car was ready for the assembly line and eliminating them in the blueprint stage.

Other great demand creators have also recognized the necessity for organizational innovation as a prelude to a successful launch. Jeff Bezos didn't hand the Kindle project over to a working team within Amazon; instead, he created Lab 126 so this unique new venture could be developed with the clear focus and fresh, independent thinking it demanded. Helmut Maucher of Nestlé made a similar move when he created a separate skunkworks to shepherd the Nespresso project through the harsh reality of an unproven market for home espresso machines in the 1980s.

Another odds-raising innovation used by Toyota involved "accelerated evolution"—creating a plethora of varieties ("mutations"), subjecting them to tough-minded competition ("external pressure"), and then selecting the very best design options ("natural selection"). Toyota tested some eighty different types of hybrid engines early in the life of the project. Through extensive computer-based testing, the engineers at Toyota narrowed the eighty possibilities down to eight, then to four (it took months). Then they had an intense bake-off among the four. The survivor of all these brutal comparisons was a highly evolved and tough engine.

A similar accelerated evolution was applied to the car's overall styling. Toyota maintains seven separate styling studios, each normally working on a different vehicle category—small cars, trucks, minivans, and so on. But for the high-stakes Prius, all seven studios were asked to submit designs, which were judged by a panel of fifty people of various ages.

And all these innovative steps to increase the odds—in addition to a series of unprecedented technical breakthroughs—were conceived and implemented in record time. (Speed itself is another odds-raising move. Every additional month a launch slips creates new opportunities for the market to shift, for competitors to make preemptive moves, for technologies to change, for customer tastes to evolve in a different direction.)

Two years into the process, Uchiyamada and his team presented Toyota's new president, Hiroshi Okuda, with their projected completion date for the Prius: late 1998 or early 1999. Okuda quietly overruled them. The Prius needed to be on the market by the end of 1997.

Uchiyamada would later describe his consternation in understated Japanese style: "I have to admit that we were against the decision. Our team believed it was too demanding." But then they returned to the *obeya* and set about implementing it. In the end, the Prius NHW10 was launched in Japan in October 1997—two months *ahead* of Okuda's impossible schedule.

The Prius NHW11 was introduced in the American market in

2000, seven months after the Honda Insight. At first, sales lagged. Toyota seemed to be succumbing to exactly the same law of failure as Honda had.

However, Toyota didn't stop. It kept redesigning the car, improving its efficiency but also going beyond the functional to the emotional. It created a new design that stood out, that let everyone know it was a Prius, not a Corolla look-alike—which meant highlighting the green sensibility and forward-thinking mindset of the driver. The new model was launched in 2004, and sales took off.

Today, nearly half of Prius's worldwide sales come from the United States. And in 2009, sixteen years after development began, the Prius became the bestselling car in Japan for the first time. By managing the launch process differently, Toyota found the demand that Honda didn't.

The Toyota story also illustrates a truth that all the demand creators recognize: the power of second chances. Like the Prius, many new products don't create significant new demand when they first enter the marketplace. But great demand creators keep talking to customers and redesigning. As a result, their products often reach escape velocity on the second or third try.

Many great products are built on a solid foundation of failure— but it must be *organized* failure, as Toyota and other launch masters exemplify.

LAUNCH IS a mind game. Success and failure hinge on how people think, and the degree to which they can overcome business as usual—and the innate proclivities of human nature. Great demand creators, like Uchiyamada and his team at Toyota, have developed a complete array of distinctive mental habits that distinguish them from most launch practitioners.

We've identified seven of these habits that appear to have the greatest impact on the odds of a successful launch. Let's consider them one by one.

1. The first is the instinctive drive to conduct a *fatal flaw search*, seeking out the crucial weakness (or the two or three crucial weaknesses) that will undermine a business design and kill the value of a launch. Examples of such flaws include the misunderstanding of American grocery shoppers' attitudes toward price on the part of Fresh & Easy, or the excessive cost of most of the eighty different hybrid engines that Toyota tested, or one of the early envelope designs at Netflix that made the DVDs prone to loss or breakage.

The Netflix team achieved a successful launch in part because the DNA of their style of thought incorporated this drive—in spades. For that reason, they were obsessive about searching for the best solution to the shipping problem, even after they'd tried and tested scores of reasonably good versions.

Finding the fatal flaw early—once, twice, or even several times—is a key step in practically every successful launch. If you find it and can fix it, fix it. If you find it and realize that you can't fix it, it's time to ask: "Should the launch proceed?" And if the honest answer is no, then shut it down.

Unfortunately, this is the opposite of how we ordinarily think. The genetic code of business as usual conditions us to look for confirmatory evidence—data that suggests we're on the right track. That's human nature, isn't it? The Semmelweis Reflex. Success at launch requires us to recognize that reflex—and take conscious steps to reverse it.

2. The second habit practiced by great launch masters is *competing inside the organization*. The idea is simple: Make accelerated evolution work for you. Create meaningful vari-

ations and have internal groups or alternatives compete, then select the strongest to compete in the outside world. It's the thinking behind Toyota's excess-options program for the engineering and design of the Prius.

In similar fashion, Apple's designers create ten pixel-perfect, unambiguous mockups of every feature for each new product. Their goal is to produce many very good, yet very different, implementations of the idea. Using specified design criteria, these ideas are narrowed down to three options. These three options are developed and perfected in parallel for months. One final option is ultimately selected for production.

This means that Apple throws away 90 percent of its design work. Wasteful? Not really. This system gives Apple's designers enormous latitude for creativity that breaks past traditional organizational and psychological restrictions. When you know that the design you are crafting is one of ten rather than *the one,* your willingness to cut loose and try something a little wild—and perhaps a little brilliant—is that much greater.

Competing internally requires a large pool of variations, and an unreasonable degree of iteration. But it is that endless iteration that leads to perfection—and is quite contrary to the business-as-usual genetic code, according to which organizations compete externally only.

3. Masters of launch understand the value of *imitating to be unique*. This refers to the *selective* role of innovation in the work of launch masters. Great demand creators don't innovate in everything. Instead they lavish creativity on the most critical variables; everywhere else, they borrow and steal shamelessly. They follow the dictum (often attributed to artist Pablo Picasso) "Good artists borrow; great artists steal."

The reason is simple: When you're running a launch, there is never enough time, money, talent, or emotional energy to analyze, master, and control all the thousand-and-one details that you *have* to get right to create significant demand. This is true even when a major corporation like Toyota or Apple is involved. After all, even a big company is really made up of a thousand tiny budgets—a million dollars here, half a million there—each of which is run by a manager who is under scrutiny and pressure to be as cost-effective as possible. And of course the smaller organizations most of us belong to, from a mom-and-pop stationery store or a local art gallery to a fifty-person tool-and-die maker, are often operating at the edge of solvency with little or no room for waste.

So investing resources in reinventing the wheel is a formula for failure. This is why great demand creators ruthlessly prioritize the handful of crucial elements when planning a launch and invest their resources in those. Everywhere else, they creatively recycle, reinvent, and reuse and so save money, time, and effort. Shakespeare didn't invest time and emotional energy to invent a fresh plot for *Hamlet*; he borrowed the story from a thirteenth-century history chronicler named Saxo Grammaticus and devoted his energies to developing profound character insights and soaring poetry in which to express them. Developing his first movie on a stingy budget, Orson Welles rummaged the back lots at RKO in search of old sets, props, and furniture he could adapt to his purposes, concentrating his efforts on developing an audacious script and eliciting brilliant, unconventional acting from a company of relative unknowns. The result, as critic Pauline Kael explained, is an epic historical drama produced at a fraction of the normal cost—*Citizen Kane*.

Following the same principle, because Uchiyamada and

his engineering team at Toyota knew they had a near-impossible array of technical problems to solve in designing the hybrid Prius, they opted to use the familiar and successful Corolla body design rather than creating a brand-new platform from scratch. They also collaborated with Matsushita on the crucial battery design rather than trying to develop it in-house. Netflix used some similar moves, emulating Amazon's website rather than designing one from scratch and partnering with Sony, Toshiba, and Panasonic to generate awareness about its new business model and build its customer base.

4. Great demand creators always remember to *emotionalize the offer.* We generally behave as if customers and their behavior are rational. But the truth is that soft and fuzzy elements—emotions, impulses, urges, tastes, aesthetics—are often what separate winning offerings from their almost-but-not-quite-equally-cool competitors. Emotionalizing your offering turns "very good" into "magnetic."

Zipcar started off promoting itself as a "car-sharing" service. Problem: Nobody really wants to "share" a car. Zipcar got traction with customers when it began promoting its super convenience instead. Who doesn't love convenience? Honda engineered a great hybrid—but nobody fell in love with it the way they fell in love with the Prius. Sony produced a technically wonderful electronic reader—but it didn't excite people the way the Kindle did. The ZEN music player was nice, but the iPod was cool. Nokia made great smartphones for years, but the iPhone turned people on.

Product design is a powerful emotional trigger. That's why, when Samsung wanted to vault past Sony and Matsushita in the world of electronic devices, it tripled the number of designers working on its products. What's more, it officially gave the designers precedence over the engineers—a gutsy move for an engineering company.

5. The fifth mental habit focuses on the *unique organizational equation*. This means looking for the managerial, structural, and communications strategies that are especially appropriate for *this* launch, at *this* time, under *these* circumstances. It's an important corrective to the business-as-usual genetic code that generally leads people to employ their existing organizational structure as the default choice, even when a launch project that absolutely demands organizational innovation is under way.

At Toyota, for example, a successful launch for the Prius meant, among other things, creating the *obeya*, harnessing two-thirds of the company's design capabilities to the Prius project, and creating reverse resident engineers to solve manufacturing problems in the design phase, long before those problems even had an opportunity to take shape.

At Lotus in the early 1990s, June Rokoff led the development of version 3.0 of Lotus *1-2-3*, the legendary spreadsheet program that was the first "killer app," transforming the personal computer from a cool kid's toy into a must-have purchase for any business. Rokoff was knowledgeable about feeds, speeds, product features, and technological twists and turns. But she wasn't obsessed with these things. Instead she was obsessed with the fuzzy but critical organizational questions, such as, "Do I have the right people, in the right numbers, organized into the right teams?" "Are they aiming at the right targets—not just in general, but specifically?" and "Are my people getting the recognition they deserve as well as the (pointed and forceful) feedback they need?"

Most of us take a fingers-crossed approach to the organizational equation, tackling issues as they arise and hoping for the best. June Rokoff was the opposite, looking under rocks to find problems and address them. Over months of anguished struggle, the task force she assembled to tackle the troubled but crucially important Version 3.0 project grew to three hundred people. She ordered endless quantities of pizza, stayed and worked with her programming teams through the night, and when everybody got sick of pizza she instituted "guest chef" nights at which company executives, including CEO Jim Manzi, had to come and cook a gourmet dinner for the entire team. Rokoff rewarded project breakthroughs with personalized recognition—handshakes from the top brass, posters honoring individual accomplishments, even a rock video she commissioned starring the entire team. Thanks to Rokoff's prodding, hand-holding, cajoling, and encouragement, Version 3.0 was completed ahead of a seemingly impossible schedule—and it saved the company.

Rokoff's colleagues at Lotus and admirers from throughout the industry gave her affectionate nicknames ranging from "The Iron Lady" to "St. June," but none of these monikers accurately captured the complex blend of toughness and understanding that made her unique. Rokoff listened to people—not just with her ears, but with her heart and her gut. She had a genuine interest in those around her, which is a quality you can't fake and which often prompts people to respond with amazing feats of creativity.

It's critical to emotionalize the product. Rokoff emotionalized the process as well.

6. Sixth, we've found that masters of launch maintain an artful *balance between confidence and fear.* Think of what is arguably the most famous statue in the world—Michelangelo's *David* in the Galleria dell'Accademia in Florence. It depicts a

beautiful male nude in the prime of his youth. It is, of course, also the classic depiction of an underdog—the inexperienced David, armed only with a slingshot, about to challenge the heavily armored Goliath, the giant Philistine warrior.

The statue reveals Michelangelo's insight into the drama of the confrontation between David and Goliath. When you enter the gallery, your first view is a side view. From this perspective, the larger-than-life-size David exudes total confidence, bordering on arrogance. But as you walk to the right, you gradually confront David face to face. Now you see that his eyes are turned upward, to a point in space about forty feet above where you are standing. He's gazing, of course, at the unseen adversary—Goliath. And you see in David's eyes a look of total, abject fear.

Contrast that with the genetically coded optimism that many people carry over to business from the world of sports. (You might think of it as the "You Gotta Believe!" approach to leadership.) Confidence is important, but fear is critical. Fear helps you to fully develop the imagination of disaster— at a time when you can actually do something about it. Fear gets the adrenaline pumping and forces you to double down on every element to ensure survival—and success.

7. Finally, launch masters remember the reality that a successful launch is rarely a one-day or even one-month affair. They think in terms of *series, not event*—a series of assaults on the indifference of the market. Do you recognize the following lines of poetry?

> To be or not to be, aye, there's the point
> To die, to sleep; is that all? Aye, all.
> No, to sleep, to dream, aye, marry, there it goes,
> For in that dream of death, when we awake,

And borne before an everlasting judge,
From whence no passenger ever returned,
The undiscovered country, at whose sight
The happy smile, and the accursed damned. . . .

Your reaction might be, "Well, some of the phrases are vaguely familiar. But there's something wrong with most of them. In fact, it just sounds goofy—a bad excuse for poetry."

And you'd be right. Because what you just read is Version 1.0 of what theater-lovers often call the greatest speech in any play ever written. You're more familiar with Version 3.0:

To be, or not to be: that is the question:
Whether 'tis nobler in the mind to suffer
The slings and arrows of outrageous fortune,
Or to take arms against a sea of troubles,
And by opposing end them? To die: to sleep;
No more; and by a sleep to say we end
The heart-ache and the thousand natural shocks
That flesh is heir to, 'tis a consummation
Devoutly to be wish'd. . . .

This is the immortal soliloquy from Shakespeare's *Hamlet* that has mesmerized generations of theater-goers. By contrast, Version 1.0 was just awful. (It comes from the early edition of the play known to scholars as the First Quarto, sometimes referred to—understandably—as "the bad quarto.") But it was a start.

The first version of your product is likely to be no better than Shakespeare's. Practically all great products are built on a foundation of failure. Fortunately, you can use the same technique Shakespeare used to unlock his own genius: revision—relentless, repeated revision.

The first version of the Prius produced results that were under-whelming. Only the second version succeeded in capturing the public's imagination. Something similar is true of the Kindle, where version 2.0 achieved a much greater marketplace breakthrough than version 1.0. And consider how the sequence of Apple iPod models released in the ten years after the product's original launch in 2001 gradually captured every corner of the market, from high end to low end.

The seven modes of thinking we've dissected above are just a sampling of the "how to think" DNA found in any great demand-creating organization. If you're an aspiring demand creator, think about your own experience and your own team. Consider the dimensions above and locate yourself somewhere on the evolu-tionary scale for each. Is your mental DNA closer to business as usual? Has it mutated to resemble that of the launch master? Or is it somewhere in the middle? Perform this analysis point by point. Do you like what you see?

But there's an even simpler way to check your organization's readiness to mount the kind of launch that makes demand creation possible. Answer these four questions:

- How strong is the leader?
- How strong is the team?
- How strong is the resourcing?
- How strong is the fear?

The better the answers, the better your odds of success.

❑   ❑   ❑

A GENERATION AGO, when the demographic, technological, social, and economic cards were stacked quite differently, we could live with a world in which most people understood very little about the daunt-ing challenges of a project launch and even less about how to meet them. Today, with much of the economy struggling for traction and demand flagging, we can't afford the mind-boggling waste of failed projects any longer. We need to spark demand much more effectively, and that includes taking the steps necessary to raise our project success rate from 10–20 percent closer to 60–80 percent. Hard to do? Absolutely. Doable? Without question.

As we've seen, the 20-to-80 shift starts with changing the way we think and the questions we ask. It requires fully understanding the customer hassle map and being able to identify all the backstory elements that *must* be in place if we hope to improve that map and make the lives of customers appreciably better. It continues with having a process for business and organizational design that's as disciplined as the ones that the most innovative companies already have for product design. It includes driving accelerated evolution through internal competition, practicing creative frugality with every product element that's not crucially important, and investing the extra time and resources required to turn your good-enough product into a got-to-have-it product, with the intense emotional appeal required to turn fence-sitters into customers.

Above all, it requires a kind of mental, emotional, and spiritual toughness that is very different from our business-as-usual energy levels. Recall how Toyota used the Apollo moon mission as a reference point for their own low-percentage project. The winning spirit of launch is exemplified in the title of NASA manager Gene Kranz's book, *Failure Is Not an Option*, as well as in the story it tells.

You remember Gene Kranz from the movie *Apollo 13*, where he was depicted by actor Ed Harris. Kranz was the director of the Houston space center who played a critical role in saving the three astronauts who were nearly marooned in lunar space aboard their crippled spacecraft. He made crucial decisions regarding the timing of rocket firings, the management of scarce energy resources, and the seat-of-the-pants repair of the damaged air filtration system. All these decisions were made under intense pressure; any one of them, if mismanaged, could have been fatal both to the astronauts and to NASA's long-term scientific mission.

The heroism Kranz displayed in that situation wasn't physical heroism, military heroism, or political heroism, but *organizational heroism*, which is arguably every bit as important but which often gets short shrift. Compounded of tenacity, imagination, shrewd judgment, self-awareness, and sheer willpower, it's a form of heroism that's desperately needed today and that is in especially short supply in most failed launch attempts.

Thanks to Ron Howard's award-winning movie, the Apollo 13 mission will probably always be viewed as NASA's finest hour. But people within the space agency know something most civilians don't—that Gene Kranz's legacy to NASA was cemented years before Apollo 13. The day after the tragic launchpad fire in January 1967 that killed three astronauts and almost derailed the space program, Kranz gave a speech to the assembled staff at the space center that has since become legendary. Known as "Kranz's Dictum," it set forth the standards of discipline, professionalism, and thoroughness that would become the North Star for NASA's future efforts at space exploration:

> Spaceflight will never tolerate carelessness, incapacity, and neglect. Somewhere, somehow, we screwed up. It could have been in design, build, or test. Whatever it was, we should have caught it. We were too gung ho about the schedule and we locked out all of the problems we saw each day in our work. Every element of the program was in trouble and so were we. The simulators were not working, Mission Control was behind in virtually every area, and the flight and test procedures changed daily. Nothing we did had any shelf life.
>
> Not one of us stood up and said, "Dammit, stop!" I don't know what [Floyd L.] Thompson's committee will find as the

cause, but I know what I find. We are the cause! We were not ready!

We did not do our job. We were rolling the dice, hoping that things would come together by launch day, when in our hearts we knew it would take a miracle. We were pushing the schedule and betting that the Cape would slip before we did.

From this day forward, Flight Control will be known by two words: "Tough" and "Competent."

Tough means we are forever accountable for what we do or what we fail to do. We will never again compromise our responsibilities. Every time we walk into Mission Control we will know what we stand for.

Competent means we will never take anything for granted. We will never be found short in our knowledge and in our skills. Mission Control will be perfect.

When you leave this meeting today you will go to your office and the first thing you will do there is to write "Tough and Competent" on your blackboards. It will never be erased. Each day when you enter the room these words will remind you of the price paid by [Virgil] Grissom, [Edward] White, and [Roger] Chaffee. These words are the price of admission to the ranks of Mission Control.

Sending a human being to the moon and returning him safely to earth was an incredibly difficult challenge. The odds of success were dismal. The same is true of many of the project launches we participate in. In most cases, thankfully, human lives aren't at stake. But the success of our companies or nonprofit organizations and the livelihoods of thousands of people often are. Those stakes are far from trivial.

So the next time we are working feverishly on the launch of any project, perhaps we should stop to remember Gene Kranz's words.

Perhaps we shouldn't allow ourselves to get caught up mindlessly in the process to the point where, someday, we may find ourselves looking back and remembering, *We were rolling the dice, hoping that things would come together by launch day, when in our hearts we knew it would take a miracle.*

We don't need to work that way. We don't need to roll the dice and hope for a miracle. Instead we can cultivate the courage to figure out the real odds—and to do what it takes to change them.

8.
Portfolio

"Nobody Knows Anything"

I F ENGINEERING ONE successful launch is like winning a bet against long odds, achieving a *series* of such successes is like picking the winning number at roulette—not once, not twice, but over and over again. No wonder many people are convinced that it simply can't be done.

Screenwriter William Goldman, after decades observing how box-office winners and losers are created in Hollywood, summed up this belief in his famous dictum, "Nobody knows anything." Judging strictly by the numbers, Goldman's Law seems inarguable—not just in the movie business, but in any activity. No one is capable of consistently predicting which products will create demand, still less of producing a string of such products, year in and year out.

Almost no one, that is.

In December 1998, John Lasseter, the creative director of Pixar Animation Studios, returned to California after an extended trip with his family to Asia. The trip had served a dual purpose: It gave Lasseter an opportunity to spend some much-needed time with his wife and kids, while he also participated in the triumphal international press tour promoting Pixar's second movie, *A Bug's Life*.

At the time, Pixar was exuding a growing sense of confidence. Its first feature, *Toy Story*, had been a huge hit, generating both critical acclaim and an enormous flow of box-office demand. Now *A Bug's Life* was off to an equally impressive start. Two feature films—two major hits. Not a bad start for a fledgling company that was trying to ride a new, unproven technology—computer-generated animation—to success in an industry where "nobody knows anything." Lasseter and his colleagues were beginning to suspect that maybe—just maybe—they were capable of turning out hit movies, not just occasionally, but on a regular basis.

But when Lasseter returned to his office in Emeryville, his mood changed.

One of the first things he did was to watch the reels containing Pixar's new work in progress, *Toy Story 2*. And as the scenes unfolded, he experienced a growing sense of dismay. "I felt like the wind had just been knocked out of me," Lasseter later recalled. The new movie simply wasn't very good. All the familiar, beloved characters from the original *Toy Story* were there—Woody, Buzz Lightyear, Mr. Potato Head, and the rest. But the excitement was missing. By comparison with Pixar's first two hits, *Toy Story 2* felt predictable, uninspired, even a little boring.

Hollywood veterans will tell you that sequels virtually *always* fall short of the originals. But for John Lasseter, and for his colleagues at Pixar, a team of talented and ambitious artists eager to reshape the world of animation, releasing *Toy Story 2* in anything like its current form wouldn't be just a disappointment—it would be a devastating setback.

Pixar's business partners at Disney—the venerable studio that had practically invented feature-length animation way back in the 1930s—were less worried than Lasseter. Colleague Tom Schumacher remembers one of the Disney executives watching the early reels of *Toy Story 2* and remarking offhandedly, "Well, it's okay." Having lived through decades of film history, including both triumphs and fiascos, the management of Disney didn't believe that releasing one less-than-brilliant movie would be disastrous. But Lasseter considered that casual "It's okay" a crushing indictment.

Yet fixing the problem would be far from simple. The scheduled release was just nine months away. Promotional campaigns had been mapped out, toys were being manufactured, the revenues had already been written into company budgets. Disney made it clear that canceling the picture, or even delaying it significantly, was *not* an option.

The standard fallback position at most studios would have been to repackage the picture as a direct-to-video release—a low-risk, low-expectations strategy commonly used for sequels in the animation arena (for example, Disney's own *Return of Jafar,* a direct-to-video sequel to *Aladdin*). But Lasseter firmly rejected that idea. He'd attracted dozens of the best young creative talents in movies, software, computer graphics, music, and other fields by establishing an implausibly high standard of excellence for everything Pixar did. Creating a second-tier standard for selected projects and relegating some of his brightest performers to laboring under it would depress morale, fracture the unity of the team, and unleash a wave of jealousy and political infighting. Lasseter wasn't about to let that happen.

Confronted with such painful and unyielding constraints, Pixar seemingly had no good options. So they chose to do the impossible: to rebuild *Toy Story 2* practically from scratch, and to do it not over two years as normally required but within the existing nine-month deadline.

Lasseter called an emergency two-day story summit in Sonoma, California. "I realized at that point that *Toy Story* was us," he said. "It's us sitting around that table." Lee Unkrich, Andrew Stanton, Ash Brannon, and a host of other young Pixar veterans who had worked on the original *Toy Story* and knew the characters intimately gathered in a room and began tossing around ideas for energizing the narrative of the second film. Concepts they'd had to drop from the first picture due to lack of time were revived, reimagined, and experimentally integrated into the new story. Imaginative twists were invented, with voices around the table rising as people vied to build on one another's brainstorms.

The energy of the entire company was suddenly focused around a single goal—to make *Toy Story 2* great. But would it work?

◻   ◻   ◻

THE ELEVENTH-HOUR DECISION to rework *Toy Story 2* from scratch was far from business as usual in Hollywood. But then, Pixar has never been a typical movie studio.

Founded in 1979 as part of the computer division of Lucasfilm, Pixar struggled to market its core product, the Pixar Image Computer. Threatened with shutdown, it fell back on a secondary competency and began producing computer-animated commercials for client firms like Tropicana, Listerine, and Life Savers. People loved them, and these small-scale successes ultimately led to a $26 million deal with Disney to produce three feature-length computer-animated films, beginning with a movie about kids' playthings that come to life—*Toy Story*.

When *Toy Story* was released in 1995, it was an immediate hit with both critics and audiences, and it ended up grossing an impressive $362 million worldwide. Pixar followed it with *A Bug's Life* in 1998, which also generated tremendous demand. And in the process of making these first two features, creative director Lasseter, Pixar president Ed Catmull, and the rest of the company team began building the business culture and creative system that would make Pixar unique.

In creative fields like film, it's easy to fall back on language that is vague and mystical when struggling to define the secrets of success—to use words like *genius, inspiration,* and *magic.* There *is* an element of the ineffable and the indescribable in what Pixar does, and there's surely no formula that other filmmakers could apply to reliably churn out Pixar-like hits. But there are many specific strategic and managerial characteristics of the Pixar organization that feed its success at creating an entire *portfolio* of products that have attracted huge audience demand.

Several of these characteristics are vividly illustrated by what ultimately happened to Pixar's third feature film, the seemingly ill-fated *Toy Story 2*.

Every successful moviemaker recognizes the importance of a great story. But few take the challenge with the seriousness of Pixar. In a speech at the 2009 Cannes Film Festival, John Lasseter spelled out the company's philosophy. "We will stop production if we have to, to get the story right," he said. "It takes four years to make a movie at Pixar, and three and a half of those years are spent on story." In order to rescue *Toy Story 2* while working within an impossible deadline, Pixar had to find a way to squeeze thirty months' worth of story development into a mere nine months. Their solution was to pull talent away from every other activity, sequester them in a room together, and bring the pot to a boil—a bit like applying heat to a chemical mixture in order to accelerate the reaction.

Over the course of the emergency weekend summit at Sonoma, Pixar's creative team hammered out the details of a revised story. The new narrative had greater emotional punch, a stronger moral arc, and better character development. To clarify and heighten the personal dilemma faced by protagonist Woody, Oscar-winning composer Randy Newman was enlisted to write a heartrending love song to be sung by the character of Jessie, the yodeling cowgirl. Some basic elements of the original story were retained, but the rewritten tale was far less predictable, more engaging, and more psychologically compelling.

It's doubtful the same ultrahigh-speed creativity would be possible on a "normal" project—for example, one where the main characters weren't already deeply familiar to everyone around the table. It's impressive that Pixar was able to pull it off. But even more impressive, perhaps, was the company's commitment to story—even at the price of jettisoning a perfectly adequate narrative, late in the day, in order to replace it with a *brilliant* one.

The remaking of *Toy Story 2* also illustrates Pixar's unique style of teamwork. Hollywood can be a hierarchically driven place, where

the word of a top executive is all-powerful. But Pixar prides itself
on maintaining a spirit of openness, self-criticism, and experimentation, deliberately avoiding the inhibiting rules and rigidly enforced
dicta from on high that plague some studios. In John Lasseter's words,
"No note is mandatory," and "Nothing is standard operating proce-
dure for us."

A former Pixar team member describes the company's reliance
on what she calls the "Yes, and" principle. In most organizations,
outside-the-box ideas tend to get shot down quickly by people
pointing out their weaknesses and explaining why they don't work.
Pixar employees are taught to respond to fresh ideas with a "Yes,
and" response:

> Suppose someone says, "We should make a movie about bal-
> loons." Instead of responding with, "No, that would be too hard to
> animate," you might say, "Yes, and what if we made them into
> animal shapes. Then we could tell a story about balloon ani-
> mals." The result is a constructive, collaborative approach to
> idea generation that plays out throughout the company.

Another Pixar-esque term for the process is "plussing"—constantly
adding input from every possible source. "It's always assumed there's
a way to make it better at every stage," in the words of director Pete
Doctor. "John [Lasseter] is great at saying, 'Well, what if you did this
extra little gesture?' And suddenly it really sparkles and comes to
life."

The power of teamwork plays an especially crucial role
whenever—as happened with *Toy Story 2*—a project is in danger of
leaving the rails. In a process that has now become routinized,
when the director/producer team in charge of a particular project
needs or wants assistance and insight, a company "brain trust" con-
venes, consisting of John Lasseter and Pixar's eight directors. They'll
study the work in progress and offer ideas aimed at improving the

film. But importantly, the brain trust has no overriding authority—the director and producer remain unambiguously in charge of the project. As Ed Catmull explains, this stipulation "liberates the trust members, so they can give their unvarnished expert opinions, and it liberates the director to seek help and fully consider the advice."

True to this spirit, the emergency summit that remolded *Toy Story 2* drew on the ideas and insights of dozens of Pixar team members. Remember, Lasseter didn't say, "*Toy Story* was me." He said, "*Toy Story* was us"—and the difference is crucial. "We just got together and started laughing hysterically at all these ideas," Lasseter continued, "building upon the foundation of the story."

When the crew returned to the studio, armed with their transformed story and a renewed sense of purpose, they were energized to perform amazing feats of productivity, starting with rewriting and reboarding the entire picture in a month—an unheard-of feat.

Toy Story 2 came out on time and proved to be one of the most acclaimed pictures of the year. The pivotal new song, "When She Loved Me," as performed by pop artist Sarah McLachlan, was nominated for the Oscar for best movie song of the year. The website Rotten Tomatoes, which aggregates and summarizes published reviews from newspaper, magazine, and broadcast critics, reported that *Toy Story 2* was reviewed favorably by 147 out of 147 critics—an astonishing 100 percent thumbs-up. *Toy Story 2* went on to be not only Pixar's third straight theatrical hit but the company's highest-grossing film to that point.

❏   ❏   ❏

OPEN-MINDEDNESS, TEAMWORK, single-minded focus on story—these are just a few of the crucial elements that have enabled Pixar to produce hit movies with greater regularity than virtually any other studio in history.

Another is Pixar's unusual emphasis on originality. Pixar deliberately eschews the play-it-safe strategies many studios follow. Instead they push the envelope as strongly as possible. It's hard to imagine another animation company green-lighting the concept for Pixar's dark, futuristic, practically dialogue-free eco-drama *WALL-E* (2008), which Catmull aptly described as "a robot love story set in a post-apocalyptic world full of trash." Not your typical animated children's fare—yet *WALL-E* ended up grossing $534 million, winning the Academy Award for best animated feature (one of twenty-four Oscars won by Pixar to date), and being named number one on *Time* magazine's list of best movies of the decade. American audiences struggled with the title of *Ratatouille* (2007), and industry experts scoffed at the idea of building a cartoon around the character of a curmudgeonly old man, as Pixar did with *Up* (2009)—yet both films created enormous demand.

This unwavering insistence on originality is reinforced by the unusual degree of freedom granted to the creative team, which is both a source and a product of the studio's artistic success. If the Pixar animators experienced two or three costly failures in a row, it's likely their creative freedom would begin to be challenged by those on the business side. The fact that they keep turning out winners earns them continued license to do their own thing—which in turn results in even more winners.

In line with this spirit, Pixar prides itself on its research and development department—no other movie studio has one like it. Pixar artists are encouraged to play with ideas they like, the more outlandish the better, and embody their findings in short, low-cost, experimental movies. It's a unique opportunity for Pixar artists to test concepts and expand their skills without creating undue financial risk for the studio or career risk for themselves. Some of the studio's hit pictures have originated in shorts produced as R&D projects. And Pixar's leaders also encourage connections with the smartest minds in academia so the studio will stay abreast of the best new ideas about computer animation and programming.

The company also prides itself on encouraging long-term partnerships among its talents—another unique element in twenty-first-century Hollywood, where the norm is for collections of artists (actors, screenwriters, directors, producers) to be assembled on an ad hoc basis for individual pictures, then quickly broken up. As members of an enduring team, Pixar employees tend to subjugate their creative egos in favor of a mutual esprit de corps unlike any other in the industry. For example, Andrew Stanton, who played a key role in creating *Finding Nemo* and who directed *WALL-E*, willingly resumed his role as an ordinary studio employee after helping to shape those two megahits, exhibiting a modesty that would be rare in any business, much less show business.

In return for this unusual degree of loyalty, Pixar rewards employees by promoting their long-term career development. For example, every employee, from animators and accountants to security guards, is encouraged to devote up to four hours a week to his or her education. That may include some of the more than 110 courses offered at Pixar University—"the equivalent of an undergraduate education in fine arts and the art of filmmaking," in the words of its dean, Randy Nelson. "Why teach drawing to accountants?" Nelson rhetorically asks. "Because drawing class doesn't just teach people to draw. It teaches them to be more observant. There's no company on earth that wouldn't benefit from having people become more observant."

Even more important, Pixar encourages and rewards artistic contributions from every member of the organization. This philosophy is driven not by some feel-good notion of egalitarianism but by a clear-eyed understanding of the intense demands created by what Ed Catmull calls the "long, arduous process" of creating an exceptional film. He goes on to observe:

> A movie contains literally tens of thousands of ideas. They're in the form of every sentence; in the performance of each line; in the design of characters, sets, and backgrounds; in the locations of the camera; in the colors, the lighting, the pacing. The director and the other creative leaders of a production do not come up with all the ideas on their own; rather, every single member of the 200- to 250-person production group makes suggestions.

Catmull is accurately describing the reality of filmmaking, which one critic has described as "the most collaborative major art form since the building of the great cathedrals in the Middle Ages." In an industry that traditionally lionizes a few individuals anointed as "creative," such honesty is rare, as is the readiness to respect and honor the contributions made by people at every level of the organization. (Once again, we sense the presence in a great demand-creating organization of social norms, supplementing and enriching the market norms that predominate in most companies, and making a deeper form of partnership among team members possible.)

Perhaps John Lasseter's enthusiasm for honoring contributions from every member of the Pixar team is, in part, a reaction to a crushing disappointment early in his own career. A lifelong animation enthusiast, it was a dream come true for Lasseter to join the team at Disney right after college. But as a rookie working under the most distinguished animators in the world, he found he was expected to work hard and say little. When he inadvertently offended his boss in his eagerness to pitch a movie idea based on the newfangled concept of computer animation, he was fired—such a painful episode that he never mentioned it to anyone until years later.

Ironically, in 2006, Lasseter would be named the new COO of Walt Disney Feature Animation, the very studio that had dismissed him decades earlier—an honor he earned largely because of Pixar's ability to learn from even the most junior members of its creative team. As Lasseter has said, "Working at Pixar is like being a trapeze artist, where you're looking across at the other guy to catch you." That's elevating teamwork to an almost unprecedented level.

But perhaps the most central pillar of the Pixar system—and the one that ties together all the specific creative strategies they employ—is to start the movie development process by asking a simple question: What movies would my family and I like to see?

Anyone with a spark of creativity can provide an insightful and potentially valuable answer to that question—which is why Pixar encourages the flow of ideas from everyone in the company. Asking that question at every opportunity, and following the answers wherever they may lead, is a Hollywood version of the practice all great demand creators share—having the guts to talk with customers and take what they say seriously.

By practicing these principles, Pixar has architected an extraordinary system for understanding how demand happens, and then making it happen—to the tune of *eleven* blockbuster hits in a row—movies that have earned both critical acclaim, industry honors (including those astounding twenty-four Oscars and twice as many nominations), and commercial success (see table below).

PIXAR'S BLOCKBUSTER PORTFOLIO (1995–2010)

Film	Release	Domestic Gross (in Millions)	Worldwide Gross (in Millions)
Toy Story	1995	$192	$362
A Bug's Life	1998	$163	$363
Toy Story 2	1999	$246	$485
Monsters, Inc.	2001	$256	$525
Finding Nemo	2003	$340	$865
The Incredibles	2004	$261	$631
Cars	2006	$244	$462
Ratatouille	2007	$206	$624
WALL-E	2008	$224	$521
Up	2009	$290	$415
Toy Story 3	2010	$415	$1,063

Pixar has managed to defy Goldman's Law largely by finding ways to elicit and activate the personal genius of every one of its employees. "Nobody knows anything"—but when you combine the intellectual and creative resources of *hundreds* of Hollywood's most talented minds, the result is a body of insight that is far more robust than what the greatest single genius could produce.

❐   ❐   ❐

REPEATED LAUNCH SUCCESS—the kind it takes to build an entire portfolio of successful products—is not a function of the economic landscape, or the available technology, or even the types of products a company makes. Success returns to those who build *systems* to create demand.

Driven by Goldman's Law, most organizations launch *multiple* projects aimed at creating potential future demand, on the same theory that the lottery player buys a handful of tickets rather than a single one. Similar strategies are employed outside of business as well: Foundations and government agencies sponsor numerous pilot projects in fields like medical research and economic development; departments of education support many charter schools testing a variety of teaching methodologies. In each case, they're hoping for the one blockbuster that will tap a significant level of demand and compensate for numerous failures—a blockbuster whose identity can rarely be predicted in advance.

Of course, the hundred-bets strategy complicates life for the would-be demand creator. As your perspective broadens from a single project to an entire array of projects, the portfolio often seems like a weed-choked garden in which the most valuable plants are hard to distinguish from the worthless ones. Bottlenecks clog the system, preventing resources from getting to the crucial projects in time.

Quantity without quality won't work. To revert to the garden metaphor, the would-be demand creator needs to plant many promising projects, but then weed and winnow them with a sharp eye for quality. Legendary portfolio master Warren Buffett says investors should pretend they have a punch card good for twenty investments—to last their whole life. The point is that when you invest, you must make it count—easy enough to say, but hard to do, and nearly impossible to do consistently. It takes a mind-set, system, and culture that are dedicated to an all-hands-on-deck mentality to maximize the chance of creating a winner, project after project after project.

Consider two companies in two very different industries—pharmaceuticals and venture capital—that have created systems for decades-long success in meeting the challenge of new demand generation. As with Pixar, the systems employed at Merck in the 1980s and 1990s and at Kleiner Perkins Caufield & Byers throughout its four-decade history are designed to generate an enormous quantity of high-quality ideas that are then winnowed down to a very few truly terrific ideas, which magnetize the focus of their respective organizations.

It's a simple idea, but a difficult one to practice, as shown by the fact that companies with remarkable portfolios like those of Pixar, Merck, and Kleiner Perkins are so rare.

❏   ❏   ❏

LIKE OTHER MAJOR drug companies, Merck has always been financially dependent on the flow of demand to its newly invented, patented medicines. When successful, these drugs play the same role for "Big Pharma" as blockbuster movies do for Hollywood studios: they pay the overhead and compensate for the losses incurred when other drugs in development prove ineffective or simply fail to attract the expected demand. Blockbuster drugs keep pharma companies afloat, create jobs for thousands of scientists, engineers, and manufacturing workers, and, most important, improve the longevity and quality of life for thousands or even millions of patients.

When Roy Vagelos, a physician and biochemist with a research stint at the National Institutes of Health (NIH) under his belt, joined Merck in 1975, he found the traditional R&D process ineffective and unsatisfyingly random. "The process of discovery," Vagelos has noted, "was empirical, whether it was conducted in a laboratory or by simple folk observation of what happened when people ingested a substance. This is how aspirin, morphine, digitalis, and vitamin C came into use. The empirical process works, but it depends on luck and takes an enormous amount of time to bear results."

Vagelos's experiences at NIH had suggested to him a more efficient way of developing drugs. It was based on identifying specific naturally occurring enzymes involved in disease processes. "Once we identified a target enzyme," Vagelos has said, "the medicinal chemists would search for inhibitors in the laboratory, and the microbiologists and natural product chemists would look for inhibitors in nature." These inhibitors, adapted for medicinal use, would stop the operation of the enzymes and thereby retard or reverse the progress of the disease. Vagelos's new approach might be much faster than the traditional method, since hundreds of experiments could be done per day, and it would produce drugs with fewer side effects, since the molecule-to-molecule matchups sought by the researchers were highly targeted and specific.

It took time for Vagelos to convince his colleagues at Merck to adopt the new approach, but once they did, the results were dramatic. In effect, Vagelos and Merck converted the random trial-and-error structure of traditional pharma research into a *system*. And having a system, while it did not guarantee success, increased the odds significantly.

In his years as Merck's head of research (1975–1985) and later as CEO (1985–1994), Vagelos took other steps to leverage the demand-creating advantage produced by his research system. The most crucial focused on recruiting, retaining, and energizing the very best talent available—an easy objective to articulate but nearly impossible to implement.

In the early 1970s, the smartest young scientists gravitated to universities; conventional wisdom held that only second-rate talents chose industry. Finding this attitude "depressing," Vagelos set out to change it. He encouraged Merck scientists to publish research papers and lecture about their work in academic settings. He also gave them unprecedented freedom to pursue basic science interests and to work collaboratively in interdisciplinary teams, giving Merck's labs an atmosphere of creative ferment that was unique in the industry. The goal was to show young scientists that applied research could be both intellectually exciting and personally fulfilling, leading to new medicines that could improve lives for millions.

Vagelos's campaign gave Merck a magnetic allure for hundreds of young research scientists. And as a physician and experienced researcher himself, Vagelos was able to personally vet both these new hires and the work they produced, interviewing potential job candidates, regularly scanning clinical test results, encouraging the most talented researchers, and suggesting new approaches that often paid dividends.

The case of Dr. Arthur Patchett is a vivid illustration of how Vagelos's system unlocked the scientific potential of Merck. Patchett had joined the company shortly after obtaining his PhD from Harvard. An outstanding researcher, he quickly rose to become head of the entire synthetic chemistry operation. He was a poor manager, however, and was "banished" to a decaying old lab where his boss relegated him to mixing random peptides, work with minimal creative or productive potential. He had been doing this for two years when Vagelos arrived at Merck.

During one of Vagelos's Saturday strolls through the laboratory, he came across Patchett. Listening to him "free-associate" about research ideas and sketch connections on a whiteboard, Vagelos realized that Patchett was a "genius in chemistry."

Vagelos offered to work with Patchett to design a project for him to spearhead. Ready for a change, Patchett eagerly agreed. Within a few years, Patchett and his team had successfully explored a new treatment for high blood pressure and had made vital contributions to cholesterol research. Vagelos later observed, "Art Patchett was one of the most innovative chemists [at Merck], but he had to be allowed to be productive—not told what to do." Stories like this one have a way of traveling throughout an industry, and they helped make Merck under Vagelos *the* place to be for talented, ambitious scientists.

By 1988, Merck plowed fully 11 percent of its revenues into R&D—a higher percentage than any other company, and a greater than fivefold increase from just under 2 percent in 1976. Special investment emphasis was focused on research areas where the potential demand was greatest—areas where chronic conditions required ongoing therapy, current treatments were not very effective, and large numbers of patients could benefit. Scientists don't often think about demand in shaping their agendas. Vagelos always did.

Guided by these principles, Merck focused on cardiovascular disease, AIDS, cancer, arthritis, Alzheimer's, and osteoporosis. Like all pharmaceutical companies, Merck had dozens of drug candidates in its pipeline. Vagelos successfully narrowed his organization's focus to between six and eight of the highest-potential candidates. He succeeded in getting the organization to focus obsessively on drug projects that addressed the biggest needs, and gave them the critical mass of resources, attention, and emotional energy that they needed to achieve breakthroughs.

The final dimension of Vagelos's approach was a contrarian attitude toward the Food and Drug Administration (FDA), the national agency whose approval was required before new drugs could be brought to market. For most pharmaceutical companies, the FDA was the antagonist, the enemy. Vagelos thought differently: "Let's treat the FDA as a customer—a very important customer."

And Merck did. The new orientation shifted attitudes within Merck. Rather than asking, What do we have to do to get the FDA off our backs with as little trouble as possible? Merck researchers began asking, What information does this important customer need to make their decisions? Then they took whatever steps were required to provide it. Submissions and presentations were overprepared, and FDA approvals began to flow more quickly than ever.

As a result of Vagelos's innovative portfolio management system, Merck produced more blockbuster drugs during his tenure than the next three competing pharmaceutical companies combined (see the table below). By streamlining the process of identifying the most promising projects, emphasizing the importance of attracting and motivating talented people, and turning the FDA approval process into a matter of customer service, Vagelos transformed drug development from a shot-in-the-dark game into a system that produced consistent results.

"Nobody knows anything"? Tell it to Roy Vagelos.

MERCK'S BLOCKBUSTER PORTFOLIO (1978–1993)

Drug	FDA Approval	Condition Treated	Revenue (in Billions, 1993–1998)
Timoptic/XE	1978/1993	Glaucoma	$2.268
Ivermectin	1981*	Parasitic infections	$3.244
Vasotec	1985	High blood pressure	$14.112
Primaxin	1985	Bacterial infections	$3.210
Pepcid	1986	Ulcers and heartburn	$5.882
Mevacor	1987	High cholesterol	$6.996
Prinivil	1987	High blood pressure	$2.735
Prilosec	1989	Acid reflux	$10.001
Zocor	1991	High cholesterol	$14.490
Proscar	1992	Enlarged prostate	$2.175

*Ivermectin is a group of veterinary medications for which FDA approval is not required; 1981 was the year it first went on sale.

After Vagelos's retirement, the system that worked so well for two decades began to experience neglect and decline. One wonders how different the results for demand creation at Merck would have been if that unique system had been protected and continued to evolve.

❐   ❐   ❐

ONE POWERFUL demand-generation system that *has* continued to evolve is that of Kleiner Perkins. Founded in 1972, Kleiner Perkins is the leading venture capital firm in the United States and has achieved enormous success as a demand creator in a very unusual world, that of start-up investing.

Investing in *existing* companies, as everyone knows, is notoriously difficult. Even when companies are mature, markets are well defined, and multiyear track records are available, the vast majority of active investment managers (by some measures as many as 80 percent) fail to match average market returns.

Now imagine a different investment arena—one in which there are no company track records and no well-defined markets, where you must invest in companies that are five to ten years away from selling a single product. During that painfully long trek to market, most companies fail, some spectacularly so. The reasons are innumerable, but four main risks stand out:

- The technology didn't work.
- The management team didn't work.
- The company ran out of money.
- There was no demand for the product.

Venture capital is supposed to be a highly glamorous business. But the fact is that most venture capital firms earn mediocre returns, and even the few successful firms experience results that are frighteningly volatile.

In this strange parallel universe of punishingly low odds and brutally long cycles, Kleiner Perkins stands out. It has returned more than a billion dollars to its investors in each of the last ten years, and its list of major successes (see the table on page 294) looks magical to anyone who understands the harsh realities of the arena in which they operate.

How do they do it?

Many have delved into the history of Kleiner Perkins, and the conventional explanations for their success are intuitive and appealing. Some attribute it largely to the personality of their leading partners. For example, there's John Doerr, who is indeed a fascinating, colorful character. After graduating from Rice University and Harvard Business School, he joined Intel in 1975 as an engineer and project manager, then switched to system sales, an arena in which his powerful drive, aggressiveness, competitive zeal, seemingly endless energy, and penchant for dramatic flourishes rose to the fore. For example, Doerr supposedly once captured a new client for Intel's microprocessors by throwing a *lawn mower* into the deal.

A magazine profile once described Doerr as "a rail-thin man in a rumpled blue blazer, with a lick of hair falling across his forehead, rushing to a conference, simultaneously holding a conversation with three people around him and talking on his cell phone." Toss in the fact that he is widely considered the single most influential figure in the entire world of high-tech venture capital and you have a reasonably accurate portrait.

Doerr has other partners who are just as memorable. There's Ray Lane, former COO and president of Oracle, then the second-largest software company in the world and a famously opinionated, outspoken authority on technological innovation. Lane and Doerr have an ongoing friendly rivalry over who can amass the largest collection of business contacts. At last count, Lane was in the lead with more than six thousand names and numbers, including such outré characters as Olafur Ragnar Grimsson, president of Iceland since 1996.

KLEINER PERKINS'S BLOCKBUSTER PORTFOLIO (1972–2010)

Company	Market Cap (in Billions, 2009)*
Google	$147.0
Genentech	$47.0
Amazon	$36.0
Cerent	$7.3
Electronic Arts	$6.9
Sun Microsystems	$5.9
Netscape	$4.2
Lotus	$3.5
AOL	$2.4
Brio Technology	$0.143
Compaq	$25.0
Intuit	$13.7
LSI	$2.65
Macromedia	$3.4
Quantum	$0.316
Tandem	$3.0

*Several of these companies have been acquired by others: Genentech by Hoffman-LaRoche (2009); Cerent by Cisco Systems (1999); Netscape by AOL (1998); Lotus by IBM (1995); Brio Technology by Hyperion (2003); Compaq by HP (2002); Macromedia by Adobe (2005); and Tandem by Compaq (1997).

Then there's Bill Joy, a famous whiz kid whose many intellectual exploits veer unknowably between the factual and the legendary. He could read at age three and play chess at four, and during oral exams for his PhD degree he improvised a sorting algorithm so brilliant that one of his examiners later compared the experience to "Jesus confounding his elders." Joy later became an awe-inspiring hacker at Berkeley whose exploits earned him a *Fortune* magazine cover story dubbing him "Edison of the Internet," and then, for good measure, he cofounded Sun Microsystems.

Doerr, Lane, and Joy are just three of Kleiner Perkins's thirty-six partners. Celebrity statesmen like former vice president Al Gore, another Kleiner partner, and former secretary of state Colin Powell, a "strategic limited partner," add further luster and clout to this remarkable team.

But the success of Kleiner Perkins is based on more than Doerr's salesmanship, Lane's intelligence, Joy's technical brilliance, or anyone's Rolodex. Others say the key is Kleiner Perkins's brand: They have the best reputation in the world of venture capital, and that means they see all the most promising business plans before anybody else. This theory is intuitive, appealing—and quite misleading.

Yes, Kleiner Perkins does have a strong brand and great deal flow. But all of that is just one aspect, and perhaps the least important aspect, of the fascinating, multifaceted demand creation process that Kleiner Perkins has built.

Kleiner Perkins knows that of the Big Four risks that ventures face—technology, team, finances, and demand—demand is the toughest, and they conduct themselves accordingly. They don't focus on companies, but on market sectors, looking for big break points that will lead to major new explosions of demand. They first looked for those break points in semiconductors, later in the Internet, and today in energy and water.

Kleiner Perkins partners sit on hundreds of boards and interact with thousands of entrepreneurs, and the singular focus of all those interactions is to develop unique insights on how demand will evolve. "We are on the board of everything from Sun to AOL to Excite. As a group, we have developed a sense of how to forecast the future before the market researchers can," says Vinod Khosla, a former partner.

Against that backdrop, they seek out companies that are customer-centric. John Doerr explains what convinced him of the enormous potential in the then-nascent financial software company called Intuit: "At the first Intuit board meeting I attended, I was surprised: more than half the meeting took place at Intuit's tech support center, listening to tech reps answer customers' product questions and fix their problems. Founder Scott Cook's uniquely intense focus on happy customers and first-hand customer feedback impresses me to this day."

Doerr shares our awareness of how rare it is for company leaders to have the guts to talk to customers and to respond to the uncomfortable truths they learn. Scott Cook not only listened to customers, but brought board members into the process, completely changing the nature of the conversation that took place at the board level. For Doerr, this was a crucial clue that *this* company was on the verge of creating significant new demand.

Being obsessed with demand is a great beginning. The next step is to generate the maximum number of good ideas to address that demand. The process begins by listening to the thousands of voices in Kleiner's network. It then quickly goes "outbound." Kleiner partners scour the nation's leading universities, looking for the better idea, and not just waiting for referrals but wearing out shoe leather like investigative reporters or peristent detectives. Partners like Doerr, Ray Lane, and Brook Byers spend enormous amounts of time prowling university labs: Doerr focuses on Stanford, Lane on Carnegie Mellon, and Byers on the University of California at San Francisco. They use the connections they make to learn about innovative research projects, build long-term relationships with top scientists, and encourage collaboration and connection among the very brightest.

The shoe leather strategy extends past the conventional university sources and beyond national borders. In support of their energy investments, Kleiner Perkins partners have found worthy ideas not just in Massachusetts, Florida, Texas, Pennsylvania, New York, New Jersey, and Georgia, but also in Israel, Germany, and China.

Referrals play their part. Doerr sees them as a guarantor of quality:

> Look, this is not a matter of odds, like a lottery. It's a matter of quality. Here's a key: Kleiner Perkins has invested in over 250 ventures. In almost every case, the project was referred to the partnership by someone—a CEO, an engineer, a lawyer, friend, or another venture capitalist—known to both the founders and our partnership.

So placing a hundred bets may be necessary—but they're not blind bets, like buying a hundred lottery tickets and hoping for the best. The firm applies a set of very tough, demanding criteria before an idea passes the entrance exam to Kleiner Perkins's rarefied world of funding. The overall approach is straightforward:

$$\begin{matrix} \text{Maximum number of} \\ \text{high-quality ideas} \end{matrix} \quad \times \quad \begin{matrix} \text{Maximum} \\ \text{selectivity} \end{matrix} \quad = \quad \text{Best odds}$$

For example, in evaluating software investments, here are the admissions criteria Kleiner Perkins uses to rate a potential product:

- Instant value to customers—solve a problem or create value with the first use
- Viral adoption—pull, not push. No direct sales force required
- Minimum IT footprint, preferably none. Hosted SaaS ["Software as a Service"] is best.
- Simple, intuitive user experience—no training required
- Personalized user experience—customizable
- Easy configuration based on application or usage templates
- Context aware—adjust to location, groups, preferences, devices, etc.

The rigor and clarity of these criteria are a bit reminiscent of the simplicity and power of Warren Buffett's investment criteria. He looks for a business to invest in (a) that sells a product for a dollar, (b) that costs a penny, (c) for which the demand lasts forever, (d) that has a huge moat surrounding it, and (e) that has a great management team.

Lots of software innovations can meet two, three, or four of Kleiner Perkins's criteria. Meeting all seven is almost impossible. And that's the point. Out of a hundred high-quality ideas in an emerging market sector, there may be just one really, really good one. *That's* the one that gets the Kleiner Perkins investment—or, if the idea is promising enough, multiple investments. For example, Kleiner Perkins currently has three investments in green auto technologies, three in fuel cells, five in solar photovoltaic systems, and multiple investments behind batteries and biofuels. After all, even if the demand is real (as Kleiner Perkins believes it is), the technology, the management team, or the financing may still fail. Doubling down on the bets that pass the most rigorous scrutiny is another key component of the Kleiner Perkins system.

The final piece of the puzzle may be the most unique. It's not enough to maximize the ideas and maximize the selectivity. Kleiner Perkins also excels at managing the upside potential of every investment it makes. The firm adds value to its investments through various kinds of "golden interventions." It may help a company find the right executive—the perfect marketing director, technology officer, financial expert, or CEO to help lift the company's performance to the next level. It may provide connections to important customers (including, perhaps, other Kleiner Perkins ventures). When an unexpected technical problem arises on the path from concept to market, a Kleiner Perkins partner may be able to suggest experts from other firms who have wrestled similar problems into submission. Kleiner Perkins even invested in the company Visible Path partly because its social networking tools could be used to help Kleiner Perkins's network of fledgling firms stay connected with one another, and ultimately help them reach full flight potential.

The Kleiner system continues to evolve. If there is a great idea but no company that embodies it, Kleiner partners believe that "our job is to go out and help create one." And they do. Led by partner Bill Joy, Kleiner Perkins has constructed a "Map of Grand Challenges"—an enormous matrix of some forty squares reflecting major opportunities for future demand growth in areas like energy storage, water, electricity generation, transportation, and others. There are many blank spots on the map, denoting ideas that should be possible and could generate huge positive changes in the market. The map has one purpose: to help Kleiner Perkins partners know what to look for. As John Doerr says, "I don't think anyone has ever really done venture capital this way."

That constant pursuit of a different and better way has generated a unique set of results. Collectively, companies in the Kleiner Perkins portfolio have created more than 250,000 jobs, generated more than $100 billion in revenue, and produced $650 billion in market capitalization. That's an extraordinary record of new demand creation emerging from the financial and creative backing of a single firm with a unique modus operandi.

❐   ❐   ❐

AS WE'VE SEEN, every portfolio master, from John Lasseter to Roy Vagelos to John Doerr, has developed a unique system for creating demand through successful launch of many products over time. But all these systems have several key dimensions in common.

They all work to maximize the flow of high-quality product ideas, whether by making short experimental films, by searching for promising enzymes to target, or by seeking out rapidly evolving market sectors with high potential for future demand. Then, having created a rich collection of product candidates, they apply an extreme degree of selectivity, as with Pixar's one-blockbuster-per-year production strategy, Merck's focus on the top six to eight drug candidates, or Kleiner Perkins's obsession with "quality" rather than "lottery."

The lesson for organizations interested in consistent, large-scale demand creation is the need to focus on two simple questions: What's the overall size and quality of our portfolio of ideas? and, How can we do a better job of choosing the best candidates from our portfolio to invest in?

Notice how radically this mind-set differs from the way most of us think. Living in a world where Goldman's Law is assumed, most of us deal with unknowability by saying, Success is a lottery, a matter of placing a lot of bets; you have to take high risks to get high returns.

Great demand creators think differently. They think not lottery, but quality. They don't want to place a bet—they want to make every swing count: each film, each drug, each investment. They play the portfolio process the way Warren Buffett plays the investment process, with his twenty-investment punch card; or the way Ted Williams played baseball, batting .400 by letting the bad pitches go by and swinging only when the ball crossed his sweet spot.

Many organizations could benefit from the emergence of a John Lasseter, a Roy Vagelos, or a John Doerr. But achieving consistent demand isn't a matter of hoping for the emergence of a lone genius with a "magic touch" for picking or creating winners. Rather, it's about creating a mind-set and a system. It might begin by applying a customized version of the general methods illustrated by Lasseter, Vagelos, and Doerr. But in the end, each organization needs to develop its own unique set of techniques.

The list of serial demand creators—organizations with ten or more blockbuster successes in a row—is not limited to these three exceptional firms. Disney did it twice, in the 1940s and the 1980s. Pfizer did it in the 1990s, and Toyota and Apple are each halfway there. They all had systems with elements we can emulate.

Others have invented their own techniques to achieve comparable results. TV and film producer Jerry Bruckheimer, whose products have generated a cumulative $13 billion in revenues, worked with Don Simpson, his late coproducer, to create his own system for developing films that audiences would love. One of the most important elements of the system? Watching the audience. Bruckheimer faces *away* from the movie screen, watching the audience as they laugh, cry, roll their eyes, drift off, or sit on the edge of their seats. You can ask people what they like and don't like, but their answers rarely provide the full truth; watching them intently can often tell you much more.

"The guts to talk to customers" is important. Bruckheimer goes further—he has the guts to *watch* customers, too.

Practically every demand creator can benefit from lessons like these—and that includes not just the corporate manager or the technology entrepreneur but the small business owner who dreams of opening not just one or two new stores but a dozen scattered across three counties, the community theater manager who hopes to mount a hit show every season for the next decade, and the app developer who aspires to produce a string of hits.

If they focus on developing a mind-set, culture, and system centered on improving the quality of their portfolio and then rigorously choosing and supporting the best potential winners, all these aspiring demand creators will have a good shot at defying Goldman's Law and creating powerful new streams of demand—not just once or twice, but repeatedly, over a period of decades.

9.
The Biggest Spark
Scientific Discovery and the Future of Demand

AVING LOOKED BACK at many of the great demand-creation achievements of the last two decades, we return to the question with which we started: Where will *tomorrow's* demand come from?

We have no crystal ball. But a crucial clue lies in the obvious yet easy-to-overlook fact that hassles come in all sizes.

Some hassles are small-scale, like the hassles of video rental that Reed Hastings fixed through Netflix, or the difficulty of finding a decent lunch in downtown London that spurred Julian Metcalfe to found Pret A Manger.

But other hassles are large-scale—national or global in scope, persistent, and exacting a heavy toll in money, time, energy, even human lives. The dysfunctions of the U.S. health care system that CareMore is striving to remedy and the failure of American schools to properly educate at-risk youth that Teach For America seeks to overcome are two current examples.

Those who fix small hassles climb the foothills of demand. They make life better in modest ways for thousands or millions of people, and often build successful organizations in the process.

But those who fix giant hassles are the demand equivalents of Edmund Hillary and Tenzing Norgay. They conquer the Himalayas of demand, performing seemingly impossible feats that radically improve life for entire societies and often founding industries that drive economic growth for decades.

But are there any unscaled Everests of demand on today's horizon—or, as some believe, have all the big opportunities for demand creation already been tapped?

One answer comes from a little-known yet highly knowledge-able source.

In 2008, the National Academy of Engineering polled 25,000 engineers to create a list of what they dubbed the Grand Challenges of the twenty-first century. In effect, they were seeking the world's greatest unsolved scientific and technical problems—the biggest global hassles from which spring countless everyday hassles (money-wasters, time-wasters, risk-increasers, and many more). The top four-teen vote-getters in the academy's poll:

1. Make solar energy economical
2. Provide energy from fusion
3. Provide access to clean water
4. Reverse-engineer the brain
5. Advance personalized learning
6. Develop carbon sequestration methods
7. Engineer the tools of scientific discovery
8. Restore and improve urban infrastructure
9. Advance health informatics
10. Prevent nuclear terror
11. Engineer better medicines
12. Enhance virtual reality
13. Manage the nitrogen cycle
14. Secure cyberspace

A serious effort to solve any one of these problems would create hundreds or thousands of new scientific and technological concepts. Winnowed down through the pressure of competition and the challenge of prototype development, the best of these ideas could lead to the development of major new industries that would generate both vast new demand and the high-income jobs to pay for it.

Most important, such breakthroughs would help reduce the hassles faced by hundreds of millions of people and entire societies around the world—hassles ranging from the mundane (unstable gas prices, delayed medical diagnoses, identity theft) to the catastrophic ("water wars" driven by climate change, global pandemics, cyberterrorism).

The fact is that scientific and technological innovation is the foundation of demand creation. Brilliant demand creators need brilliant material to work with. You can't connect the dots if the dots aren't there in the first place.

That's why the greatest surges of demand, those that play out over decades and leave vast new industries and huge explosions of economic activity in their wake, originate in fundamental scientific discoveries and technological breakthroughs.

Which leads to yet another crucial question: How do such discoveries and breakthroughs actually happen? The answers aren't obvious. But getting them right will be essential if our world is to enjoy the kind of economic growth and improvement in living standards we all want in the decades to come.

❑   ❑   ❑

A LOT WAS happening in the postwar world on July 1, 1948, as reflected in the headlines from page one of the *New York Times*. "Last British Unit Leaves Palestine," announced one story. (The newly proclaimed state of Israel was already engaged in its first war for independence and survival.) "Truman Sets Feb. 1 As 'Freedom Day,'" declared another. (The advent of the Cold War had created demand for new patriotic holidays to promote the benefits of democracy.) "Shift at Midnight" described the first-ever increase in the New York City subway fare—from the traditional nickel all the way to a dime. (By the end of 2010, a ride would cost you $2.50.)

But, in retrospect, the biggest news story of the day was nowhere on the front page. Buried on page 46, at the bottom of a column headed "The News of Radio—Two New Shows on CBS Will Replace 'Radio Theatre' During the Summer," it read:

> A device called a transistor, which has several applications in radio where a vacuum tube ordinarily is employed, was demonstrated for the first time yesterday at Bell Telephone Laboratories, 463 West Street.
>
> The device was demonstrated in a radio receiver, which contained none of the conventional tubes. It also was shown in a telephone system and in a television unit controlled by a receiver on a lower floor. In each case the transistor was employed as an amplifier, although it is claimed that it also can be used as an oscillator in that it will create and send radio waves.

The birth announcement was modest, but the infant technology would transform what we as consumers would demand in the next six decades. By the mid-fifties, transistors would be employed to manufacture pocket-sized radios that every teenager craved—first by a Dallas company called Texas Instruments, then by a little-known Japanese firm named Sony. In the 1960s, Sony began building color TV sets using transistors, marking the start of the slow decline of the U.S. electronics industry and the rise of Japan to global economic prominence. Scientists soon learned to pack hundreds, then thousands and millions of transistors onto tiny slivers of silicon called integrated circuits; by 1971, the functions of an entire array of such circuits were combined in the first microprocessors. In the decades that followed, as the powers of these silicon chips multiplied, the size and cost of information technology were steadily reduced, enabling a cascading series of new developments—electronic calculators, personal computers, cellular telephony, the Internet. The "several applications in radio" referred to by the *Times* turned into millions of applications whose larger impacts—technological, economic, social—are still unfolding.

It's understandable that the newspaper editors misgauged the significance of their first glimpse of the transistor. The breakthrough emerged not from a massive government program like the Manhattan Project that produced the atomic bomb, but rather from the obscure tinkerings of a handful of scientists and engineers working in a corner of Bell Labs they'd playfully dubbed "Hell's Bells Laboratory."

A brilliant young theoretician named William Shockley, assigned the task of building on wartime semiconductor research that had led to the development of radar, had assembled a team that included experimental physicist Walter Brattain and theoretical physicist John Bardeen, recruited from the University of Minnesota. When Shockley's first attempt to build a "semiconductor amplifier" to replace the bulky and unreliable glass vacuum tubes failed, he assigned Brattain and Bardeen to figure out why.

They spent two years on the project. Working with razor blades, tape, and soldering irons on an ordinary workbench in a small New Jersey lab, they built tiny gadgets using metal plates thinly coated with silicon and cylinders made of various metals; they tried dunking the devices in tubs of water to see if moisture would improve the signal amplification. Finally, in December 1947, Bardeen noticed that a crystal layer on the surface of the unit was impeding the flow of electrons. Altering their latest experimental design, he and Brattain built a one-inch device using strips of gold foil on a plastic triangle, connected by copper wires to a battery and pressed down by hand to make contact with a slab of germanium. They called it a "point-contact transistor," and it succeeded in boosting an electrical signal almost a hundred times.

When Brattain and Bardeen informed Shockley of their breakthrough, he was delighted—and startled to find himself consumed by jealousy. As he later recalled, "I experienced frustration that my personal efforts, started more than eight years before, had not resulted in a significant inventive contribution of my own."

The ego blow spurred Shockley to a creative response. He holed himself up in a hotel room in Chicago for four weeks with pens and pads of paper, skipping the New Year's Eve parties his colleagues were attending between sessions of a scientific conference. He emerged with the design for an improved device that was more rugged and easier to manufacture than Brattain and Bardeen's version. It was this transistor that Bell Labs debuted before a handful of reporters on June 30, 1948, that won a Nobel Prize in physics for all three scientists in 1956, and that laid the foundation for the computer age.

In time, the fathers of the transistor parted ways. Brattain and Bardeen moved on to academia; Bardeen won a second Nobel Prize for his work on superconductivity at the University of Illinois. Shockley left Bell Labs to found Shockley Semiconductor in his hometown of Palo Alto, California—the first electronics firm in a sleepy apricot-growing region that would soon become known as Silicon Valley. Scientists and engineers Shockley hired eventually launched their own firms, including Fairchild Semiconductor and Intel.

As we've discovered, there are always many unseen factors that drive the creation of demand. But the single greatest factor is the kind of scientific discovery that leads to the development of new industries, simultaneously creating demand for new products and the high-income jobs to pay for them. From television to compact discs, calculators to cell phones, computers to the Internet, Shockley's little baby has now spawned untold offspring, creating thousands of companies, tens of millions of jobs in virtually every country on earth, and trillions of dollars' worth of demand.

Today, more than sixty years later, the fourth- and fifth-generation offspring of Shockley's baby are continuing to stimulate new forms of demand around the world, producing benefits the Bell Labs pioneers could never have envisioned.

In the introduction, we described the Nokia 1100, the world's bestselling consumer electronics device. It's a cheap, rugged, versatile cell phone that is transforming life for tens of millions of rural people in India, nearly half of whom now have access to mobile

telephony. In the process, cell phone service itself is being rein-
vented, enhanced by functions for addressing many of the most
pressing problems facing the Indian farmer. Cell phones like the
Nokia 1100 are becoming multifaceted business tools for rural Indians, providing dozens of ways for them to overcome the hassles of
doing business in the developing world and improve their chances
of escaping poverty.

The impact on an Indian farmer can be remarkable, as a January
2009 study by agricultural researchers revealed. One farmer surveyed,
identified only as Mr. Jagdish, raises *gwar*, a grain used as livestock
fodder, in a village in Rajasthan near the Pakistani border. Jagdish
attributes a 25 percent increase in his annual earnings to the cultivation practices he learned from his IKSL cell phone feed. A group
of flower cultivators in Maharashtra in central India has begun using
daily market reports to adjust the quantity of perishable blooms they
transport to town, thereby reducing waste and maximizing the value
of their crops.

Besides having created the quintessential cell phones for the
developing world—sturdy, simple, inexpensive wedges of plastic
with a hundred well-designed functions—Nokia is vigorously supporting the development of information services like these, thereby
expanding the usefulness of its phones for rural customers.

Nokia Life Tools, for example, includes an array of applications
designed to appeal to people in the developing world. Created in
collaboration with Reuters, it offers services like weather reports,
market prices for various commodities and agricultural inputs (like
seeds, fertilizers, and pesticides), English-language lessons, test-prep
programs for students, and even selective entertainment functions
such as horoscopes, cricket scores, and ring tone downloads.

Mail on Ovi is another Nokia breakthrough. It's an e-mail application based on Ovi, Nokia's broad-based Web-services portal (the
company's answer to Apple's iTunes Store). Mail on Ovi lets users of
Internet-enabled cell phones like the Nokia Classic 2323 set up and

use an e-mail account without access to a computer. And while the 2323, currently priced at around $50, may be a trifle pricey for the typical Indian farmer, it fits nicely into the multiple-owner cell phone model that many in the developing world practice.

Nokia is also investing in Obopay, a mobile-phone cash-transfer system that lets mobile phone users access bank accounts, pay bills, borrow money, and repay loans electronically. Based in Redwood City, California, Obopay operates in India and uses cell phone software or text-messaging programs to transfer funds from one account to another, collecting a small usage fee for each transaction.

Meanwhile, Nokia continues to innovate around the phone itself. One methodology has been the creation of what the company calls Open Studios in shantytowns in Mumbai (India), Rio de Janeiro (Brazil), and Accra (Ghana), where users are invited to work with Nokia designers to create their own concepts for the ideal mobile phone. More than two hundred local residents have produced unique phone designs, proposing new features that include a sensor to test water quality and a screen that flashes the word "Peace" as a way of defusing conflicts.

The information revolution in Indian farming has led to a whole new layer of demand whose origins can be traced back to Shockley's invention. Demand for cell phones, of course—but also demand for cars, schooling, better houses, improved diets, and all the other benefits of middle-class life that India's newly empowered farmers are increasingly able to afford.

The question for today—more than sixty years after Shockley's breakthrough—is this: What institutions in contemporary society are fostering the culture of discovery that will lead to the *next* transistor?

◻   ◻   ◻

NOT SO LONG AGO, the core skill of the United States was new industry creation. And at the same time—not coincidentally—the country boasted the world's largest and fastest-growing economy. During the

1920s, 1930s, 1940s, 1950s, and 1960s, scientific and technological breakthroughs from the United States produced a steady stream of extraordinary new industries and products. These industries stimulated consumer demand and, by providing high-paying jobs, enabled it.

That stream of basic discoveries was produced not mainly by self-funded geniuses in backyard garages but rather by a quite unusual and focused machine for discovery and innovation—a network of institutions deliberately founded, organized, and run for the purpose of fueling scientific and technological insight. Including such legendary institutions as Bell Labs, Xerox PARC, RCA Laboratories, DARPA, and others, this network consisted of public, private, nonprofit, and for-profit efforts working in combination. Programs with clear commercial potential were supported alongside efforts at "pure science," with the two streams resonating with and feeding off each other. This discovery and innovation machine existed because of a business and political culture that supported invention independent of immediate practical applications, as being "good for the country."

The contributions these institutions made to science, technology, and the economy—including the creation of millions of high-paying jobs and entire industries—are both enormous and difficult to quantify.

Consider Bell Labs, for example. Founded in New York City in 1925 under the leadership of research director Frank B. Jewett as a joint venture of American Telephone & Telegraph and Western Electric to develop equipment for the Bell System telephone companies, the labs grew to include facilities in New Jersey, the Chicago area, and several other locations. Supporting both pure scientific research and technological developments with immediate applications to telecommunications, Bell Labs spawned or supported a startling number of scientific breakthroughs that played pivotal roles in the history of twentieth-century technology and that created entire new industries with millions of high-paying jobs. The invention of the transistor by Shockley, Bardeen, and Brattain is only the most dramatic and important example. Some others:

- The first public demonstration of fax transmission (1925)
- Invention of the first synchronous-sound movie system (1926)
- First transmission of stereo signals (1933)
- First electronic speech synthesizer (1937)
- Research underpinning the development of the photovoltaic cell (1941)
- First description of the laser (1958)
- Development of metal oxide semiconductor field-effect transistor, basis for the large-scale integrated circuits that make modern IT possible (1960)
- Creation of the UNIX operating system (1969)
- Development of cellular network technology for cellular telephony (late 1960s to 1971)
- Creation of C programming language (1973)

Seven Nobel Prizes in physics were awarded for work completed at Bell Labs. And the number of companies and entire industries built on the foundations laid at Bell Labs is almost incalculable.

However, over the last two decades, funding and staffing of Bell Labs has been drastically reduced. The number of researchers has fallen from 3,400 to fewer than 1,000. And in August 2008, its parent company, Alcatel-Lucent, announced it would be pulling out of some of its last remaining areas of basic science—material physics and semiconductor research—to focus on projects that promise more immediate payoffs.

Financial pressures made this decision inevitable. But it cost our economic system a unique asset whose value is literally incalculable, since pure scientific research often has long-term benefits that are impossible to predict.

Here's one example. In 1948, Bell Labs scientist Claude Shannon, who is widely acknowledged today as the founder of modern information theory, published his paper "A Mathematical Theory of Communication" in the *Bell System Technical Journal*. At the time, it was a piece of "pure science," with no obvious or immediate practical payoff. But years later, physicists applying Shannon's ideas to the mathematics of data transmission discovered ways of sending digital information at ultrafast speeds over copper wires, making DSL connections possible. Today those connections bring high-speed Internet service into 160 million homes.

Thus the downsizing of Bell Labs isn't simply a loss for scientists interested in knowledge for its own sake. It eliminates one powerful mechanism for pursuing new concepts whose potential practical benefit we will never know.

In similar fashion, the other great U.S. research institutions of the twentieth century, such as RCA, DARPA, and PARC, have also been downsized and redirected.

Formed in 1935 and based since 1942 in Princeton, New Jersey, RCA Labs (formally known as the David Sarnoff Research Center) was even more focused on wireless communication than Bell Labs. RCA Labs helped to perfect the science of black-and-white TV and laid the technical foundations for both the color television broadcast network and its system components. This new industry generated enormous demand and millions of jobs in programming, advertising, manufacturing, and TV station operation. RCA Labs went on to make discoveries that enabled space communication, satellites, disc recording, low-power MOSFET and CMOS technology, liquid crystal displays, and a host of other breakthroughs.

RCA Labs differed from its rivals in one fundamental way. Its growth was driven by David Sarnoff, a tough-minded leader who played enormous roles in the creation of a series of major twentieth-century industries. Way back in November 1916, a twenty-five-year-old Sarnoff had proposed to his boss, E. J. Nally of the Marconi Wireless Telegraph Company Ltd., that radio broadcasting of music, news, and sports would one day entertain and inform millions, and urged that Marconi quickly get into the business of manufacturing "radio music boxes." When Marconi rejected the idea, Sarnoff convinced General Electric to fund the development of a prototype through its investment in RCA. In 1921, he helped arrange for the live broadcast of the Dempsey-Carpentier heavyweight championship fight, which drew hundreds of thousands of listeners. It was an early indication that radio would soon become a powerful force in sports and entertainment, a trend that helped propel Sarnoff to the presidency of RCA in 1923.

Sarnoff deeply believed in the long-term value of basic science, even when developed by a single company. Sarnoff bid for government contracts to defray costs and pursued patenting and licensing deals aggressively. This combination of moves generated powerful revenue streams that helped cover the direct costs of the basic science work, and the huge industry wins in the manufacturing of TV components and other products were all upside. (We wonder what the returns might have been if this business model of for-profit basic research had been applied at Bell Labs or at Xerox PARC.)

Sarnoff long retained his visionary grasp of the power of technology. In the mid-fifties he predicted that biotechnology, aquaculture, and computers would eventually transform the world. In the mid-1970s, even after Sarnoff's retirement in 1970, RCA Labs proudly announced it was generating as many patents as the larger Bell Labs. But a gradual decline had already begun. In 1986 RCA was sold to GE, which donated RCA Labs to SRI International.

The Defense Advanced Research Projects Agency (DARPA) was originally launched in 1958 as a response to the Soviet launch of Sputnik, the first artificial satellite. DARPA's focus was primarily on projects that could meet the demands of the military sector, but those demands were defined as broadly as possible—fortunately for the nation and the world.

Under the leadership of J. C. R. Licklider, the first director of IT research at DARPA, the agency (either directly or through programs it funded and promoted) helped launch an amazing array of information technologies we now take for granted, including such breakthrough inventions as time-sharing, computer graphics, microprocessors, very large-scale integration (VLSI) design, RISC processing, parallel computing, and local area networks.

Countless commercial applications can be traced directly to DARPA projects. A small example: The Sun Microsystems workstation would not have existed except for half a dozen major technologies developed at universities and companies that were funded and supervised by DARPA. And a huge example: DARPA's interagency information-sharing network laid the foundation for the Internet, which exploded into a full-blown industry around 1995—the last major new industry created in the United States, now a full decade and a half ago.

Today, DARPA's focus and methods have changed dramatically. Partly in response to the trauma of 9/11, DARPA has shifted its emphasis from broad-based scientific inquiry to projects with short-term military applications. Funding has been moved from universities to military contractors; publicly available research designed to spur further advances by others in the field has given way to classified programs conducted in secrecy.

PARC, Xerox's Palo Alto Research Center—the original gestation place for the technology that ultimately gave rise to E Ink, the Kindle, and a growing array of related products—offers another, somewhat different example of the challenges now facing America's discovery and innovation machine.

In the 1970s, PARC thrived thanks to generous funding by its corporate founder and sponsor, as well as a hands-off philosophy that encouraged independent, farsighted work regardless of immediate applications. Note that PARC was established in 1970 some three thousand miles away from Xerox's headquarters in Connecticut—a move that both symbolically and practically emphasized its freedom to establish its own direction.

In its heyday, PARC employed some 280 researchers. It was a powerful magnet for many of the most brilliant and creative minds in its fields. And as at Bell Labs, the discoveries and breakthroughs made at PARC fed on one another, creating a uniquely valuable upward spiral of creativity and innovation. Fueled by the extraordinary talent that had grown up doing DARPA projects in the 1960s, PARC produced perhaps the greatest set of discoveries in the shortest time of any innovation engine in history: the graphical user interface, the personal computer, the Ethernet, WYSIWYG (what-you-see-is-what-you-get) design software, laser printing, and many others.

Ultimately, through the midwifery of Steve Jobs, Bill Gates, and the Silicon Valley venture capital community, these discoveries produced a multidimensional demand explosion even greater than that of the color TV. And they simultaneously produced a high-income explosion (in the millions of high-paying jobs) that helped pay for the demand unleashed by the PC revolution.

Today, the number of researchers at PARC is about 165. The focused profile and business goals of today's PARC typify the fate of America's once-enormous, well-funded research institutions. Although smaller versions of the great industrial labs continue to operate, the gigantic research infrastructure filled with freewheeling, visionary scientists has been dramatically reduced.

◻   ◻   ◻

THE DECLINE OF the twentieth-century discovery engines forces the question: Who is going to produce the scientific breakthroughs that will create the new industries on which *tomorrow's* demand will be based?

The hopeful news: The creative spark once embodied in places like Bell Labs still burns—on a smaller scale, but as intensely as ever—at a handful of institutions that are pioneering new approaches to scientific discovery and technological innovation.

The first is a twenty-first-century microcosm of Bell Labs—a corporate-sponsored research institution that is focused not on projects with obvious commercial viability and short-term payoff but on open-ended exploration of diverse technological challenges.

One of its proudest creations: ASIMO, a humanoid robot that boasts an amazing array of capabilities. ASIMO, whose name refers not to Isaac Asimov (the science fiction writer whose "Three Laws of Robotics" have inspired generations of futurists) but rather stands for Advanced Step in Innovative Mobility, can walk, turn, stop, and climb stairs; push a cart or carry a tray; switch on a light or open a door; and detect moving objects and avoid obstacles. ASIMO can even recognize facial expressions and obey spoken commands. First unveiled in 2002, and still the world's most advanced humanoid robot, ASIMO has become an international traveler and celebrity, seen on the slopes in Switzerland, riding in the Rose Bowl parade, and hobnobbing with Hollywood royalty at Sundance.

You might think that ASIMO is the natural product of playful PhDs in some Silicon Valley start-up. But ASIMO was invented by the Honda Research Institute (HRI), a division of the automaker with facilities in the United States, Japan, and Europe. Why would a car company be involved in such a project? And what does this have to do with demand?

As for the first question: We think of Honda as a car company, but it's always been an engine company, producing engines for everything from lawn mowers to ultralight jets. Honda's past has been largely shaped by the century-old motorcycle and automobile industries, but its future (like everyone's) has yet to be shaped. That helps to explain how Honda got into the robot business—as a way to explore some of the emerging technologies that may foster the next great industry through which Honda hopes to create large-scale new demand.

Driven in part by Honda's intense interest in mobility, the company's engineers set out in 1986 to create a walking robot that could duplicate the complexities of human motion. They went to zoos to study how animals walked; they observed the structure and function of beetle legs, and compared them to the joints in human limbs.

Honda's first complete humanoid robot, P1, had the build of an NFL lineman—six foot, two inches tall and 386 pounds, much of the weight due to a built-in backpack that held wiring and a large battery. Subsequent models became increasingly svelte and graceful. ASIMO himself—the robot boy king—is a petite four foot three and 119 pounds, which allows him to walk at a speedy 3.7 miles per hour. There are around a hundred ASIMO robots in the world today, demonstrating their capabilities in research settings and serving as ambassadors for Honda.

Basic research has deep roots in the culture of Honda. Company founder Soichiro Honda once observed that "the true value of research and development lies in the exploration of uncharted waters," and historically each of Honda's CEOs has come from the company's R&D division. Honda's current president and CEO, Takanobu Ito, for example, who serves simultaneously as director of R&D, was initially attracted to Honda because of its ambitious research in aviation and robotics.

Today the Honda Research Institute focuses on open-ended exploration of diverse technological challenges, with the explicit goal of "contributing to society." Top researchers are recruited and given the resources to pursue their own projects, even if they have no direct value to the corporation's current product line—or bottom line. At HRI, it's the future that counts.

And HRI's open-ended research has led to a number of new businesses for Honda, through such diverse innovations as high-yield rice genes, powerful fuel cells, and the design for a business jet whose fuselage is made of composite plastics lighter than aluminum. Honda was even once named the top organic soybean producer in Ohio, a business it entered partly to fill containers rather than ship empties back to Japan after delivering cars to the United

States. That led them into a business selling fermented soybeans that help dissolve blood clots.

As these examples illustrate, basic research is not a straight-line process. Scientists look for A, but find B—and in the process they make breakthrough C, which pays off in both societal benefits and corporate profits. It's the same zigzag model we've seen since Louis Pasteur's search for a way to stop milk-borne diseases led to theories about the immune system and the technology of vaccination.

In similar fashion, ASIMO's systems for monitoring and controlling robotic movements have yielded technologies now being used in developing Honda's Walk Assist devices to improve the mobility of people who are elderly, frail, or disabled, such as hip/leg pads that respond to signals from the walker to provide support as needed. Just count the number of people over the age of seventy-five, and you can begin to sense the magnitude of the potential.

ASIMO also spawned DiGORO, a robot that learns how to clean and keep house by imitating human movements glimpsed through a camera on its head. And back in the auto industry, ASIMO technology has also led to Honda's Lane Keeping Assist System, which uses cameras and steering controls to help keep cars from drifting.

Thus ASIMO and the other projects under way at HRI have the potential to solve consumer hassles and human problems on a global scale—and to unlock a series of huge streams of twenty-first-century demand for Honda.

A MULTINATIONAL CORPORATION that invests in basic science is an echo of the glory days of Bell Labs and RCA Labs—but it's not the only effective discovery-producing model for the twenty-first century. A second is the "demo or die" research model exemplified by the famed MIT Media Lab.

The Media Lab is a scene of marginally controlled chaos, with hundreds of research projects visible from multiple vantage points in a glimmering new glass building. As you take in the scene, someone whizzes by on a GreenWheel, an electric bike with an integrated electric motor and battery in the wheel hub designed to overcome hills and travel longer distances, making cycling accessible to those who normally would not ride a bike. A couple of students nearby are tinkering with a foldable electric motor scooter called the Robo Scooter, below a huge photo of a prototype CityCar, a stackable, foldable two-passenger vehicle designed for shared use in dense urban areas. These vehicles are designed for a new use model called Mobility on Demand, which places electric vehicles at charging stations throughout the city. Users simply walk up to the closest charging station, swipe an access card, and drive to any other station.

Ryan Chin, a PhD student, explains: "We design all kinds of urban mobility devices to respond to the extreme density in today's cities. The main problem is a last-mile, first-mile problem. To get to the train from your house, or from the train to your destination, is a problem. That's why people drive: access to public transit is just too inconvenient and inflexible. But Mobility on Demand systems will begin to solve that."

As described by William Mitchell, the late dean of the MIT School of Architecture and Planning, and head of the Media Lab's Smart Cities research group, the approach to innovation is holistic, with the CityCar representing the confluence of four big ideas: the transformation of vehicles from internal combustion to electric-drive; the use of the Internet to enable vehicles to process enormous amounts of data; the integration of vehicles with smart electric grids that use renewable energy; and the creation of real-time systems with dynamically priced markets for electricity, road space, parking space, and shared-use vehicles. The nurturing of such high-quality, big-picture ideas in which demand creators can play is a hallmark of the Media Lab.

Every great lab has a distinctive culture. In the Media Lab's new glass building, researchers working on a range of projects, including cars, robots, biomechatronic limbs, hyperinstruments, and early

education projects can all watch and interact with one another—
a "fish-scale model" of overlapping disciplines that reinforces the mul-
tidisciplinary nature of the lab.

Considering its relatively small size—an approximately $35
million operating budget supporting some 40 faculty members, senior researchers, and visiting scholars, and close to 140 graduate
students—the lab's output is prodigious and broad. In twenty-five
years, more than eighty start-up companies have been spun out of
it. The lab's E Ink spin-off (1997), for example, is the key to legible,
low-power-consumption e-readers. One Laptop per Child, a Media
Lab spin-off, was the spark that inspired ASUSTeK's Eee netbook.
Another spin-off, Sense Networks, uses cell phone data to map the
real world, much as Google indexes the Internet. Harmonix (the
music technology behind Rock Band video games) and TagSense
(RFID and wireless sensing) also came from the lab. Other products and projects have been codeveloped with industry, including
WebFountain, an architecture for text analysis of billions of pages
for IBM, and wireless mesh networks for Nortel.

Will any of these innovations become the basis for a major new
industry creating millions of jobs? It's too soon to tell, but the Media
Lab is focused on questions that lead them in that direction.

"The Media Lab is looking at the forces that will transform society over the next ten years," says Frank Moss, director of the lab from
2005 to 2011. "Whether the research is called science or engineering,
applied or pure, it does not matter to us. The question is: Can it
lead to something important that will affect people and society?
The business model for innovation in the U.S. is broken. What
we have here is the bones of a new way of thinking. Research at
the Media Lab is highly creative but finds its way into the world via
industry."

The next frontier for the lab is creating stronger connections
and synchronization among humans, digital machines, and the real
world. The more than 350 projects currently in progress include

cars that sense their environment and one another to provide real-time data about traffic patterns, smart prosthetics that can read social-emotional cues, and interactive wallpaper that allows you to control your environment—light a lamp, play a tune, control your toaster. Then there's SixthSense, a wearable, gestural interface device that turns any physical object into a kind of touch-screen computer: to take a picture, frame a camera with your fingers; to check the time, draw a circle on your wrist; outline an "@" symbol, and you are shown your e-mail.

The Media Lab is, in many ways, the antithesis of a corporate R&D lab. It focuses on human needs, but has no blinders—no time constraints or deadlines, no shareholders to please. It celebrates openness and collaboration between different disciplines and entities. But it winnows ideas quickly because of the emphasis on testing concepts through prototype building. The discoveries that work find their way into the world, with E Ink as exhibit A.

A would-be demand creator looking for a wealth of ideas from which to glean a handful of possibilities for building our next big industry could do a lot worse than spend a few months hanging around the Media Lab, soaking up insights and absorbing a culture in which freewheeling innovation is celebrated.

❑   ❑   ❑

A RESEARCH LAB is a great place for generating breakthrough ideas. But labs don't always do a good job of turning their ideas into products. Most labs, that is. SRI International is different.

Founded in 1946 in Menlo Park, California, as the Stanford Research Institute, SRI is now the largest nongovernmental lab in the United States, with roughly $500 million in government- and corporate-funded projects. Like the Media Lab, SRI stretches the R&D horizon far beyond the typical corporate three-to-five-year view. But SRI shows that a research lab armed with a *system* for commercialization of ideas can successfully cross the so-called valley of death that separates the lab from the marketplace—a route littered with unread papers and long-forgotten patents describing products that never connected with customers.

Siri, a virtual personal assistant for the iPhone, is one of SRI's latest spin-offs. When users speak to their phones, Siri understands the question or command, performs research, and responds. Over time, Siri adapts to users' individual preferences, making a tailored, concierge-like experience possible. Siri can find you the nearest ATM, discover who's playing at a local jazz club, check the status of a flight or the weather at your destination, or buy tickets to an upcoming basketball game. Even multistep tasks, like making a dinner reservation—including searching nearby restaurants, browsing reviews, booking a table, alerting companions, and setting up a reminder—are handled seamlessly.

The development of this supersophisticated virtual assistant would not have been possible without almost $200 million in DARPA funding for artificial intelligence research spread over twenty-five universities. Then the disparate research findings were pulled together under the auspices of SRI's CALO (Cognitive Assistant that Learns and Organizes) project. One application born from the research project was shaped for the market by Dag Kittlaus. A former research engineer at Motorola who was frustrated by the slow pace of commercialization in a large corporate environment, Kittlaus found SRI a fast and effective launchpad for vanguard products. After roughly half a year at SRI, Kittlaus spun off Siri in 2009 with $24 million in venture capital backing; a year later, the company was bought by Apple for an undisclosed amount thought to be in the $200 million range.

SRI held a stake in Siri and enjoyed one of its best investment returns ever. It's an unusual financial model for a research lab, but one that SRI has perfected. In the last fifteen years, SRI has spun off more than forty companies, creating new industries and billions of dollars in market value. Three of the spin-offs—Nuance, Intuitive Surgical, and Orchid Cellmark—have been taken public, with a combined market cap of nearly $20 billion and more than six thousand employees.

How do they do it? CEO Curtis Carlson, himself a brilliant technological innovator, helps to set the tone. Before joining SRI in 1999, he worked as a physicist in the imaging division of RCA Labs, where he led the team that developed the high-definition television system that became the U.S. standard, for which they received an Emmy Award. Now he drives the managerial, intellectual, and social system by which SRI winnows promising scientific concepts, seeking out those with the greatest demand-creating potential for fast-tracking. "You can invent by yourself," Carlson likes to say, "but you can't innovate that way." To bring great ideas to fruition takes the guidance and support that a great institution like SRI can provide.

Each quarter, an SRI Commercialization Board meets to pore through dozens of the best market-ready ideas, looking for disruptive market opportunities and a "golden nugget" solution that meets SRI's criteria for value creation—and has a champion who has assembled a team. Once an idea is selected, SRI recruits an entrepreneur in residence—someone like Siri's Kittlaus—who works on-site for three to eight months to prepare the venture for funding and spin-off. Throughout this period, SRI's nVention advisory board provides close ties with Silicon Valley venture capital funds, a set of connections whose value is difficult to overstate. Out of many candidates, the Commercialization Board moves about ten opportunities a year through its pipeline—winnow, winnow, winnow—and actually launches two to four ventures.

One of the biggest successes to emerge from the SRI commercialization system is Intuitive Surgical, which sells the da Vinci Surgical System for robotic-assisted minimally invasive surgery.

In 1995, Intuitive Surgical was spun off from SRI with venture funding from Morgan Stanley Dean Witter, Mayfield, and Sierra Ventures. In 1999, the first da Vinci Surgical System was declared market-ready, and in July 2000, the FDA cleared da Vinci for use in laparoscopic surgery. Da Vinci's first beachhead market was with urologists, who found robotic surgery effective in prostate surgery and allowed for much shorter patient recovery times. But da Vinci Systems have been used for a variety of chest and abdominal surgeries, including heart surgery. Today there are more than 1,600 da Vinci Systems in place worldwide, and Intuitive Surgical has a market value topping $13 billion.

Two very different business creation myths have long coexisted in Silicon Valley's business culture. The better-known narrative is that of the venture-funded entrepreneur in a garage whose invention leads to an IPO. The older, now largely forgotten, story is one of the government-funded initiative, like the DARPA projects that led to personal computers, networking, and the Internet. SRI has helped build companies following both pathways, and is arguably the first institution to meld them into one coherent and potentially more powerful narrative of innovation for the twenty-first century.

Carlson sometimes worries about the long-term future of the SRI model. One reason for his concern is America's flagging production of new scientific talent. "If it were not for our foreign-born researchers," he observes, "America's growth would stop." And he points out that China today has more honor students than the United States has students. Partly as a result, America's strategy for innovation is "inadequate." "Solar cells were invented here," he says, "but most of the value is going to China. Compared to America, China is buying forty-one times more manufacturing equipment for solar cells."

Part of Carlson's response would be a shift in national immigration policy: "I would let in all the smart, educated folks I could find," he recommends—and he adds with a smile, ". . . and all the chefs."

Despite the dwindling number of young scientists being groomed in American schools, Carlson and SRI are continuing to drive the commercialization of science. SRI's business model offers a powerful set of tools for reducing the time it takes to traverse the valley from discovery to funding to market, the ultimate goal, in Carlson's words, to "make the world a better place by augmenting and extending human intellect."

A lab with a business model? Shades of David Sarnoff's RCA! It's as unusual as a car company that creates new varieties of rice. And it's unexpected sources like these that are likely to spawn the new ideas from which tomorrow's demand will grow.

❐   ❐   ❐

ACCORDING TO HOARY legend, Charles Duell, commissioner of the U.S. Patent Office, is supposed to have said, in 1899, that "everything that can be invented has been invented." Researchers have failed to unearth evidence that Duell said any such thing, and in fact he appears to have been quite bullish about the prospects for twentieth-century technological innovation—and rightly so.

But there's this much truth in the Duell myth: Despite the brilliant work of today's great demand creators, we are living largely off inherited riches. Many of the breakthroughs on which today's demand is based came from four sources: RCA Labs, Bell Labs, DARPA, and PARC. The transistor, on which so much of today's demand depends, was invented way back in 1947.

We've seen how frustratingly unpredictable industry-creating discoveries can be. But when we had Bell, RCA, and PARC, we invested, as a society, a modest share of our resources in a set of powerful discovery tools that made the odds tremendously better.

Do we need to build new discovery engines of equal or even greater potency? Can we dare to imagine a dozen Honda Research Institutes? A score of Media Labs? Several SRIs? How might a proliferation of institutions like these affect the frequency of new industry-creating discoveries?

There's no shortage of challenges that have large-scale human, social, and economic implications and—equally important for the true scientist—offer fascinating lifelong work for those who choose to tackle them. The list of Grand Challenges for the twenty-first century created by the National Academy of Engineering testifies to that. But exactly when and where will tomorrow's big breakthroughs finally appear? The answer is still unknown—and it depends, in part, on our readiness to do two things: rebuild the engines of industry-creating discovery, and make science prestigious again, in a way that encourages the best minds to take up the challenge that only they can meet—to make the basic discoveries that lead to tomorrow's new industries and tomorrow's new forms of demand.

Coda: The Demand Creators

D RIVEN BY CURIOSITY and by the nagging suspicion that the origin of demand is both seriously misunderstood and deeply important, we began our research hoping to discover a formula for demand creation. It turned into a multiyear quest that made us realize that there is no formula for demand any more than there is a formula for human creativity itself. Yes, there are common elements and unmistakable patterns shared by most stories of demand creation, as we've explained and illustrated in these pages. But just as the hassles that complicate life are endlessly varied, so is the artistry of hassle-fixing that underlies demand creation, making our topic not only vitally important to economic and social progress but also uniquely fascinating.

To our delight, we've also discovered that great demand creators are endlessly varied. They include Fortune 500 CEOs and Nobel Prize–winning scientists as well as corner store proprietors, aspiring entrepreneurs, and frontline employees in modest-size companies and nonprofit organizations. They range from Reed Hastings, dreaming up a new way of renting movies that grew into a multibillion-dollar business, to Yoona Kim, teaching kids in a Harlem classroom how to measure the perimeter of a pentagon; from Danny Wegman, sending a cheese manager to Europe to learn more about the delicious products she sells, to a CareMore clinician, visiting an elderly patient's home to make sure the area rugs won't cause her to slip and fall; from Robin Chase, dreaming of a world where millions of people can enjoy the freedom of driving without the expense, inconvenience, and environmental costs of car ownership, to Tracy Gingell, climbing a ladder to make sure the chandelier in his Pret A Manger store is sparkly enough to meet his exacting standards for cleanliness; from Henk Kwakman, recruiting designers to make the Nespresso coffee maker not just fast and easy but stylish and sexy, to Joe Skenderian, noticing a young mom's swollen leg and helping her remedy a potentially dangerous blood clot; and from Jonathan Dean, introducing fifth graders to the magic of opera as he leads them in a new production of *Siegfried and the Ring of Fire*, to Russ Wilcox, working for almost a decade to achieve the breakthrough that would turn the vision of an electronic book into a practical reality.

Looking at this remarkable roster of quiet heroes and so many others like them, it's hard to imagine a more varied group—except that all are amazing demand creators, making life better for their fellow human beings in ways big and small, and helping to spur economic growth and social progress in countless forms.

So the next time you find yourself fretting over the latest discouraging news on cable TV or in your local newspaper, and perhaps wondering, "Where will we find the demand we need to make our nation grow, expand prosperity, and give the next generation the same chance at a better life that we enjoyed?" we hope you'll think about the demand creators profiled in these pages, and take a leaf from their book.

Don't look up. Look in the mirror.

SOURCE NOTES

For each story told in this book, we provide below a list of books, articles, websites, and other sources from which significant information was drawn. These sources are listed in chronological order by date of first publication. Other specific factual details, quotations, or ideas that readers may be interested in tracking are cited by source, linked by brief phrases (in italics) to the main book text.

"Author interviews" refers to interviews with named individuals conducted by either or both of the two listed authors or by one or more members of our research team, whose names appear in the acknowledgments. "Oliver Wyman consumer interviews" refers to interviews with individuals conducted by one or more members of our research team as part of the continuing background study of consumer behaviors, preferences, and opinions by Oliver Wyman, a leading global management consulting firm, of which author Adrian J. Slywotzky is a partner.

INTRODUCTION: THE MYSTERY OF DEMAND

2   Netflix story: "Netflix CEO Reed Hastings Profile," interview with Lesley Stahl on *CBS 60 Minutes,* reprinted by *Technology Wire,* December 4, 2006, online at http://www.accessmylibrary.com/coms2/summary_0286-28805727 _ITM. Also see chapter 4, "Trigger," below.

4   Nokia 1100 story: Kevin Sullivan, "For India's Traditional Fishermen, Cell-Phones Deliver a Sea Change," *Washington Post,* October 15, 2006. Also see chapter 9, "The Biggest Spark," below.

1. MAGNETIC

14 Zipcar story: Fred Bayles, "A Hot Import: Communal Cars for Congested Streets," *USA Today,* July 21, 2000; Kit J. Nichols, "A New Option for Drivers

Who Don't Want to Own," *Consumers Research*, August 1, 2003; Shawn Mc-
Carthy, "Zipcar a Vehicle for Thrifty Urban Existentialism," *Globe and Mail*
(Toronto), April 11, 2005; Brian Quinton, "Zipcar Goes the Extra Mile," *DI-
RECT*, September 15, 2005; Stephanie Clifford, "How Fast Can This Thing
Go Anyway?" *Inc.*, March 1, 2008; Mark Levine, "Share My Ride," *New York
Times Magazine*, March 8, 2009; Paul Keegan, "The Best New Idea in Busi-
ness," *Fortune*, September 14, 2009; Zipcar website, http://www.zipcar.com/.

16   *Mary Morgan, a journalist in Ann Arbor, Michigan:* Mary Morgan, "MM Does
Zipcar," *Ann Arbor Chronicle*, March 9, 2009.

17   *As a deadly accurate 2000 headline: The Onion*, http://www.theonion.com
/articles/report-98-percent-of-us-commuters-favor-public-tra,1434/.

19   *Not-for-profit car-sharing services:* See *Bringing Carsharing to Your Community*, City Car Share, http://www.citycarshare.org/download/CCS_BCCtYC
_Short.pdf.

20   *One early adopter remarked: Carpundit* (blog), April 11, 2005, http://
carpundit.typepad.com/carpundit/2005/04/zipcar_a_review.html. Other
user comments in this paragraph from *Insiderpages*, http://www.insiderpages
.com/b/3715573336/zipcar-incorporated-cambridge.

23   *"This has to be a lifestyle choice":* Quoted in Lisa van der Pool, "Scott Griffith:
Zipping Ahead," *Boston Business Journal*, August 27, 2007.

24   *As one Zipcar member told us:* Oliver Wyman consumer interviews.

26   *Suddenly people by the thousands began to discover:* Comments in this paragraph and the four that follow are from Oliver Wyman consumer interviews.

28   *As one Zipster puts it, "I like the idea of being green":* Oliver Wyman consumer interviews.

29   *Even seemingly unpredictable hassles:* Stories in this paragraph and the three
that follow are from Oliver Wyman consumer interviews.

32   *"We use information as a competitive advantage":* Scott Griffith, "Zipcar:
Selling Cars, One Ride at a Time," *What Matters*, October 27, 2009, McKin-
sey & Company, online at http://whatmatters.mckinseydigital.com/internet/
zipcar-selling-cars-one-ride-at-a-time.

34   Wegmans story: Beverly Savage, "Want a Wegmans? Many Shoppers Do,"
New York Times, April 27, 2003; Matthew Swibel, "Nobody's Meal: How Can
87-Year-Old Wegmans Food Markets Survive—and Thrive—Against the
Likes of Wal-Mart?" *Forbes*, November 24, 2003; "Wegmans Tops Fortune's

'100 Best Companies to Work For' List," *Progressive Grocer,* January 11, 2005; Matthew Boyle, "The Wegmans Way," *Fortune,* January 24, 2005; Warren Thayer, "Wegmans Still Rules," *Refrigerated & Frozen Foods Retailer,* May 16, 2008, http://www.rffretailer.com/Articles/Cover_Story/2008/05/16/Wegmans -Still-Rules; Joe Wheeler, "Wegmans Food Markets: How Two Halves Make More Than a Whole," *Progressive Grocer,* August 11, 2009; Wegmans website, http://www.wegmans.com/.

36 *If you ever have the opportunity to meet our friend Stephen:* Oliver Wyman consumer interviews.

39 *From 1950 to 1976, the stores multiplied:* See "Robert B. Wegman: A Great Merchant 1918–2006," Wegmans website, http://www.wegmans.com /webapp/wcs/stores/servlet/ProductDisplay?storeId=10052&partNumber =UNIVERSAL_2706&catalogId=10002&langId=-1.

39 *When the economic downturn hit in 2008:* "Profile: Danny Wegman," from "SN Power 50, 2009," *Supermarket News,* online at http://supermarketnews .com/profiles/danny-wegman-2009/.

46 *The difference lies in what social psychologists:* See Dan Ariely, *Predictably Irrational: The Hidden Forces That Shape Our Decisions* (New York: HarperCollins, 2008), chapter 4, "The Cost of Social Norms," pp. 67–88.

48 *In early 2008, Wegmans launched an online shopping tool:* See "Wegmans Revamps Online Shopping Tool," *Brandweek,* February 5, 2009, http://www .brandweek.com/bw/content_display/news-and-features/shopper-market ing/e3id425eb6001d58ee74c7da4827b5afcc3.

50 *Wegmans is equally innovative beyond technology:* See "Wegmans Reverses Supermarket Supply Chain, Starts Organic Farm," GreenBiz.com, September 12, 2007, http://www.greenbiz.com/print/1498.

52 *The explanation for Wegmans' economic success:* See William J. McEwen and John H. Fleming, "Customer Satisfaction Doesn't Count," Gallup Organization, March 13, 2003, http://www.adobe.com/engagement/pdfs/gmj _customer_satisfaction.pdf.

2. Hassle Map

55 1908 New York–Paris auto race: Julie M. Fenster, *Race of the Century: The Heroic True Story of the 1908 New York to Paris Auto Race* (New York: Crown, 2005).

58 *Or consider another observer's comment:* "Steve Jobs Speaks Out: On the Birth of the iPhone," *Fortune* website, http://money.cnn.com/galleries/2008/fortune/0803/gallery.jobsqna.fortune/index.html.

65 Bloomberg story: Ken Auletta, "The Bloomberg Threat," *New Yorker*, March 10, 1997; Davis S. Bennahum, "Terminal Velocity," *Wired*, February 1999; Felicity Barringer and Geraldine Fabrikant, "Coming of Age at Bloomberg L.P.," *New York Times*, March 21, 1999; Michael R. Bloomberg, *Bloomberg by Bloomberg* (Hoboken, NJ: Wiley, 2001); Ken Kurson, "Emperor Mike," *Money*, October 1, 2001; Carol J. Loomis, "Bloomberg's Money Machine," *Fortune*, April 5, 2007; Jon Meacham, "The Revolutionary," *Newsweek*, November 3, 2007; Ian Austen, "The New Fight for Financial News," *New York Times*, June 23, 2008; Seth Mnookin, "Bloomberg Without Bloomberg," *Vanity Fair*, December 2008; Bloomberg website, http://www.bloomberg.com/.

72 CareMore story: Author interviews (August 18, 2010, and October 28, 2010) with CEO Alan Hoops, Dr. Charles Holzner, nurse practitioner Peggy Salazar, Dr. Balu Gadhe, Dr. Ken Kim, Dr. Henry Do, and Dr. Sheldon Zinberg. Other sources: "Delivering Integrated Patient Care for Seniors," CareMore, November 2008; Gilbertson Milstein, "American Medical Home Runs," *Health Affairs*, September/October 2009; Bonnie Darves, "Physicians Who Work with Health Plans Are Testing a Wide Range of Post-Discharge Innovations," *Today's Hospitalist*, February 2010; "The Way Healthcare Should Be Delivered," CareMore, February 25, 2010; "Palliative Care Extends Life, Study Finds," *New York Times*, August 18, 2010; CareMore website, http://www.caremore.com/.

86 *One of the chief goals of the Extensivist:* Lisa Girion, "Keeping Tabs on Patient Can Cut Costs," *Los Angeles Times*, September 20, 2009.

3. BACKSTORY

92 E Ink and Kindle: Author interviews (December 17, 2009) with E Ink CEO Russ Wilcox and E Ink team members Pete Valianatos, Harit Doshi, Joanna Au, Lynne Garone, Karl Amundson, and Jenn Vail. Author interview (February 27, 2010) with Yoshitaka Ukita of Sony. Other sources: Iddo Genuth, "The Future of Electronic Paper," *The Future of Things*, October 15, 2007; David Talbot, "E-Paper Comes Alive," *Technology Review*, November 20, 2007; Erich Schwartzel, "E Ink Writes a New Chapter," *Boston Globe*, September

1, 2008; Maureen Farrell, "Is E Ink Publishing's Savior?" Forbes.com, September 15, 2008; "Insight Into E Ink," *Printed Electronics World*, September 25, 2008; Wade Roush, "Kindling a Revolution: E Ink's Russ Wilcox on E-Paper, Amazon, and the Future of Publishing," *Xconomy Boston*, February 26, 2009; Michael V. Copeland, "The End of Paper?" *Fortune,* March 3, 2009; Julia Hanna, "E Ink's Wild Ride," *HBS Alumni Bulletin,* September 2009.

100 *He summarizes his business strategy this way:* Julia Kirby and Thomas A. Stewart, "The Institutional Yes: The HBR Interview—Jeff Bezos," *Harvard Business Review,* October 2007.

100 *They apply this principle even when:* Alan Deutschman, "Inside the Mind of Jeff Bezos," *Fast Company,* December 19, 2007.

103 *One reviewer wrote in 2007:* Nate Anderson, "Down with Paper: A Review of the Sony Reader," Ars Technica website, http://arstechnica.com/hardware/reviews/2007/11/sony-reader-review.ars/3.

110 Tetra Pak: Author interview (March 1, 2011) with Phil Mazza and Nick Marsella, Byrne Dairy. Author interview (March 14, 2011) with Matthew Cain, president of J. Soif, Inc. Other sources: "Tetra Pak and Chef Creations Whip Up Solution for Creamy Gourmet Specialties," CulinaryConceptsInc.com, May 2004, http://www.culinaryconceptsinc.com/new_1_popup.htm; Clara Carlsson and Johan Rasmusson, "Control and Synergies in the Outsourced Supply Chain: Recommendations for How to Improve and Organize Tetra Pak's Supply Chain," Lund Institute of Technology, Industrial Management and Logistics, Lund University, Lund, Sweden, January 17, 2005; Jon Bonne, "Wine in a Box, One Serving at a Time," MSNBC, April 19, 2006, http://www.msnbc.msn.com/id/12374800/; Joel Stein, "New Wine in . . . Uh, Juice Boxes," *Time,* August 30, 2007; Finn Iljott Christensen and Torben Vilsgaard, "Churning Out Cold Treats," *Asia Food Journal,* August 1, 2008; "The History of an Idea," Tetra Pak, February 2009, http://www.tetrapak.com/Document%20Bank/About_tetrapak/the_history_of_an%20_idea.pdf; "MJR Media Crafts a Striking Vendange Wine Rendering on Tetra Pak's Aseptic Prisma?" *Package Design,* April 2009; Kelly Kass, "Tetra Pak Gives Employees a Programme to LiVE For," Simply Communicate website, September 17, 2009, http://www.simply-communicate.com/news/tetra-pak-gives-employees-programme-live; "All That Is Fluid Becomes Solid," Meijling.net,

http://meijling.net/fluid_solid.html; "Tetra Pak Expands Support for School Milk Programmes Around the World," company press release, September 29, 2009; "Turnaround at Tetra Pak Converting Technologies (CT)," *Dilipnaidu's Blog*, March 21, 2010; Tetra Pak website, http://www.tetrapak.com/Pages/default.aspx.

115 *The first Tetra Pak Classic Aseptic machine outside Europe:* "Tetra Pak— Development in Brief," Tetra Pak, June 2008, http://www.tetrapak.com/Document%20Bank/About_tetrapak/9704en.pdf.

116 *Chief among them is the early U.S. adoption:* David Landes, *The Unbound Prometheus: Technological Change and Industrial Development in Western Europe from 1750 to the Present* (Cambridge: Cambridge University Press, 1969), pp. 438–39; Richard S. Tedlow, *New and Improved: The Story of Mass Marketing in America* (Boston: Harvard Business School Press, 1990), p. 347.

121 *For an example of how Tetra Pak's unique design:* See "Tetra Harmony Together With the Dairy Industry Chain," Frbiz.com, December 4, 2008.

121 *Ulla Holm, the director of Tetra Pak's Food for Development program:* Dean Best, "When CSR and the Need for New Business Meet," Just-Food website, August 23, 2007, online at http://www.just-food.com/the-just-food-blog/when-csr-and-the-need-for-new-business-meet_id1314.aspx.

123 *Talk to Tetra Pak customers and you begin to get a sense:* Author interview, op. cit.

124 *Hear me, know me, grow me:* Janet Shaner and Kamran Kashani, *Tetra Pak (B): Hear Me, Know Me, Grow Me: The Customer Satisfaction Initiative* (Lausanne, Switzerland: International Institute for Management Development, 2002).

124 *As CEO Dennis Jönsson points out:* Calle Froste, "Rausings nya stadare" ["Rausing's New City"], *Affars Varlden*, March 14, 2006, online at http://www.affarsvarlden.se/hem/nyheter/article271169.ece.

125 *One approach has been to seek a foothold:* See "History of Soy Products," Soyfoods Association of North America website, http://www.soyfoods.org/products/history-of-soy-products.

126 *Soon thereafter, Kate Murphy:* Kate Murphy, "Thinking Outside the Can: A Fresh Look at Food in a Box," *New York Times*, March 14, 2004.

127 *Marketing director Chris Kenneally describes the mission:* Chris Kenneally, "Making an Impact: How Package Design Influences Consumer Choice,"

Food Engineering & Ingredients, September 1, 2009, online at http://www
.fei-online.com/featured-articles/making-an-impact-how-package-design
-influences-consumer-choice/index.html.

128 *The story of Tetra Recart is a particularly vivid example:* Kevin T. Higgins,
"Diced Tomatoes in a Carton? Now, That's Italian," *Food Engineering*, March 1,
2007, online at http://www.foodengineeringmag.com/Articles/Departments
_and_Columns/BNP_GUID_9-5-2006_A_10000000000000059828.

128 *Matthew Cain, founder and president of wine importer J. Soif, Inc.:* Author
interview, op. cit. Also see "Yellow + Blue Make Green: A New Organic Malbec in TetraPak," *Dr. Vino* (blog), April 21, 2008, http://www.drvino.com
/2008/04/21/yellow-blue-make-green-a-new-organic-malbec-in-tetrapak/.

129 *In fact, for a time, Tetra Pak and other companies:* Dennis Jönsson and Warren Tyler, "Thinking Out of the Box: Competitors Join Forces to Save an Industry," *Chief Executive*, June 1997.

4. TRIGGER

134 Netflix: Author interviews (March 8, 2010, and January 11, 2011) with Steve
Swasey of Netflix. Other sources: Jim Cook, "Five Customer Focused Lessons
from the Netflix Startup Story," *Allbusiness*, July 25, 2006, http://www.allbus
iness.com/operations/3878629-1.html; "Reference Guide on Our Freedom &
Responsibility Culture" ["The Netflix Culture Pack"], slide presentation, Netflix, 2009, http://www.slideshare.net/reed2001/culture-1798664; Christopher
Borrelli, "How Netflix Gets Your Movies to Your Mailbox So Fast," Chicago
tribune.com, August 4, 2009; Daniel Roth, "Netflix Inside," *Wired*, October
2009; "An Evening with Reed Hastings, in Conversation with Michael Eis-
ner," video, February 25, 2010, http://www.youtube.com/watch?v=gKba6
FWYSz4.

144 *Netflix worked on designing a unique, ingenious envelope:* See G. Pascal Zach-
ary, "The Evolution of the Netflix Envelope," *Business 2.0*, April 21, 2006,
http://money.cnn.com/2006/04/20/technology/business2_netflixgallery
/index.htm.

151 *The consumer review website Gizmodo:* Jason Chen, "Blockbuster Gimps
Total Access Plan, Now Only 5 Free Exchanges a Month, $1.99 Each After,"
Gizmodo, July 27, 2007, http://gizmodo.com/#!283286/blockbuster-gimps
-total-access-plan-now-only-5-free-exchanges-a-month-199-each-after.

154 Nespresso: Author interviews (February 9, 2011) with former Nespresso CEO
    Henk Kwakman and CEO Richard Girardot. Other sources: Thyra Porter,
    "Nespresso's Caffe Battle," *Business and Industry*, February 9, 1998; Joyce
    Miller, *Innovation and Renovation: The Nespresso Story* (Lausanne, Switzer-
    land: International Institute for Management Development, 2000); Reg Butler,
    "The Nespresso Route to a Perfect Espresso," *Tea & Coffee Trade Journal*, May
    20, 2000; Richard Tomlinson, "Can Nestlé Be the Very Best?" *Fortune*, No-
    vember 13, 2000; "Planet Nestlé . . . and the Seven Commandments You
    Need to Observe to Live There," *Facts*, May 12, 2004; Jennifer White, "Some-
    thing's Brewing," *Business and Industry*, March 21, 2005; Jennifer White,
    "Pouring It On," *Business and Industry*, October 9, 2006; Edouard Tintig-
    nac, *Nespresso, What Else? Nespresso's Customer Profile and Behavior* (Ge-
    neva, Switzerland: IFM University, 2007), http://www.zamaros.net/Nes
    presso_What_Else.pdf; Rob Sharp, "The Cult of Nespresso," *Independent*,
    October 4, 2007; John Gapper, "Lessons from Nestlé's Coffee Break," *Finan-
    cial Times*, January 2, 2008; Matthew Saltmarsh, "A Cup of Coffee, Enriched
    by Lifestyle," *New York Times*, February 20, 2009; Viviane Menétrey, "Jean-
    Paul Gaillard: 'I Do Not Copy, I Innovate,'" *Le Matin*, March 14, 2010;
    Christina Passariello, "Nestlé Stakes Its Grounds in a European Coffee War,"
    Wall Street Journal, April 28, 2010.

155 *Thanks to features like these:* Comments from Oliver Wyman consumer in-
    terviews.

161 *Gaillard took a deep breath and declared:* Enrollment numbers cited in Luca
    D. Majer, "Clooney's Clones," Foodservice.com, April 2, 2010.

162 *In a survey of French Nespresso customers:* Oliver Wyman consumer inter-
    views.

5. TRAJECTORY

176 *Novelist and social critic Aldous Huxley:* Quotation from *Island* (New York:
    Harper Perennial, 2009), chapter 9.

177 Netflix Prize: Dan Frommer, "No Winner Yet in Netflix $1 Million Coding
    Contest," *Silicon Valley Insider*, December 10, 2008; Jordan Ellenberg, "This
    Psychologist Might Outsmart the Math Brains Competing for the Netflix
    Prize," *Wired*, February 25, 2008; Steve Lohr, "A $1 Million Research Bargain
    for Netflix, and Maybe a Model for Others," *New York Times*, September 22,

2009; Farhad Manjoo, "The Netflix Prize Was Brilliant," *Slate*, September 22, 2009; "Netflix Prize: Top Eight Facts," Telegraph.co.uk, September 22, 2009; Eliot Van Buskirk, "How the Netflix Prize Was Won," Wired.com, September 22, 2009; Stephen Baker, "Netflix Isn't Done Mining Consumer Data," MSNBC.com, September 22, 2009; Ian Paul, "Netflix Prize 2: What You Need to Know," *Network World*, September 23, 2009; Michael V. Copeland, "Tapping Tech's Beautiful Minds," *Fortune*, October 12, 2009.

179 Teach For America: Author interviews with TFA team members Amanda Craft (July 8, 2010), Elissa Clapp (August 13, 2010), Lauren LeVeen (February 16, 2011), and Steven Farr (April 1, 2011), and with teaching corps members Yoona Kim and David Parker-Longmaid (February 15, 2011). Other sources: Wendy Kopp, *One Day, All Children . . .* (New York: PublicAffairs, 2001); Adam Bryant, "Charisma? To Her, It's Overrated," *New York Times*, July 5, 2009; Steven Farr, *Teaching as Leadership: The Highly Effective Teacher's Guide to Closing the Achievement Gap* (San Francisco: Jossey-Bass, 2010); "Eight Questions for Wendy Kopp," *Economist*, April 3, 2010; Brendan Lowe, "Mind the Gap," *Good*, July 2, 2010; Naomi Schaefer Riley, "What They're Doing After Harvard," *Wall Street Journal*, July 10, 2010; Michael Winerip, "A Chosen Few Are Teaching for America," *New York Times*, July 11, 2010; Dana Goldstein, "Does Teach For America Work?" *Daily Beast*, January 25, 2011; Teach For America website, http://www.teachforamerica.org/.

184 *Journalist Amanda Ripley has tracked TFA's:* Amanda Ripley, "What Makes a Great Teacher?" *Atlantic*, January/February 2010.

194 Pret A Manger: Author interview with Pret store manager Tracy Gingell (July 16, 2010). Other sources: Jamie Doward, "Between a Big Mac and a Hard Place," *Guardian*, February 4, 2001; Christian Broughton, "Bread Winners," *Independent*, February 29, 2004; Todd Benjamin, "Julian Metcalfe: A Hunger for Success," CNN, November 28, 2005, http://www.cnn.com/2005/BUSINESS/11/25/boardroom.metcalfe/; Sonia Kolesnikov-Jessop, "Spotlight: Julian Metcalfe, Founder of Pret A Manger," *International Herald Tribune*, January 26, 2007; Neil Gerrard, "The Rise of the Healthy Fast-Casual Chains," Caterersearch.com, September 2, 2010, http://www.caterersearch.com/Articles/2010/09/02/334899/the-rise-of-the-healthy-fast-casual-chains.htm; Rebecca Smithers, "Pret A Manger Chief Is Stacking Up Healthy Profits in Lean Times," *Guardian*, October 8, 2010.

202 *So in June 2009, after Julian Metcalfe saw:* Christopher Leake, "End of the Line for the Pret Tuna Sandwich," *Mail Online*, June 6, 2009.

202 *In every Pret store you'll find a box with cards: Coachbarrow* (blog), June 14, 2010, http://www.coachbarrow.com/blog/2010/06/14/pret-a-manger-2/.

203 *Here's how one critic compared Pret:* Mary Portas, "Shop! Mary Portas at Pret A Manger and Eat," *Telegraph*, May 13, 2010.

203 *In August 2009, Metcalfe received a tongue-in-cheek letter:* See Jon Swaine, "Man Invoices Pret A Manger and EAT for Time Spent Waiting in Shops," *Telegraph*, August 27, 2009.

6. VARIATION

210 Orchestra "churn project": Multiple author interviews with Martin Kon, director of pro bono research project conducted by Oliver Wyman for leading U.S. orchestras, 2007. Author interviews with Partha Bose (January 21, 2010) and Kim Noltemy (February 10, 2010) of Boston Symphony Orchestra, and with Jesse Rosen, League of American Orchestras (February 1, 2010). Other sources: Maureen Dezell and Geoff Edgers, "They Can Also Conduct Business: It's a Bad Time for American Orchestras but BSO Inc. Is Thriving," *Boston Globe*, August 10, 2003; Alan S. Brown and John Bare, "Bridging the Gap: Orchestras and Classical Music Listeners," John S. and James L. Knight Foundation, June 2003; Martin Kon, "Custom Churn: Stop It Before It Starts," *Mercer Management Journal* 17, June 2004; Ed Cambron, "Creating an Environment for Exploration," *Engaging Art* (blog), June 19, 2007, http://www.artsjournal.com/league/2007/06/creating_an_environment_for_ex.html; "Audience Growth Initiative: Summary," Oliver Wyman website, 2009, http://www.oliverwyman.com/ow/9673.htm; "Opening to a Packed House," Oliver Wyman website, 2009, http://www.oliverwyman.com/ow/9034.htm; Rebecca Winzenried, "Into Thin Air," *Symphony*, January–February 2009; Rebecca Winzenried, "The Price Is Right," *Symphony*, January–February 2010.

219 Seattle Opera: Author interviews with team members Jonathan Dean, Seneca Garber, Rebecca Chawgo, and Rian Kochel (February 4, 2010), and with Vira Slywotzky (January 25, 2010). Also see Seattle Opera website, http://www.seattleopera.org/.

223 *And Jenkins's passion makes him an untiring salesman:* Deanna Duff, "Most Influential: Speight Jenkins," *Seattle Magazine*, November 2010, online at http://www.seattlemag.com/article/most-influential-speight-jenkins-9.

224 "Corner store" experiences: Author interviews with Marc Najarian, Dale Szczeblowski, Carol Stoltz, Jane Dawson, and Joe Skenderian.

231 Eurostar: Author interview (April 12, 2011) with Richard Brown, chairman of Eurostar. Information from Oliver Wyman analysis. Other sources: Paul Mungo, "Why Eurostar Has Failed to Make the Grade," *Daily Mail*, August 19, 2002; Andrew Davidson, "The Friendly Controller," *Sunday Times* (London), January 11, 2004; Michael Harrison, "Richard Brown, Chief Executive of Eurostar," *Independent*, April 16, 2005; Katie Silvester, "Richard Brown, Chief Executive of Eurostar," *Rail Professional*, February 2008; Andrew Cave, "Eurostar Feeding on Hunger for Travel," *Telegraph*, April 12, 2009; Dan Milmo, "Eurostar Faces Rivals for Cross-Channel Route," *Guardian*, June 8, 2009; Karl West, "Rail Chief Has the Inside Track on His Rivals," *Daily Mail*, July 23, 2009; Alex Carlisle, "Richard Brown Eurostar's Debyshire Resident Chief Executive," *Derbyshire Life*, March 12, 2010.

232 *British paranoia on this theme actually persisted:* Story cited in Robert Townsend, *Up the Organization* (Greenwich, CT: Fawcett Publication, 1970), p. 75.

240 *Journalist Andrew Martin experienced the first celebratory run:* Andrew Martin, "St Pancras Is a Start, But It Takes More to Stop Us Flying," *Independent*, November 18, 2007.

7. Launch: The Achilles' Heel of Demand

250 Honda Insight: "Long-Term Test: 2000 Honda Insight," *Edmunds Inside Line*, January 1, 1999, http://www.insideline.com/honda/insight/2000/long-term-test-2000-honda-insight.html#article_pagination_top_0; Phil Patton, "Once Frumpy, Green Cars Start Showing Some Flash," *New York Times*, July 15, 2007.

252 Tesco: Mark Ritson, "Tesco Finds US Not So Easy," *Marketing*, March 4, 2009; George MacDonald, "Don't Write Off Fresh & Easy," *Retail Week*, February 27, 2009; William Kay, "Tesco Admits: We Got It Wrong in US," *Sunday Times* (London), February 22, 2009; Kerry Capell, "Tesco: 'Wal-Mart's Worst Nightmare,'" *BusinessWeek*, December 30, 2008.

253 *Actual failure statistics for project launches are hard to verify:* Probabilities of project success drawn from the following sources: Hollywood movie: Oliver Wyman analysis based on data from MPAA 2003 Statistics, MGM 2003 Operating Results, and http://www.factbook.net/wbglobal_rev.htm. Corporate

mergers and acquisitions: *Investment Dealers' Digest,* November 24, 2003, and Paul Mallette, "The Acquisition Process Map: Blueprint for a Successful Deal," *Southern Business Review,* Spring 2003. Information technology: Nicholas G. Carr, *Does IT Matter?* (Boston: Harvard Business School Press, 2004). Venture capital: Nadim F. Matta and Ronald N. Ashkenas, "Why Good Projects Fail Anyway," *Harvard Business Review,* September 2003. Food: John L. Stanton, "Most Pioneers Got Killed, but Some Got Rich," *Food Processing,* July, 2003. Pharmaceuticals: *Pharmaceutical Industry Profile,* Pharmaceutical Research and Manufacturers of America, 2004.

254 *In their 2003 article:* Dan Lovallo and Daniel Kahneman, "Delusions of Success: How Optimism Undermines Executives' Decisions," *Harvard Business Review,* July 2003.

256 *One technique that can be helpful:* See Gary Klein, "Performing a Project Premortem," *Harvard Business Review,* September 2007.

258 Toyota Prius: Author interview with Toyota executive Takeshi Uchiyamada (September 26, 2006). Other sources: James B. Treece, "Prius Got Top Support," *Automotive News,* February 23, 1998; Ikujiro Nonaka and Noboru Konna, "The Concept of 'Ba': Building a Foundation for Knowledge Creation," *California Management Review,* Spring 1998; Jeffrey K. Liker, *The Toyota Way: 14 Management Principles from the World's Greatest Manufacturer* (New York: McGraw-Hill, 2003); Peter Fairley, "Hybrids' Rising Sun," *MIT Technology Review,* April 1, 2004; James Mackintosh, "Cost Cuts Are Key to Success of the Prius," *Financial Times,* June 16, 2005, p. 28; Chester Dawson, "Why Hybrids 'Are Here to Stay,'" *BusinessWeek Online,* June 20, 2005, http://www.businessweek.com/print/magazine.content/05_25/b3938029.htm?chan=gl; Chester Dawson, "Takehisa Yaegashi: Proud Papa of the Prius," *BusinessWeek,* June 20, 2005; David Welch, "What Makes a Hybrid Hot," *BusinessWeek,* November 14, 2005; Alex Taylor III, "The Birth of the Prius," *Fortune,* February 24, 2006.

264 *Developing his first movie on a stingy budget:* See Pauline Kael, "Raising Kane," in *The Citizen Kane Book* (Boston: Atlantic Monthly Press, 1971), pp. 53–54.

266 *At Lotus in the early 1990s, June Rokoff:* Glenn Rifkin, "Profile: The 'Iron Lady' Keeping Lotus on Track," *New York Times,* January 23, 1994.

272 *The day after the tragic launchpad fire in January 1967:* See Gene Kranz, *Fail-*

ure Is Not an Option: Mission Control from Mercury to Apollo 13 and Beyond (New York: Simon & Schuster, 2000).

8. PORTFOLIO: "NOBODY KNOWS ANYTHING"

275 *Screenwriter William Goldman, after decades observing:* William Goldman, *Adventures in the Screen Trade: A Personal View of Hollywood and Screenwriting* (New York: Warner Books, 1983).

275 Pixar: Author interview with former Pixar team member Lizzi Weinberg (November 3, 2010). Other source: Karen Paik, *To Infinity and Beyond! The Story of Pixar Animation Studios* (San Francisco: Chronicle Books, 2007).

280 *Another Pixar-esque term for the process:* Alex Ben Block, "Animator John Lasseter Making Disney a Top Draw," *Hollywood Reporter,* October 23, 2008.

284 *Perhaps John Lasseter's enthusiasm:* Block, op. cit.

285 *By practicing these principles:* Box office data in Pixar blockbuster chart from http://www.boxofficemojo.com.

287 Merck: Roy Vagelos and Louis Galambos, *Medicine, Science, and Merck* (Cambridge: Cambridge University Press, 2004); Fran Hawthorne, *The Merck Druggernaut: The Inside Story of a Pharmaceutical Giant* (Hoboken, NJ: Wiley, 2005); Gordon Bock, "Merck's Medicine Man: Pindaros Roy Vagelos," *Time,* February 22, 1988; Joseph Weber, "Merck Needs More Gold from the White Coats," *BusinessWeek,* March 18, 1991; "Merck Provides Update on R&D Pipeline; Sets 2010 Targets," *IHS Global Insight,* December 12, 2007, online at http://www.ihsglobalinsight.com/SDA/SDADetail11208.htm.

290 *As a result of Vagelos's innovative:* Data in Merck blockbuster chart from J. Rubin and P. A. Brooke, "Merck: Merck Quarterly Sales Model, 1993–2004E," New York: Morgan Stanley Dean Witter, August 7, 1998, and October 22, 1999.

292 Kleiner Perkins Caufield & Byers: Roger Taylor, "Shaping the Future with Nothing but Ideas," *Financial Times,* July 19, 1999; Rodes Fishburne and Michael S. Malone, "Founding Funders: Two Venerable VCs Talk About Then and Now," *Forbes ASAP,* May 29, 2000; Katherine Campbell, "Venture Capital: Entry Is by Invitation Only," *Financial Times,* September 13, 2000; Laura Rich, "Investment Engines in Search of Their Next Moves," *New York Times,* May 3, 2004; "Q&A with Kleiner Perkins Caufield & Byers," Silicon

Beat, *San Jose Mercury News,* November 13, 2004, http://www.siliconbeat .com/entries/2004/11/13/qa_with_kleiner_perkins_caufield_byers.html; Jim Carlton, "Kleiner's Green Investment Machine," *Wall Street Journal,* December 14, 2006; Jon Gertner, "Capitalism to the Rescue," *New York Times Magazine,* October 5, 2008.

292 *In this strange parallel universe:* List of companies in Kleiner Perkins blockbuster chart from http://www.kpcb.com.

293 *A magazine profile once described Doerr:* Michael S. Malone, "John Doerr's Startup Manual," *Fast Company,* February 28, 1997, online at http://www .fastcompany.com/magazine/07/082doerr.html.

295 *Then there's Bill Joy, a famous whiz kid:* Malcolm Gladwell, *Outliers* (New York: Little, Brown, 2008), chapter 2.

9. THE BIGGEST SPARK: SCIENTIFIC DISCOVERY AND THE FUTURE OF DEMAND

303 *In 2008, the National Academy of Engineering:* "Introduction to the Grand Challenges for Engineering," National Academy of Engineering website, http://www.engineeringchallenges.org/cms/8996/9221.aspx.

305 Transistor: Michael Riordan and Lillian Hoddeson, *Crystal Fire: The Invention of the Transistor and Birth of the Information Age* (New York: Norton, 1998).

307 Nokia 1100: Sascha Segan, "Nokia 1100" (review), Pcmag.com, March 31, 2006, http://www.pcmag.com/print_article2/0,1217,a%253D174758,00.asp; Kevin Sullivan, "For India's Traditional Fishermen, Cell Phones Deliver a Sea Change," *Washington Post,* October 15, 2006; Jack Ewing, "How Nokia Users Drive Innovation," *BusinessWeek,* April 30, 2008; Sanjay Gandhi, Surabhi Mittal, and Gaurav Tripathi, "The Impact of Mobiles on Agricultural Productivity," *Moving the Debate Forward,* Policy Paper Series, Vodafone Group, January 2009; Eric Bellman, "Rural India Snaps Up Mobile Phones," *Wall Street Journal,* February 9, 2009; "OPK, Indiana Jones and 4.6 Billion Other People," *Nokia Coversations* (corporate blog), January 8, 2010, http://conversations.nokia.com/2010/01/08/opk-indiana-jones-and-4-6 -billion-other-people/.

310 *Consider Bell Labs, for example:* "Bell Labs History," Alcatel-Lucent website, http://www.alcatel-lucent.com/wps/portal/BellLabs/History; Linda A.

Johnson, "Bell Labs' History of Inventions," *USA Today*, December 1, 2006, http://www.usatoday.com/tech/news/2006-12-01-bell-research_x.htm.

312 RCA Laboratories: Kenyan Kilbon, *Pioneering in Electronics: A Short History of the Origins and Growth of RCA Laboratories, Radio Corporation of America, 1919 to 1964*, David Sarnoff Library, http://www.davidsarnoff.org /kil.html; Ross Basset, *To the Digital Age: Research Labs, Start-up Companies, and the Rise of MOS Technology* (Baltimore: Johns Hopkins University Press, 2002).

313 DARPA: Steven LeVine, "Can the Military Find the Answer to Alternative Energy?" *BusinessWeek*, July 23, 2009; Duncan Graham-Rowe, "Fifty Years of DARPA: A Surprising History," *New Scientist*, May 15, 2009; John Markoff, "Pentagon Redirects Its Research Dollars," *New York Times*, April 2, 2005.

314 Xerox PARC: Michael A. Hiltzik, *Dealers of Lightning: Xerox PARC and the Dawn of the Computer Age* (New York: HarperCollins, 1999); Brian Bakker, "The Importance of PARC," *Brainstorm*, February 5, 2009; Peter Dizikes, "Xerox PARC: On the Money Trail," ABC News, November 11, 2002, online at http://abcnews.go.com/Business/story?id=86872&page=1; Xerox PARC Fact Sheet, online at http://www.parc.com/content/newsroom /factsheet_parc.pdf; Palo Alto Research Center website, http://www.parc .com.

315 Honda Research Institute: "All Too Human: Honda's Walking, Talking Robot, ASIMO, Leads Automaker into Uncharted Territory," *Automotive News*, January 28, 2002; "Art and Science of Crash Survival," *Globe and Mail*, October 25, 2005; "Inside Honda's Brain," *Forbes*, March 7, 2008; "Honda's New CEO Is Also Chief Innovator," *BusinessWeek*, July 27, 2009; "Researchers Given Freedom to Explore," *Nikkei Weekly*, September 16, 2003; "Pragmatic Path to Globalization; Honda's Maverick Culture," *Nikkei Report*, April 2, 2009; "Interview with Masato Hirose—'Falling Down, Getting Up, and Walking On,'" *TechOn*, 2001; "Honda R&D Facility to Study Future Auto Power Systems," *Nikkei Report*, January 14, 2004; "Trumpets vs. Crumpets in a Robot Duel," *New York Times*, March 9, 2008.

318 MIT Media Lab: Author interviews (March 2, 2010) with Frank Moss, Tanya Giovacchini, John Moore, Ryan C. C. Chin, Alex "Sandy" Pentland, Deb Roy, Tod Machover, and Cynthia Breazeal. Other sources: Media Lab 25th

Anniversary celebration, October 15, 2010; MIT Media Lab website, http://www.media.mit.edu.

321 SRI International: Author interviews (December 9, 2009) with Curt Carlson, CEO; Norman Winarsky, vice president, ventures, licensing, and strategic programs; Bill Mark, vice president, information and computer sciences; Alice Resnick, vice president, corporate and marketing communications; Tom Low, director of medical devices and robotics program; Harsha Prahlad, research engineer; Kristin Precoda, director of Speech Technology and Research Lab; Doug Bercow, director of business development; and Dag Kittlaus, SIRI CEO. Other sources: SRI International Corporate Overview Packet, National Science Foundation, Division of Science Resources Statistics; Andrew Pollack, "Three Universities Join Researcher to Develop Drugs," *New York Times*, July 31, 2003; Bob Tedeschi, "What Your Phone Might Do for You Two Years from Now," *New York Times*, November 4, 2009.

324 *Carlson sometimes worries about the long-term future:* Stephen P. Wampler, "Innovation Only Path to Growth and Prosperity," account of speech by Curtis Carlson, Lawrence Livermore National Laboratory website, October 8, 2010, online at https://www.llnl.gov/news/aroundthelab/2010/Oct/Curtis_Carlson.html.

ACKNOWLEDGMENTS

Demand is based largely on the insights and wisdom we've gained from client work at Oliver Wyman and from in-depth conversations with hundreds of customers about all kinds of products (both consumer goods and business services), hassles, and new opportunities.

We owe a debt of gratitude to the business managers who have shared with us their experiences, on and off the record, in wrestling with the thorny challenge of creating new demand in today's difficult economy. We've learned an enormous amount from them and consider it a privilege to work with them.

We appreciate the time, energy, and perspectives customers have generously provided to us and to our colleagues at Oliver Wyman. Most of what we've learned about demand and how it is created has been taught to us by customers, especially those who care about making products better.

Perhaps the most exciting aspect of creating *Demand* for us has been the opportunity to meet and learn from those who listen to (and watch) customers most closely—the demand creators profiled in these pages. They are some of the most creative, thoughtful, inspiring people we've ever had the privilege to encounter. They have changed how we think, and their examples inspire. We're very grateful to them for letting us see the hidden mechanisms that make their stories so extraordinary. The list of remarkable demand creators we interviewed for this book includes Alan Hoops, Dr. Charles Holzner, Peggy Salazar, Dr. Balu Gadhe, Dr. Ken Kim, Dr. Henry Do, and Dr. Sheldon Zinberg of CareMore; Russ Wilcox, Pete Valianatos,

Harit Doshi, Joanna Au, Lynne Garone, Karl Amundson, and Jenn Vail of E Ink; Phil Mazza and Nick Marsella of Byrne Dairy; Matthew Cain of J. Soif, Inc.; Steve Swasey of Netflix; Henk Kwakman and Richard Girardot of Nespresso; Amanda Craft, Elissa Clapp, Lauren LeVeen, and Steven Farr of Teach For America, along with teaching corps members Yoona Kim and David Parker-Longmaid; Tracy Gingell of Pret A Manger; Kim Noltemy of the Boston Symphony Orchestra; Jesse Rosen of the League of American Orchestras; Jonathan Dean, Seneca Garber, Rebecca Chawgo, Rian Kochel, and Vira Slywotzky of the Seattle Opera; Richard Brown of Eurostar; Takeshi Uchiyamada of Toyota; Frank Moss, Tanya Giovacchini, John Moore, Ryan C. C. Chin, Alex "Sandy" Pentland, Deb Roy, Tod Machover, and Cynthia Breazeal of MIT Media Lab; and Curt Carlson, Norman Winarsky, Bill Mark, Alice Resnick, Tom Low, Harsha Prahlad, Kristin Precoda, Doug Bercow, Ellie Javadi, and Dag Kittlaus of SRI International.

We want to offer special thanks to our friend Yoshitaka Ukita of Sony (Yoshitaka_Ukita@terumo.co.jp), who shared his insights into the early history of the e-reader and who is now applying his legendary talents to a new career as a consultant in the field of technology.

Many other individuals have also contributed in concrete ways to the creation of this book. Our research team at Oliver Wyman not only unearthed and verified hundreds of important details and data points but also offered fresh, provocative ideas that helped us to see our subject in new ways. Those who contributed significantly to the research effort include Bernard Zipprich, Shannon Monaghan, Kara Culligan, Larissa de Lima, Simon Heawood, Heather Kaptein, Max Kasriel, Jimmy Li, Chelsea Rich, Anna Rosenblatt, Jay Schafer, Ying Wang, Elizabeth Wise, Janée Woods-Weber, and Cheng Zhang. Each one brought tenacity, insight, imagination, and infectious enthusiasm to the project, and made *Demand* a measurably better, smarter, and more interesting book.

Charlie Hoban, a good friend and former colleague, invested a great deal of time and intellectual energy in reading an early version of the manuscript, and helped to catalyze a major change in direction.

The senior leadership of Oliver Wyman—John Drzik and the management committee—provided crucial organizational support throughout the process. They believe in intellectual capital, they believe in creating great results for clients, and they are willing to invest to get there. Many Oliver Wyman partners provided substantive input, both on the major concepts of the book as well as on specific stories. They include Jacques César, Paul Beswick, and Matt Hamory, especially on retail; Olivier Fainsilber and Gilles Roucolle, especially on Eurostar and passenger rail transportation; Tom Main, especially on CareMore and the health care industry; and Martin Kon and Edouard Portellcte, especially on the challenges of the classical music business. Many, many conversations with Brian Rixner and John Marshall helped to challenge our thinking, sharpen the ideas, and evolve them in an exciting and pragmatic direction. Thanks to all for their knowledge and their generous support of this project.

Others at Oliver Wyman who read, commented on, and helped to improve the manuscript of *Demand* include our friends and colleagues Partha Bose, Steve Szaraz, Chris Schmidt, Eileen Roche, Peter Edmonston, Liz Egan, and Nicholas Sullivan. Their tough and totally accurate critiques helped trigger a second major redirection of the effort. Chris Schmidt, in particular, pulled out all the stops and helped us see what needed to be done. Partha Bose's unerring judgment helped us think through every major decision. Steve Szaraz's astute counsel helped guide our revisions throughout the process. One of the greatest benefits we derive from our work is the opportunity to learn from such an exceptional collection of individuals, and the process of developing this book has certainly underscored that fact.

Valerie Sachetta, as always, provided amazing intellectual, conceptual, and moral support and routinely solved complex administrative and organizational problems with apparent ease, unflappability, and good humor. Phyllis Greenhill transcribed our interviews with speed and accuracy.

At Crown, John Mahaney's careful reading, thoughtful commentary, and shrewd, pragmatic suggestions helped to improve this book significantly. We're grateful for the support of the other members of the Crown team, including publisher Tina Constable, marketing director Meredith McGinnis, senior publicist Dennelle Catlett, publicity director Tara Gilbride, and production editor Christine Tanigawa. A special shoutout to design director David Tran, who worked with us patiently to create a jacket design that reflects not just his creative spark but also his unusual insight into the message and meaning of the book.

Our literary representative, Mel Berger of the William Morris Endeavor Agency, was a pleasure to work with. His enthusiasm for our book helped sustain us throughout the writing process.

Karl Weber and I have worked on five books together. *Demand* has been the most challenging of them all—but also the most rewarding. We hope we've succeeded in communicating to the reader some of the excitement we experienced in exploring the mysteries of demand.

When you're trying to decipher seemingly unsolvable mysteries, there are many black days in the process. When you try to write up your discoveries, the days can get blacker still. Having a partner who can see clearly, on dark days and bright, makes all the difference. My wife, Christine, always brought that clarity of vision (as well as countless readings, edits, challenges, and suggestions). It would have been impossible without her.

Adrian J. Slywotzky
Cambridge, Massachusetts
May 2011

INDEX

accelerated evolution, 259–60, 262–63
advertising: Nespresso, 167, 170
Åkerlund, Erik, 112
Åkerlund & Rausing, 112, 113
Albert, J. D., 97
Amazon, 61, 64, 100, 146, 147, 153
    Kleiner Perkins and, 294
Amazon Kindle, 9, 64, 108, 109, 168
    development process, 101–3, 259
    success factors, 104–7, 141
Apollo 13, 271–73
Apple, 58, 61, 63, 149, 153, 169–70, 301
    design development, 263
    Siri and, 322
    See also specific products
ASIMO, 316–17, 318

backstory, 11, 96, 132, 176
    Nespresso, 171–72
    Netflix, 146
    Zipcar, 29–30
    See also Amazon Kindle; Tetra Pak
Bardeen, John, 306, 307
Barnes & Noble, 101, 108
Beecham, Sinclair, 197–98
BellKor's Pragmatic Chaos, 178
Bell Laboratories, 305, 306–7, 310–12, 325
Benjamin, Maria, 50–51
Benz, Karl, 56
Bernstein, Leonard, 219–20
Bezos, Jeff, 100–102, 105, 223, 259
    See also Amazon; Amazon Kindle
Bishop, Jack, 126
Blockbuster, 3, 135, 136–37, 149–51
Bloomberg, Michael, 59, 65–67, 69,
    70, 223
Bloomberg LP, 59, 61, 65–71
books. See Amazon Kindle; e-readers
Boston Symphony Orchestra, 213, 215,
    216, 217–18

Bouley, David, 45
Brakke, Crystal, 191
Brannon, Ash, 277
Brattain, Walter, 306, 307
Brown, Richard, 236–40, 241, 245
    See also Eurostar
Bruckheimer, Jerry, 301
Buffett, Warren, 286–87, 298, 300
A Bug's Life, 275, 278
business organization, 270, 271–74
    for new product launches, 249, 258,
        259, 262–63, 266–67
    See also specific companies
business systems design, 64, 65, 230
Bye, Gordon, 236
Byers, Brook, 297
Byrne Dairy, 123–24

Cain, Matthew, 128–29, 130
Canandaigua Wine Company, 131
CareMore Medical Group, 72–91
    Extensivists, 83–88
    founding and development, 75–83
    patient services, 72–74, 80–88, 91
    physician recruitment and relations,
        73–74, 77–78, 88
    replication, 89–91
Carlson, Curtis, 323, 324, 325
cars and car travel, 15–18, 55–57, 319, 321
    See also Honda Insight; Toyota Prius
car-sharing, 19–20, 21, 25, 57
    See also Zipcar
Catmull, Ed, 278, 281, 282, 283–84
cell phones, 5–7, 58, 320
    iPhone, 58–59, 63, 265, 322
    Nokia, 6–7, 307–9
Centerra Wine Company, 131
Chase, Robin, 14, 18–23, 33–34, 327–28
Chawgo, Rebecca, 219
Chef Creations, 125–26

Chin, Ryan, 319
China, Tetra Pak in, 121–22
Chunnel, 232
    See also Eurostar
churn rates, 211, 212
Cincinnati Symphony, 216–17
Cinematch, 147, 177–79
CityCar, 319
Clapp, Elissa, 182
Clarke, Sally, 201–2
classical music: Seattle Opera, 219–24
    symphony orchestras, 210–18
coffee, 156, 163
    See also Nespresso
Comiskey, Barrett, 97
communications technologies: Nokia,
    6–7, 265, 307–9
    notable U.S. research labs, 305–7,
    310–13
    radio, 304–7, 312–13, 325
    See also cell phones
competition, within organizations,
    262–63
confidence, 267–68
    misplaced, 254–55
Connect (Sony), 103–4
Connect by Hertz, 33
Cook, Jim, 143–44, 146
Cook, Scott, 296
Cook's Illustrated, 126
Craft, Amanda, 184–85
customer churn, 211, 212
customer input: Bloomberg, 67–68
    Eurostar, 238
    Nespresso, 170, 172–73
    Pret A Manger, 202–5, 208
    Wegmans, 48–49, 53
customer relationships, 132–33
    CareMore, 83–88
    direct marketing, 160–62
    experience design, 64–65
    Tetra Pak, 117–24, 132–33
    See also emotional connection;
    hassle reduction
customer research and data, 139, 148,
    162, 164, 248–49
    Audience Growth Initiative, 214–15
    Eurostar, 238, 240

Netlix customer ratings, 178–79
Skenderian Apothecary, 229–31
customer service: Amazon, 100–101
    Bloomberg, 70–71
    Intuit, 296
    Nespresso, 161–62
    Netflix, 147
    Pret A Manger, 198–99, 203, 205
    small businesses, 225–28, 231
    Tetra Pak, 117–24
    Wegmans, 46

Daly, Timothy, 192
Danielson, Antje, 19, 21
DARPA, 310, 313–14, 322, 324, 325
data. *See* customer research; proprietary
    information; research
David (Michelangelo), 267–68
David Sarnoff Research Center. *See* RCA
    Laboratories
da Vinci Surgical System, 323–24
Dawson, Jane, 227, 228
Dean, Jonathan, 221, 328
de-averaging, 11–12, 212
    See also demand variation
DeepBlue Ice Cream Freezer, 118
Defense Advanced Research Projects
    Agency. *See* DARPA
"Delusions of Success" (Lovallo and
    Kahneman), 254–55
demand creation systems, 278, 286–87,
    299–301
    See also portfolios
demand forecasting/analysis, 11–12, 212,
    254–55
    *See also specific companies and
    products*
demand triggers, 11, 137, 141–42, 168,
    170–71, 176
    Nespresso, 160–62, 163–64, 167
    Netflix, 153
    product trials as, 164–65, 167–70
    symphony orchestras, 215
demand variation, 11–12, 69, 210, 212
    average customer myth, 210, 211–13,
    233
    Seattle Opera audience develop-
    ment, 218–24

small business examples, 224–31
strategies for, 244–45, 248–49
symphony orchestras, 210–18
variation-based pricing, 216–17, 235,
    239–40, 242–43
Zipcar, 25–26
See also Eurostar
Deming, W. Edwards, 80
DePeters, Jack, 47–48
design, 64–65
    accelerated evolution and internal
        competition, 259–60, 262–63
    emotional connection and, 265–66
    revision, 268–70
    *See also specific companies and
        products*
diabetes care, 81–82, 85, 88
digital technologies: hassle maps and
        reduction, 57–59, 60–65
    Kleiner Perkins investment criteria,
        297–98
    social networking, 177
    streaming video, 151–53
    transistor and, 305, 309
    See also research; *specific companies
        and products*
DiGORO, 318
direct marketing, 160–62
Disney, 276, 277, 278, 284, 301
Doctor, Pete, 280
Doerr, John, 293, 296–97, 299
Dow Jones Telerate, 68–69
Duckworth, Angela Lee, 185–86
Duell, Charles, 325

Eat, 203, 208
Edgley, Richard, 235–36
Edmunds, 251
education, 191–92, 324
    See also Teach For America
E Ink, 94, 95, 97–98, 320, 321
    and Amazon Kindle, 102, 107
emotional connection, 18, 42–43, 52–54,
        122, 176
    launch process and, 265–66
    magnetism and, 18, 20–21, 42, 118
    Nespresso, 164–66
    Zipcar, 31, 43

Emotional Intelligence (Goleman), 86
employees and staffing: CareMore physi-
        cians, 73–74, 77–78, 88
    compensation and benefits, 44–45,
        46, 206
    Merck, 289
    Pixar, 282–86
    Pret A Manger, 198–99, 205–6
    teamwork, 44, 279–81, 282–83
    Tetra Pak, 120, 123, 124
    training programs, 45
    Wegmans, 44–48, 50–51
The End of the Line (film), 202
energy technologies, 296, 298, 303, 324
entropy, 194–95
environmental consciousness, 106,
        128–30, 202
e-readers, 9, 63–64, 92–95, 107–10
    E Ink and, 94, 95, 97–98, 102, 107,
        320
    See also Amazon Kindle; Sony
        Librié; Sony Reader
Ethical Coffee Company, 173
Eurostar, 231–48
    competitors, 243, 246, 247
    current status and outlook, 246–47
    customer types, 233–35, 237–40,
        242–44
    demand analysis, 233–35
    infrastructure, 231–32, 236, 240–41
    marketing, 235, 239–40, 242–44, 245
    ownership, 232, 236
    ridership, 232, 235, 236, 239, 245–46
    service problems and improvements,
        235–36, 237–42, 246–47
expansion, 51–52, 89–90, 196–97, 198,
        206–8
experience design, 64–65
experimentation. *See* innovation
Extensivists, 83–88

Facebook, 177
factor analysis, 214
Failure Is Not an Option (Kranz), 271
Farr, Steven, 185, 188, 191, 192
fatal flaw searches, 257–58, 262
Favre, Eric, 154, 157
FDA, 290, 291

fear, 267, 268
Ferrera, Mark, 45
Food and Drug Administration, 290, 291
food packaging, 113–14, 129–30
    See also Tetra Pak
forecasting. *See* research
franchising, 207
free trials. *See* product trials
Fresh & Easy Neighborhood Markets,
    252–53
Fresh Pond Market, 225–27
functionality, 20–21

Gadhe, Balu, 86
Gaillard, Jean-Paul, 158–61, 164, 171,
    173
Gapper, John, 163
Garner, Bill, 50
Gasser, Rupert, 171–72
Gates Foundation, 191
General Electric, 313
Gingell, Tracy, 194–96, 328
    See also Pret A Manger
Girardot, Richard, 172–73, 174
Goldman's Law, 275, 286, 300
Goleman, Daniel, 86
Google, 294
Google eBookstore, 108–9
Gore, Al, 129, 295
Grauer, Peter, 71
Griffith, Scott, 14, 15, 32, 34
    See also Zipcar
grocery stores and shopping, 40–42,
    52–54, 116, 225–27, 252–53
    See also Wegmans
Groupe Eurotunnel S.A., 232

hassle maps, 10–11, 12, 55, 59–60, 176,
    210
    health care, 75, 76–77
    symphony attendance, 214–15
hassle reduction, 10–11, 57–61, 176, 327
    Amazon Kindle, 102, 104–5
    Bloomberg LP, 65–71
    CareMore, 72–91
    car sharing, 19–20
    car travel, 15–17, 56–57
    cell phones, 58–59

digital technologies and companies,
    57–59, 60–65
    Eurostar, 240, 241–42, 245
    Nespresso, 165
    Netflix, 135, 147–49
    Pret A Manger, 197
    Tetra Pak, 113–14, 127–28
    Wegmans, 40–42
Hastings, Reed, 2–4, 58, 134–39, 140,
    142–43, 148
    and Netflix Prize, 177, 179
    See also Netflix
health care. *See* CareMore; HMOs
Heberle, Jim, 50
Hermé, Pierre, 45
Hertz, 33
HMOs, 75–76, 83
Holm, Ulla, 121
Holzner, Charles, 76, 77, 80, 84, 85–86
Honda, 316
Honda, Soichiro, 317
Honda Insight, 250–52, 265
Honda Research Institute (HRI), 315–18
Hoops, Alan, 89–90, 91
HRI (Honda Research Institute), 315–18
hundred-bets strategy, 286–87, 297
Huxley, Aldous, 176
hybrid cars. *See* Honda Insight; Toyota
    Prius

ice cream manufacturing, 118
IKEA, 253
imitation, 146, 263–65
immigration policy, 324
improvement. *See* trajectory
India, cell phone technologies in, 4–7,
    307–9
information technologies: Bloomberg LP,
    59, 61, 65–71
    in the developing world, 4–7, 307–9
    health care, 84–85, 87–88
    notable U.S. research labs, 305–7,
    310–15
    Zipcar and, 32, 33
    See also cell phones; digital technol-
    ogies
infrastructure, 132
    See also backstory

innovation: Wegmans, 49–51
  See also hassle reduction; research
Internal Medicine Specialists, Inc., 75–76
Internet, 314
  See also digital technologies; infor-
    mation technologies; *specific com-
    panies and products*
Intuit, 294, 296
Intuitive Surgical, 323–24
iPad, 63, 108
iPhone, 58–59, 63, 265, 322
iPod, 20, 63, 265, 270
Ito, Takanobu, 317
iTunes, 61, 63, 103

J. Soif, 128–29, 130
Jacobson, Joseph, 97, 101
Jardine Matheson, 205
Järund, Harry, 113
Jenkins, Speight, 219, 222–23
  See also Seattle Opera
Jewett, Frank, 310
Jobs, Steve, 58, 63
  See also Apple
Jönsson, Dennis, 124, 129, 130
Joy, Bill, 295, 299

Kahneman, Daniel, 254–55
Kenneally, Chris, 127
Kessel, Steve, 102, 107
Khosla, Vinod, 296
killer offers, 216–17
Kim, Yoona, 186–89, 231
Kindle. *See* Amazon Kindle
Kittlaus, Dag, 322
Kjellberg, Uno, 129
Klein, Gary, 257
Kleiner Perkins Caufield & Byers, 292–99
Kopp, Wendy, 179–81, 183, 184, 192,
    193–94, 223
  See also Teach For America
Kranz, Gene, 271–73
Kwakman, Henk, 164–68, 169, 171–72,
    174–75, 328

Lab 126, 102
Landes, David, 116
Lane, Ray, 293, 297

Lasseter, John, 275–77, 278, 279, 280,
    281, 284
  See also Pixar
launches: key success factors, 261–70
  maximizing success potential,
    270–74
  misplaced optimism, 254–55
  repeated success, 278, 286–87,
    299–301
  See also portfolios; *specific com-
    panies and products*
launch failure, 251–54
  analyzing potential for, 257–58, 262
  company failures, 292
  Honda Insight, 250–52, 265
  statistics, 254
Lessin, Leeba, 86
Librié, 9, 92–95, 98–99, 101–2, 103,
    253, 265
Licklider, J. C. R., 313–14
Lorenzo, Perry, 219–22, 223
Lotus, 266–67, 294
Lovallo, Dan, 254–55
Lucasfilm, 278

MacBook Air, 253
magnetism, 10, 17–18
  backstory and, 96
  emotional engagement and, 18,
    20–21, 42, 52–54, 118
  functionality and, 20–21
  hassle reduction and, 40–42
  Pret A Manger, 198–200
  triggers and, 142
  Wegmans, 36–38
  Zipcar, 20–21, 30–31
Mail on Ovi, 308–9
Marconi Wireless, 312–13
Marsella, Nick, 123–24
Martin, Andrew, 240–41
"A Mathematical Theory of Communica-
    tion" (Shannon), 311–12
Maucher, Helmut, 156–57, 158, 159,
    161, 259
Mazza, Phil, 123
McCrudden, Paul, 203–5
Media Lab, MIT, 97, 318–21
Medicare, 78, 79, 87

Merck, 287–92
Merrill Lynch, 67–68
Metcalfe, Julian, 197–98, 200, 201–5,
    208–9, 223
    See also Pret A Manger
Mitchell, Deborah, 257
Mitchell, William, 319
MIT Media Lab, 97, 318–21
Moonves, Alaina, 191
Morgan, Mary, 16, 30–31
Moss, Frank, 320
movies, 254, 301
    See also Pixar
Murphy, Kate, 126
music: Seattle Opera, 219–24
    symphony orchestras, 210–18
MySpace, 177

Najarian, Marc, 225–26
Nally, E. J., 312
NASA, 271–73
National Academy of Engineering, 303,
    326
National Institutes of Health, 287, 288
Nelson, Randy, 283
Nespresso, 154–75
    airline sales, 163, 167
    competitors, 173–74
    current status and outlook, 172–75
    demand triggers, 160–62
    founding and early development,
        154–59, 259
    home market development, 158–63
    Nestlé and, 154, 155–59, 160, 169,
        172, 259
    in the U.S., 174
    under Kwakman, 164–71
Nestlé, 154, 171
    Nespresso and, 154, 155–59, 160,
        169, 172, 259
Netflix, 3–4, 61, 134–53, 192–93
    competitors, 3, 136–37, 149–51, 153
    founding and development, 3,
        134–41, 262, 265
    improvement trajectory, 146–48,
        177–79, 193
    product and systems design, 64, 132,
        139–41, 143–46, 151–53

    recommendation system, 147,
        177–79
    streaming and future changes,
        151–53
    website design, 64, 132, 146, 265
Netflix Prize, 177–79
Newman, Randy, 279
New Teacher Project, 192
New York–Paris auto race (1907), 55–56
New York Philharmonic, 216, 219–20
New York Times, 126–27, 251
N-Gage, 253
NIH, 287, 288
Nokia, 6–7, 253, 265, 307–9
Noltemy, Kim, 217, 218
Nook, 108

Obopay, 309
Okuda, Hiroshi, 260
One-Click World, 62–65
    See also specific companies
opera, 219–24
Oracle, 293
organizational structure. *See* business
    organization
originality, 281–82
Ovi, 308

Pagano, Camillo, 157, 158
Palo Alto Research Center. *See* PARC
Panasonic, 146
PARC, 97, 310, 312, 313, 314–15, 325
Patchett, Arthur, 289–90
Patient Protection and Affordable Care
    Act, 84
Patient QuickView, 84–85
Pennington, Nancy, 257
Pensacola Symphony, 217
personnel policies. *See* employees and
    staffing
Pfizer, 301
pharmaceuticals, 287–92
Picasso, Pablo, 263
Pixar, 275–86
    company culture, 278–86
    employee relationships, 282–86
    founding and early successes,
        275–76, 278

releases and revenues, 285
    Toy Story 2, 276–78, 279–81
Pixar University, 283
Porter Square Books, 227–28
portfolios, 278, 286–87
    hundred-bets strategy, 286–87, 297
    key success factors, 299–301
    Kleiner Perkins, 292–99
    Merck, 287–92
    SRI commercialization system,
      322–25
    See also Pixar
Potter, Emily, 178
Potter, Gavin, 177–78
Powell, Colin, 295
premortems, 257–58, 262
Pret A Manger, 194–209
    competitors, 203, 208
    customer service, 198–99, 203, 205
    employees and staffing, 205–6,
      298–99
    expansion, 196–97, 198, 206–8
    founding and early development,
      197–98
    magnetism of, 198–200
    overcoming entropy, 194–96
    revenues, 208
pricing, variation-based, 216–17, 235,
    239–40, 242–43
product design. *See* design; *specific com-
    panies and products*
product improvement. *See* trajectory
product launches. *See* launch; launch
    failure; *specific products*
product portfolios. *See* portfolios
product trials: Nespresso, 163–65,
    167–70, 171
    trialists and customer churn, 211,
      213–17
product variations, 242–44, 248
    See also demand variation
proprietary information, 229, 230,
    248–49
    See also customer research
Pure Software, 134, 142–43, 148

quality maintenance, 51–52, 201–2, 207
    See also trajectory

Race to the Top, 191–92
radio, 304–7, 312–13, 325
Rajan, Babu, 4–6
Rausing, Ruben, 112–13, 115, 131
RCA Laboratories, 310, 312–13, 323, 325
recycling, 129, 130
research, 302–26
    before a launch, 255–56
    commercialization systems,
      322–25
    at Merck, 287–91
    at Pixar, 282
    recent declines, 311, 312, 313,
      315–18
    teacher effectiveness, 184–85
    twenty-first century challenges,
      303–4, 325–26
    See also customer research
research labs: Honda Research Institute,
    315–18
    MIT Media LAB, 97, 318–21
    notable twentieth-century work,
      309–15, 325
    SRI International, 321–25
Reuters, 68, 69, 70
revision, 268–70
    Toy Story 2, 276–78, 279–81
Rider-Longmaid, Parker, 189
robotics research, 316–17, 318
Rokoff, June, 266–67
Rubin, Jerome S., 97
Russell, Roy, 19–20
Russo, J. Edward, 257

Saccardi, Charles, 45
Salomon Brothers, 66, 67
Samsung, 265–66
San Antonio Symphony, 217
Sarnoff, David, 312–13
Schlee, Clive, 205, 206, 207
school reform, 191–92
    See also Teach For America
Schumacher, Tom, 276
Schuster, George, 55, 56
scientific discovery. *See* research
Seattle Opera, 219–24
Seikan Tunnel, 232
Semmelweis Reflex, 256, 262

Semonian, Nish, 225, 226
serial demand creation. *See* portfolios
Shannon, Claude, 311–12
Sheridon, Nicholas, 97
Shockley, William, 57, 306–7
Simpson, Don, 301
Siri, 322
Skenderian, Joe, 229–31, 328
Skenderian Apothecary, 228–31
small businesses, demand variation in,
    224–31
Sobel, Robert, 232
social networking, 177
social norms, 46–47, 206
Sony, 62, 63, 92, 146, 305
Sony Connect, 103–4
Sony Librié, 9, 92–95, 98–99, 101–2, 103,
    253, 265
Sony Reader, 9, 63–64, 103–4, 107–8
soy milk, 125, 126
SRI International, 321–25
Stanford Research Institute. *See* SRI
    International
Stanton, Andrew, 277, 283
Starck, Philippe, 238–39
Stockton Symphony, 217
Stoltz, Carol, 227, 228
Sun Microsystems, 294, 295, 314
supermarkets. *See* grocery stores and
    shopping; Wegmans
supply chains and vendor relationships,
    171–72, 173, 196, 207
Swasey, Steve, 152–53
symphony orchestras, 210–18
Szczeblowski, Dale, 227, 228

Taylor, Hamish, 236
Teach For America (TFA), 179–92,
    231
    founding and early development,
        179–80
    teacher effectiveness improvement,
        183–90
    teacher recruitment and quality,
        181–83
    and wider school reform efforts,
        191–92
Teaching as Leadership (Farr), 185

teamwork, 44, 279–81, 282–83
    See also employee *entries*
technological innovation, 33, 49–50, 57
    Netflix and, 151–52
    Tetra Pak, 118
    Wegmans online shopping applica-
        tion, 48–49
    See also communications technolo-
        gies; digital technologies; re-
        search; *specific companies and
        products*
Telerate, 68–69
television, 312, 323
Tesco, 252–53
Tetra Pak, 110–33
    company organization and employee
        relations, 120–21, 122–23, 124
    customer relationships, 117–24,
        132–33
    founding and development, 112–15,
        131
    U.S. consumer resistance, 115–17,
        123, 126
    U.S. market development, 123–31
Texas Instruments, 305
TFA. *See* Teach For America
Toshiba, 146
Toyota, 301
Toyota Prius, 251–52, 258–61, 263,
    264–65, 266, 270
Toy Story, 275, 278
Toy Story 2, 276–78, 279–81
trajectory, 11, 176–77, 192–93, 200–201
    Eurostar, 237–39
    Netflix Prize, 177–79
    Pret A Manger, 195–96, 201–2
    revision, 268–70
    See also Teach For America
transistor, 304–7, 309, 325
trials. *See* product trials
triggers. *See* demand triggers

U.S. Food and Drug Administration,
    290, 291
Uchiyamada, Takeshi, 252, 258–59, 260
    See also Toyota Prius
Ukita, Yoshitaka, 92–95, 98–99, 103
Unkrich, Lee, 277

Vagelos, Roy, 287–92
venture capital, 254, 292
    Kleiner Perkins Caufield & Byers,
        292–99
    SRI spinoffs, 323–24
Visible Path, 299
Vitasoy, 125

Walmart, 34–35, 39, 42, 149, 253
Wegman, Danny, 34, 35–36, 39–40, 47,
    50, 327
Wegman, Robert, 39, 41, 44, 49
Wegmans, 34–54
    customer engagement and relation-
        ships, 36–38, 42–43, 46, 48–49,
        53–54
    employee relationships, 44–48,
        50–51
    expansion, 51–52
    founding and development, 38–40
    hassle reduction, 40–42
    innovation, 49–51
    profitability, 52
White, Carol, 126
Whole Foods, 42

Wilcox, Russ, 94, 97, 98, 328
Windhab, E. J., 118
wine packaging, 128–29, 130, 131
Winfrey, Oprah, 107
word of mouth, 140, 161–62, 167, 170,
    171, 245

Xerox PARC, 97, 310, 312, 313, 314–15,
    325

Yaegashi, Takehisa, 258
Yellow+Blue, 130

Zehr, Gregg, 102
Zinberg, Sheldon, 75–80, 81, 88–89
    See also CareMore
Zipcar, 14–15, 18–34, 57, 132, 141
    convenience and density, 24–26,
        242, 265
    current status and outlook, 31–33
    emotional engagement, 31, 43
    founding and early years, 18–22,
        33–34
    Griffith's changes, 14–15, 23–28, 34
Zodarecky, Terri, 45

ABOUT THE AUTHORS

Adrian J. Slywotzky is a partner of Oliver Wyman, an international management consulting firm. *The Times* of London named Slywotzky one of the top fifty business thinkers, and *Industry Week* has named him one of the six most influential management thinkers, "promising to be what Peter Drucker was to much of the twentieth century: the management guru against whom all others are measured." He is the author of the bestselling *The Profit Zone* (selected by *BusinessWeek* as one of the ten best books of the year), *Value Migration, How to Grow When Markets Don't,* and *The Upside.* Slywotzky has also been published in the *Wall Street Journal* and the *Harvard Business Review* and has been a featured speaker at the Davos World Economic Forum, Microsoft CEO Summit, TED, Fortune CEO Conference, and many other events.

Karl Weber writes about business and current affairs. He has collaborated with Adrian Slywotzky on several books and with such authors as Nobel Peace Prize winner Muhammad Yunus and Loews Hotels CEO Jonathan Tisch.